# COUNTERTRANSFERENCE

# COUNTERTRANSFERENCE
## Theory, Technique, Teaching

edited by
### *Athina Alexandris*
and
### *Grigoris Vaslamatzis*

Contributors

| | |
|---|---|
| *Athina Alexandris* | *León Grinberg* |
| *Theodore J. Jacobs* | *Otto F. Kernberg* |
| *Joyce McDougall* | *Thomas H. Ogden* |
| *Hanna Segal* | *Grigoris Vaslamatzis* |
| *Vamik D. Volkan* | *Hector Warnes* |

London
## KARNAC BOOKS

First published in 1993 by
H. Karnac (Books) Ltd.
58 Gloucester Road
London SW7 4QY

Chapter five published in Great Britain in 1989 by Free Association
Books, 26 Freegrove Road, London N7 9RQ, by arrangement with
International Universities Press, Inc. First published in 1988 in
Madison, CT, USA, by International Universities Press, Inc.

**British Library Cataloguing in Publication Data.**

Alexandris, Athina
  Countertransference: Theory, Technique,
  Teaching
  I. Title   II. Vaslamatzis, Grigoris
  154.2

ISBN 1 85575 028 7

Printed in Great Britain by BPCC Wheatons Ltd, Exeter

Dedicated

*. . . to all those who provided stimulation, motivation, assistance, and support to this endeavour;*

*. . . in particular, to those who motivated the analysts to study countertransference–transference further by activating in them strong countertransference feelings;*

*. . . to the authors of this volume, who eagerly offered their important work, thus making this book invaluable to the reader*

# CONTENTS

## ACKNOWLEDGEMENTS

What prompted the publication of this volume is the presentation of the paper entitled "Some Thoughts on Insight and Its Relation to Countertransference" by the editors of this book, A. Alexandris, M.D., and G. Vaslamatzis, M.D., during the Eighth World Congress of Psychiatry (1989), in Athens, Greece. The positive comments of analysts, referring to the importance of the clinical material presented in this paper on the one hand, and the demand expressed by our own colleagues and students (psychiatrists and psychologists) to know more about transference–countertransference on the other, made us think that it would be valuable to have in one volume the views of prominent analysts about the subject. Professor Otto Kernberg was the first analyst to whom we communicated our thoughts and who strongly encouraged us to go ahead with this venture, offering his valuable advice throughout the whole process. We are, therefore, deeply indebted to Otto Kernberg, without whose support this volume would not have materialized.

Subsequently we contacted the analysts Leo Grinberg, Theodore Jacobs, Joyce McDougall, Thomas Ogden, Hanna

xi

Segal, Vamik Volkan, and Hector Warnes (names mentioned in alphabetical order), who responded with enthusiasm and also offered us their papers to be included in the book. It is understood that it is their contribution that gives this book its value.

It goes without saying that several important analysts who have written about countertransference are not present in this volume. This is by no means due to our negligence, but to the pressure of time to publish this book.

We would like to thank the psychiatrists and psychologists whose participation in our teaching stimulated our own interest to offer them something more—i.e. the present volume.

We also wish to thank Professor C. Stefanis, Chairman of the Department of Psychiatry of the Athens University, in whose department we are both teaching and supervising psychoanalytic psychotherapy. He strongly encouraged us to go on with this endeavour and offered us his support.

We express our appreciation to the secretary, Miss Olga Emmanouil, and to the I.S.C.O. Office for their assistance in preparing the manuscript.

Finally, we are grateful to those publishers who gave us permission to reprint papers.

# PREFACE

*Grigoris Vaslamatzis*

The contributors to this book invite the reader to explore with them the processes affecting the therapist's mind—and, occasionally, his body—during psychoanalytic therapy, and the reasons for which the therapist thinks, feels, and reacts in a particular way.

The full significance of these processes, referred to as "countertransference" since Freud's time, has recently been recognized, resulting in the therapist's use of additional resources so that he or she can understand and help the patient more effectively. If we, as therapists, do not deal with our countertransference, we deprive ourselves of the use of an instrument that may prove invaluable to our work. Let us here recall Freud's statement that "everyone possesses in his own unconscious an instrument with which he can interpret the utterances of the unconscious in other people" (Freud, 1913i, p. 320) and, more specifically with respect to countertransference, that the analyst "must turn his own unconscious like a receptive organ toward the transmitting unconscious of the patient" (Freud, 1912e, p.115).

A continuation of this line of thought, 37 years later, is obvious in the work of Paula Heimann (1950) for whom "countertransference is an instrument of research into the patient's unconscious" (p. 81). For several reasons, her paper may be considered a milestone insofar as it marks a major shift in therapists' conceptualization of countertransference and in their approach to the clinical situation as a whole.

Heimann stressed the fact that the therapeutic situation is primarily a relationship between two persons and maintained that it differs from other relationships not in that the therapist has no feelings (or should not experience any emotions), but in the way that the therapist sustains these feelings and works through and uses the patient's influence upon his own feelings. The aim of the therapist remains to use his countertransference in the therapeutic interest of the patient. Heimann also emphasized the conscious aspects of countertransference in addition to the unconscious aspects, which had been discussed until then.

A few years later, Heinrich Racker (1957) also maintained that the recognition and understanding of countertransference phenomena can serve as a useful tool for the analyst, indicating what and when interpretations should be made. Racker criticized all attempts to repress the countertransference and noted that the myth in psychoanalytic training, that analysis is an interaction between a person who is ill and one who is healthy, has come to an end. In actuality we have two subjects who affect one another. The analyst tries, of course, to be objective, but this objectivity is related to his perception of his own subjectivity and countertransference (1968). Racker further tried to elucidate the mechanisms by means of which countertransference develops.

For the following three decades a major impetus in psychoanalytic thinking was gained and a multitude of published material came to light. Analysts, such as Otto Kernberg (1965, 1976), Joyce McDougall (1975), Hanna Segal (1977), León Grinberg (1962, 1990), among others, explored a variety of complementary concepts: projective identification and counteridentification, and their clinical relevance; the notion of the containing function of the therapist; unusual countertransference reactions, and the relationship between the primitive aspects of the patient's personality structure and the intensity of counter-transference, and so forth. Their propositions, as well as prevailing approaches, which are at the heart of current deliberation about the nature and the meaning of countertransference, are further elaborated in this volume.

It is our hope that this book will illuminate these areas, attempting to do so in a uniquely personal fashion. The contributors share their experiences with the reader, offering fragments of their psyche and often revealing intimate aspects of their inner self. Finally, they examine the analyst's psychic fate as this is shaped by the interaction with another human being, and how this, in turn, ultimately affects the psychic fate of the patient and the outcome of therapy.

# COUNTERTRANSFERENCE

# INTRODUCTION

*Athina Alexandris*

Irma, Lucia, Ralph, Annabelle, George, She, or He could very well have featured as the title of this book, because each one of the persons behind these names has been the protagonist for a good part of our professional lives. Some of them will stay with us, challenging us, for the rest of our lives—when, for example, we question ourselves what it could be that we "missed in our understanding of them". We always try to find out what happened to them, and often we do get the information, even if it is many years later.

This silent questioning of each one of us might explain why analysts are inclined to write about those cases that had been the cause of considerable difficulties in the course of their careers, having at times a poor outcome, rather than about those cases that had a satisfactory outcome—which constitutes, after all, the analyst's only reward.

Irma, Lucia, Ralph, Annabelle are the witnesses, and they will always stand as the proof of the analyst's feelings experienced during the psychoanalytic voyage upon which both (analyst and protagonist–patient) had embarked at some time or another in life.

1

We, the analysts, will always be recognized by the way these Muses (our patients) have inspired us in creating the papers that appear in this book. (Hesiod says the Muses—daughters of Mnemosyne—sang of things present, past, and future, and their role was to inspire the poets and urge them to create their works—*Theogonia 38*).

The case studies we are concerned with in this volume are those of so-called "difficult cases" or regressed individuals. They were selected by their own authors from among numerous analysands and supervised patients. Having been objects of massive parental projections, they created particular counter-transference problems. Their powerful projections induced diverse feelings in the analysts, which acted upon their minds. This view assumes that transference is rooted in the primitive pre-verbal infantile experience and is consistent with the Kleinian concept of projective identification (Hanna Segal, chapter one). The analysts, in turn, projected into them their own fantasies, wishes, and internal objects.

It is Irma who made Freud dream of her because of his guilt. The dream fulfilled his wish that "he was not responsible for the persistence of Irma's pains, but Otto was" (Freud, 1900a, p. 118).

It is Lucia who intended to induce Otto Kernberg "into the role of an admiring and potentially corruptible as well as seductive father . . .". "It is as if Lucia had let me 'die', and I and the hospital staff let the patient's treatment 'die' in return." Irma will be the evidence of interaction between Freud, his friend Otto, and Dr M: "Otto had in fact annoyed me by his remarks about Irma's incomplete cure, and the dream gave me my revenge by throwing the reproach back on to him" (Freud, 1900a, p. 118). Similarly, Lucia will stand as a reminder of the interaction of the hospital staff, whose unresolved conflicts made them fail in her treatment (chapter eight).

It is Ralph whose comment, "I must seem pretty disgusting to you", made Kernberg feel that he was at a loss for words "because of the accuracy of his observation" (chapter eight).

It is She (the patient) who made Hanna Segal feel that she was "in the position of a helpless and rather bewildered child" (chapter one).

It is Annabelle who made Joyce McDougall feel that she was "about as useful as a cloth monkey, for all the good the patient was able to get out of their analytic work together" (chapter five).

It is She (the patient) who made León Grinberg feel as if he were "analysing a corpse", because she tried to force the dead part of herself into him (chapter three).

It is Sophia who, during the sessions, induced in her therapist terrifying bodily feelings almost unbearable to him, affecting his containing function (chapter six).

It is He (one of his borderline patients) who made Vamik Volkan feel "as though he had eaten a heavy meal", experiencing difficulties in his chest and feeling uncomfortable in his stomach, while another patient gave him the feeling of "bodily lightness" (chapter seven).

It is George who intended to seduce Athina Alexandris and turn her into a passive listener by narrating his myths to her in order to make her fail in her role (chapter four).

It is Katerina who managed to terrify her therapist and make him feel guilty because he changed an appointment (chapter nine).

It is Stavros who shook off his therapist when he made him aware of his unconscious feelings of rejection toward him (chapter nine).

The "exacting demands" of Hector Warnes' patient caused him to feel "imprisoned" and to experience "devaluation in his capacity to care". This motivated him to evaluate the efficiency of the frame he had provided for his patient (chapter ten).

We could go on and on, pointing out all the countertransference feelings and reactions experienced, but I would rather let the reader enjoy their full account and the way countertransference reactions develop in relation to the transference taking place during the psychoanalytic session.

Similar transference–countertransference interactions "play a role of importance in supervision, as they do in analytic therapy", writes Theodore Jacobs. "For this complex set of interactions Racker coined the term 'indirect countertransference'", to mention one. The supervisee, Mr G, had caused in the supervisor Theodore Jacobs "the stirring of these old ghosts", due to the fact that the supervisor's father "had something in common" with the supervisee (chapter eleven).

It is the supervisee who, by reporting to her supervisor Grigoris Vaslamatzis her dream of him, forced him to deal with transference–countertransference issues that he was avoiding (chapter twelve).

All the authors of this volume discuss primitive transference and primitive communication, including the importance of non-verbal communication when analysing the so-called "difficult" or regressed cases. In her illuminating paper, Joyce McDougall mentions that primitive communication is an appeal, ". . . in a sense a demand to be understood without passing by the normal verbal channels, to be understood by mere signs". Communication seeks "to restore the primary mother–child unity". Annabelle's words "had partially lost their communicative aim". Her intention to speak "was to arouse feelings in the analyst". Words used as actions, ". . . as weapons, . . . as a desperate cry for help . . ." (chapter five).

This was also evident with Sophia, who was using the word 'menos' (meaning fury) as a weapon against her therapist, causing him agonizing bodily feelings (chapter six).

León Grinberg's patient also used non-verbal means to communicate to him that she had a dead object inside her. Another of his patients transmitted to him non-verbally with her "ring game" that she was waiting for him "to intervene and talk," while with her "baby game" she was saying that she needed to hear his voice "in order to engender 'word–babies'" (chapter three).

Primitive non-verbal communication is very powerful and plays a decisive role in the outcome of the analysis. According to Hanna Segal, it is something constantly present—a constant interaction in which the patient acts on the analyst's mind. It takes many forms—either as a predominant form of communication or as an attack on communication.

While it is by non-verbal channels that patients transmit their psychic state to their analyst, all authors here agree that it is mainly through countertransference reactions that this communication may be detected. These reactions will act as a guide to a further understanding of the patient's inner psychic state. The sum-total of these very reactions, as well as the feelings experienced by the analyst toward his patient, constitute the most common definition of countertransference adopted by the majority of authors of this volume. The reactions and feelings implied are both conscious and unconscious, with the emphasis on those that are unconscious.

During analytic therapy, attention should be given to understanding the reactivation of the patient's projective identification. To quote from Thomas Ogden's "Mr C, Supervised Case": "It was becoming clear to the therapist that the patient was having great difficulties accepting the loss of Mr J and that projective identification . . . was being used in part as a defence against feelings of loss". In my opinion, when analysts encounter difficulties in understanding the reactivation of projective identification as a defence against loss, it is because they are under the great impact of their patient's projective identifications.

Joyce McDougall, on the other hand, talks of the difficulty of some patients to mourn: "Annabelle lived out defensively an unelaborated depression." "It is impossible to mourn the loss of an object one has never possessed, or whose existence has never been truly recognized as distinct from one's own, or as an integral part of one's inner world". McDougall stresses the importance of understanding and eventually helping the patient to mourn losses, such as the loss of the idealized omnipotent analyst and of the self.

Athina Alexandris illustrates in her paper how the patient denied the losses and thus avoided going through the process of mourning by using massive projections and other defensive means. She also delves on the way the inability to mourn and defensive measures against losses may be transmitted from one generation to the other through the parent–child relationship (chapter four).

During the analytic voyage it is, therefore, important for the analyst to discern how and when the persecutory anxiety gives way to the depressive one due to object losses as well as to losses due to the projected parts of the self, which are felt to be lost. Otto Kernberg illustrates the sudden activation of projective identification "in the patient's defensive repertoire" and how it is related to shift from concordant to complementary identification in his countertransference and its relation to empathy.

Projective identification, as the authors of this book assert, is instrumental in the understanding of transference as well as of countertransference. Otto Kernberg's case, Lucia, shows how the interaction of projective identifications becomes more complex in the hospital milieu (chapter eight).

Another aspect investigated by all the contributors to this monograph is that in working with severely "regressed", "difficult", "borderline" cases, it is the mother–child relationship within the analyst that is reactivated and put to the test, since our capacity to contain the infantile parts of the patient depends on our own capacity to contain the infant part of ourselves (Hanna Segal, chapter one). However, in some cases and under special circumstances it becomes apparent that the father–son relationship comes to the fore, as in the hospital treatment of Lucia, Otto Kernberg's case. The same was observed in the supervised case of Thomas Ogden, in which therapist, patient, and supervisor were all male, as well as in Theodore Jacobs' case, where the supervisee, Mr G, projected his feelings for his step-father onto the supervisor, thus reactivating Jacobs' relationship with his own father.

The same could be said of the male patient Stavros and his male therapist, who wanted to "abandon" him because he was "unanalysable", just as the patient's father had abandoned him at an early age (chapter nine). When this problem of the father–son relationship is settled, it is certain that the mother–child relationship will surface.

It has been my experience that when male analysts reach an impasse in the treatment of their male patients, they often seem to choose to come to a female analyst for supervision. Obviously, the unconscious demand in this case is for the mother (female analyst) to settle the problem between them (father and son).

All authors emphasize the fact that in order to be able to help their patients, analysts should try to contain and live with the feelings induced by them—an equivalent to the function of a mother containing the infant's projections (Bion). Analysts have to observe their feelings, consult them, and use them for the understanding of their patients; but they must never be swayed by them. The reader will be informed throughout this volume of the circumstances and conditions under which countertransference—and therefore the capacity to contain—becomes disturbed. In such cases, particular countertransference difficulties could arise, such as the projective countertransference described by León Grinberg, which is caused by some patients who, as infants, have been subjected to heavy parental projections (chapter three).

In order for therapy to continue and in an ultimate effort to contain the patient rather than dropping him altogether, Dr Alexandris suggests that a detour—a defensive manoeuvre—might take place in the therapist's countertransference, as described in chapter six.

We should, however, keep in mind that the patient's perception of his analyst does not consist solely of projections; patients do react to aspects of our personality. In a good functional countertransference situation we have a double relation to the patient: one perceptive, containing and understanding the patient's communication, the other active, producing or giving understanding, knowledge, or structure to the patient in the form of interpretation. It is very important for us to be aware that countertransference is the best of servants but the worst of masters (Hanna Segal, chapter one).

Vamik Volkan describes the "common" countertransference reactions that are evoked in analysts by transference, such as drowsiness experienced at times during the analysis of patients with full-blown narcissistic personality organization or typical "split" transference, when treating borderline personality organization, or feeling uncomfortable, having difficulties with breathing, etc. Further, Volkan writes, ". . . 'common' countertransference reactions occur in the treatment of a borderline patient when the analyst regresses to meet his already regressed patient" (chapter seven).

Joyce McDougall also describes general countertransference reactions, such as "boredom", "irritation", "remaining silent", "feeling aggressive" when the analyst cannot decode communication.

The countertransference affect is often the first signal, alerting the analyst to the patient's inner experience as well as of his own countertransference—as in the case of Otto Kernberg's first signal of the countertransference affect—the feeling of "disgust" in relation to Ralph and the role that it played in the better understanding of his patient. Athina Alexandris was alerted when she caught herself deriving "satisfaction" from her patient's narrations. The investigation of this first signal made her aware that the patient wished to repeat with her his relationship with his mother and that she, the analyst, was inclined to accept the appointed role and thus repeat with the patient her own past experience.

Thomas Ogden draws our attention to the "masochistic misuse of the concept of containment" as it took place with his supervisee, Dr S, who "masochistically contained her patient due to her unconscious wishes to serve as a martyr of a parent–child relationship".

Hector Warnes discusses countertransference reactions in the light of frame theory and draws our attention to the fact that "the analyst should accept the patient's frame because it contains the non-solved symbiotic part of the personality". Warnes informs us of the patient's various projections to the "frame" and how important it is for the analyst to understand these projections (chapter ten). Talking of "frames"—I believe that the "frame" that we provide for our patients in our private offices is part of our countertransference, and it also speaks of our personalities.

Theodore Jacobs throws light on several problems taking place in supervision, and he tells us how the supervised patient can be affected. He makes an interesting remark regarding the ending of supervision: "It could be perceived by the supervisor as a loss and followed by his or her defences against it." The supervisee could also react to the ending of supervision and attempt to prolong it, as, for instance, in the case described in chapter twelve by Grigoris Vaslamatzis.

All of the above are only a few examples of the difficulties experienced by analysts in analytic treatment. To recognize our failures and try to learn from them is very important indeed. It is true that if transference is the most difficult part of analysis, then countertransference must come a close second. When finding ourselves in a transference–countertransference impasse or before a cross-roads, then countertransference becomes a priority. It has to be dealt with first and adequately before the psychoanalytic process resumes its course. The cases presented by Alexandris in chapter four and McDougall's Annabelle case in chapter five are good examples of this realization.

The clinical concept of countertransference may well be one of the most crucial matters of concern in psychoanalysis over the past fifty years. There has been a growing body of writing on the subject, which reflects the analyst's increasing interest in knowing more about this phenomenon and having the opportunity to exchange views with other colleagues. Writing about our analysands is an effort—a final attempt—to understand better what has gone on between ourselves and our patients. Our selection of cases is indicative of our intention to search further for the truth about their unconscious—and for the truth about our own unconscious—in the hope that we will continue our own personal self-analysis in areas that have either thus far escaped analytical scrutiny or require to be worked through more fully.

As young analysts, we are fascinated by our patients and by the stories they bring us (transference), to the extent that we talk about them "all over the place". As we grow older and gain experience, we begin to pay closer attention to our feelings towards patients (countertransference), and finally we come to focus on the transference–countertransference relationship. And when we have reached full maturity, we may come to question what the analyst's profile might be: transference–countertransference, or countertransference–transference? How might one sketch out the analyst? We shall let the reader draw his own conclusions.

From the study of the papers included in this volume it can be concluded that countertransference in its own unique way promotes and shapes psychoanalytic thinking, technique, and teaching. Let it be understood that here we talk not only of our countertransference as analysts towards our analysands, as supervisors towards our supervisees or supervised patients, but also of our countertransference towards our colleagues, hospital authorities, and all others who are related in one way or another to our patients or to our supervisees.

The special value of each paper lies in the presentation of clinical material from patients treated or supervised by the authors themselves. In this fashion the analysts reveal fragments of themselves. We are here concerned with the analysis of the relationship between two persons, in which the analyst participates with his own psychic strengths and weaknesses, believing that he understands something of what his patient is experiencing. At times he identifies with him, at other moments he experiences the thoughts and feelings of the internal objects of his patient. His most precious guide in this difficult voyage is his countertransference.

Each paper, in its unique way, offers elucidation of difficult concepts, theoretical knowledge, its application and management in clinical practice, suggestions, and advice with reference to psychoanalytic technique in relation to various types of patients, and so each teaches all of us how to transmit our knowledge and experience to younger generations in a more effective way. It is hoped that this volume will fulfil its task as a source of further and deeper understanding of transference–countertransference interaction in clinical practice.

# PART ONE

# COUNTERTRANSFERENCE: THEORETICAL AND TECHNICAL ASPECTS

CHAPTER ONE

# Countertransference

*Hanna Segal*

A s analysis developed, transference, at first considered a major obstacle in treatment, came to be seen as the fulcrum on which the psychoanalytic situation rests. Similarly, countertransference, first seen as a neurotic disturbance in the psychoanalyst, preventing him from getting a clear and objective view of the patient, is now increasingly recognized as a most important source of information about the patient as well as a major element of the interaction between patient and analyst. In her pioneering paper on the subject, Paula Heimann (1950) drew attention to the fact that, though not recognized as such, countertransference had always been a guide in psychoanalytical work. She suggested that Freud's discovery of resistance was based on his countertransference, his feeling that he was meeting a resistant force in the patient. Once our attention is drawn to it, this view of countertransference seems almost obvious.

Reprinted by permission from Hanna Segal, 'Countertransference'. In: *The Work of Hanna Segal* (North Vale, NJ: Jason Aronson, 1981).

To take a single example, I had a patient who evoked in me a whole gamut of unpleasant feelings. It would have been very foolish of me to ignore these feelings or consider them my own neurotic reactions, since this patient's principal complaint was her terrible unpopularity. Obviously, the way she affected me was a function of her psychopathology—a function of utmost importance to her, and one that it is crucial for us to understand.

This view of countertransference as a function of the patient's personality is not universally accepted. It is still often contended that ideally countertransference should be eliminated, though it is recognized that in practice this might not be possible. On the other hand, the view of countertransference as an important part of the psychoanalytic process is widely recognized. The literature on the subject is far too vast to discuss in this short paper, but, to mention only a few, there are papers on the subject by Winnicott (1949), Money-Kyrle (1956), León Grinberg (1962), and a book by Heinrich Racker (1968). Many authors simply take countertransference for granted and describe the uses to which they put it, as Bion (1967) does in his account of his work with psychotics.

Our changing views on countertransference are, in part, related to changes in our views on transference. Originally, the analyst was seen as a mirror *onto* which the patient projects his internal figures and to whom he then reacts. As Enid Balint put it succinctly in a paper read in the British Society, "We now have a more three-dimensional view of the transference". We do not think of the patient projecting *onto* but, rather *into* the analyst. This view assumes that transference is rooted in primitive pre-verbal infantile experience and is consistent with the Kleinian concept of projective identification. We see the patient not only as perceiving the analyst in a distorted way, reacting to this distorted view, and communicating these reactions to the analyst, but also as doing things to the analyst's mind, projecting *into* the analyst in a way that affects the analyst.

We are all familiar with the concepts of acting in, which can happen in quite a gross way; I speak here, however, not of gross acting but of something constantly present—a non-verbal constant interaction in which the patient acts on the analyst's mind. This non-verbal activity takes many forms. It may be underlying and integrated with other forms of communication, giving them depth and emotional resonance. It may be the predominant form of communication, coming from pre-verbal experiences that can only be communicated in that way. Or it may be meant as an attack on communication; though when understood, even this can be converted into communication. Of course, all communication contains an element of desire for action. We communicate in order to produce some effect on the other person's mind; but the degree to which action occurs, whether non-verbal or apparently verbal (using words to act rather than to communicate), varies enormously from situation to situation and patient to patient. As a general rule, the nearer we are to the psychotic processes, the more this kind of acting takes precedence over symbolic or verbal communication. If we look at transference in this way, it then becomes quite clear that what Freud describes as free-floating attention refers not only to intellectual openness of mind, but also to a particular openness of feelings—allowing our feelings, our mind to be affected by the patient to a far greater degree than we allow ourselves to be affected in normal social intercourse—a point stressed by Paula Heimann (1950).

By speaking of these free-floating feelings in the analyst, am I saying that there is no difference between transference and countertransference? I hope I am not saying anything of the kind, because at the same time as the analyst is opening his mind freely to his impressions, he has to maintain distance from his own feelings and reactions to the patient. He has to observe his own reactions, to conclude from them, to use his own state of mind for the understanding of the patient but at no point be swayed by his own emotions. The analyst's capacity to contain the feelings aroused in him by the patient can be seen as an equivalent to the function of a mother containing the infant's projections, to use Bion's model (1967). Where the parents react instinctively, however, the analyst subjects his state of mind to an examination—a reflection, albeit much of the time preconscious.

In the past we have thought of an ideal analyst as cold, objective, having no feelings, etc. Am I presenting here, in the analyst's perfect containment, a similarly unattainable ideal? I think so. This would be an idealization of the analyst's capacity. In fact, this capacity for containment can be breached in many ways. There is a whole area of the patient's pathology (I am ignoring for the moment the analyst's pathology), which specifically aims at disrupting this situation of containment, such as invasion of the analyst's mind in a seductive or aggressive way, creating confusion and anxiety, and attacking links in the analyst's mind. We have to try to turn this situation to good account and learn about the interaction between the patient and ourselves from the very fact that our containment has been disturbed. It is from such disturbances in the analyst's capacity to function that one first gets an inkling of such psychotic processes as, for instance, attacks on links, again a subject with vast literature.

There is a particular countertransference difficulty (described also by Grinberg [1962] as projective counteridentification) produced by some patients who, as infants, have themselves been subjected to heavy parental projections. I shall give an example here from the second session with a patient—a mild example of the kind of thing I have in mind. In the first session the patient had spoken about the various ways in which she felt she had been a great disappointment to her parents and to herself. In the following session she seemed extremely depressed, spoke in a hardly audible voice, and went on at fairly great length describing how terrible she felt. She was depressed, she felt dead, terribly weak, she had an awful headache, perhaps it was due to her period which was about to start. The session went on for a time, and I felt unduly affected by it. I wondered whether I had done something wrong in the previous session. I felt helpless and very eager to understand her. In answer to a question the patient said that, no, she did not usually have headaches with her periods, but her mother had that symptom. I knew that at that point the patient was identifying with her mother, but somehow this knowledge did not help, and I felt that there would not be much point in interpreting it to her. I was more puzzled by my own overreaction and slowly came to realize that now I felt that I was a disappointment both to her and to myself. I was in the position of a helpless and rather bewildered child, weighed down by projections coming from a depressed mother, and it was an interpretation emphasizing that aspect which produced a change in the situation.

Later on the patient related that she had perfect pitch, but that although she was trained and encouraged and apparently gifted enough to become a soloist, she could never do it and so had specialized as an accompanist. When she was a child, her mother sang, and she used to accompany her on the piano. It seemed to me that this patient had developed perfect pitch for her mother's depression and found a way of getting on with her some of the time, but only as an accompanist. I also understood that my quite unwarranted concern in the second session that I did not understand my patient perfectly arose because, somehow, she managed to make me feel, right at the start, that I must now be the child with the perfect pitch. I shall return to the problem of the perfect pitch. This situation can be compared and contrasted with a much more violent though similar one.

The patient mentioned earlier, who complained of unpopularity, was particularly able to disrupt my capacity to function. The experience of closeness with her has been an experience of almost unceasing discomfort or pain. She has evoked anxiety, confusion, guilt, anger, irritation; occasions on which I felt more relaxed were dangerous. I was immediately and unexpectedly assaulted in some way or other. Her stream of accusations was almost incessant. This patient is the child of parents who had hated one another at the time of her birth. So far as I can reconstruct, from infancy on she was flooded with extreme anxiety by her mother (an anxiety neurotic) and with the hatred derivative of her mother's hatred for her father. The father, on the other hand, a near psychotic, flooded her with either aggressive accusations or gross sexuality. She described how once she was older and her parents divorced, her father would pour accusations and complaints about her mother at her and how, when she was with her mother, the mother on a few occasions pinned her to the armchair and made her listen to violent attacks on the father. This latter situation probably reproduced what was originally a non-verbal but violent experience of projection from both parents. In the countertransference, it may be this experience that she tried to inflict on me, often with success. I frequently felt with her that I was pinned into my armchair and forced to listen to violent outpourings of accusations against some third person. I felt attacked; I did not want to hear them, and could not defend myself against them. The experience is not that of a parent bombarded by infantile projections, but of an infant bombarded by overpowering projections, often beyond its understanding. This lends to the countertransference feelings of a particular kind of helplessness, and there is always a danger of reacting by withdrawal, omnipotence, hatred of the patient, etc.—in other words, of mobilizing our own infantile defences against helplessness. We are all familiar, of course, with patients reversing roles and putting us in the position of a helpless child. But here I think is an infrequent added dimension. This patient is a borderline case, and her method of projecting infantile experiences into the analyst may be what protects her from psychosis.

The cases of these two patients may be compared and contrasted. From the "unpopular" patient it is exceedingly difficult to obtain any kind of non-destructive communication. In defending herself against projections, she projects violence and in turn experiences her objects as projecting it back in a vicious circle of increasing distress and violence. The first patient, the one with the perfect pitch, had obviously developed some kind of satisfactory communication with her mother, albeit one based on a split and at great cost to her own personality (becoming an accompanist).

But I knew that her perfect pitch would cause other big problems. One was her expectation, projected into me, that I, too, should have perfect pitch (hence my discomfort in the second session). Another was the early indication of her perfect pitch in relation to me. In the third session she spotted some minor change in my expression—one unnoticed by other patients. If we think of the transference/countertransference situation as an interaction, we must take into account that the patient's perceptions of us are not all projections. Patients do, indeed, react to aspects of our personalities, changes of mood, etc., whether these are a direct response to their material or come from some other source, and patients with perfect pitch present a particular problem in that way. I think this perfect pitch is a function of the patient's dependence. It is the extremely dependent patient who develops an unusual sensitivity to the slightest change in the analyst's attitude. Usually, the pitch is only selectively perfect. We are all familiar with the misleading perfect pitch of the paranoid patient, who most correctly perceives anything negative and is totally blind to any evidence of positive attitudes, or with that of the depressive patient, who is most sensitive to any sign of weakness or illness. Be that as it may, one must be aware of the patient's pitch, or responsiveness to what comes from us, and not deny it in ourselves. I am not advocating here breast-beating or confessions of countertransference, just awareness of the nature of the interaction and recognition of it in the interpretation.

Of course, all this is easier said than done. I have noticed that when people speak of transference, they recognize that the major part of the transference is unconscious, while, when speaking of countertransference, they apparently speak as though countertransference referred only to the analyst's conscious feelings. Of course, the major part of the countertransference, like the transference, is always unconscious. What we do become aware of are conscious derivatives. The way I visualize it is that at depth, when our countertransference is, say, in a good functional state, we have a dual relation to the patient: one is receptive, containing and understanding the patient's communication; the other is active, producing or giving understanding, knowledge, or structure to the patient in the interpretation. It might be analogous to the breast as containing and the nipple as feeding, or to the maternal/paternal functions. This does not exclude our own infantile experience, since our capacity to perceive and contain infantile parts of the patient depends on our capacity to contain the infant part of ourselves. We must not, however, equate that analytic function with the parental function. We give over part of our mind to this experience with the patient, but we also remain detached from it as professional analysts, using professional skills to assess the interaction between the patient and the parental parts of ourselves. In other words, we are deeply affected and involved but, paradoxically, uninvolved in a way unimaginable between an actual good parent and a child. When our countertransference works that way, it gives rise to a phenomenon called empathy or psychoanalytic intuition or feeling in touch. It is a guide to understanding. When breaches in this attitude occur, we become aware of disruption in our analytic functioning, and we must, in turn, try to understand the nature of the disruption and the information it gives us about our interaction with the patient. When such disruptions occur, there is always an internal pressure to identify with our countertransference, and it is very important to be aware that countertransference is the best of servants but the worst of masters, and that the pressure to identify with it and act it out in ways either obvious or very subtle and hidden is always powerful.

Countertransference has become a very abused concept, and many analytic sins have been committed in its name. In particular, rationalizations are found for acting under the pressure of countertransference, rather than using it as a guide to understanding. I often find myself telling supervisees that countertransference is no excuse; saying that the patient "projected it into me", or "he made me angry", or "he put me under such seductive pressure" must be clearly recognized as statements of failure to understand and use the counter-transference constructively. I do not contend here that we must—or, indeed, can—be perfect, merely that we will not learn from our failures unless we clearly recognize them as such.

# CHAPTER TWO

# The analytic management and interpretation of projective identification

*Thomas H. Ogden*

Projective identification is *not* a metapsychological concept. The phenomena it describes exist in the realm of thoughts, feelings, and behaviour, *not* in the realm of abstract beliefs about the workings of the mind. Whether or not one uses the term or is cognizant of the concept of projective identification, clinically one continually bumps up against the phenomena to which it refers—unconscious projective fantasies in association with the evocation of congruent feelings in others. Resistance on the part of therapists and analysts to thinking about these phenomena is understandable: it is unsettling to imagine experiencing feelings and thinking thoughts that are in an important sense not entirely one's own. And yet, the lack of a vocabulary with which to think about this class of phenomena seriously interferes with the therapist's capacity to understand, manage, and interpret the transference. Projective identification is a concept that addresses the way in which

Based on articles originally published in Thomas H. Ogden, *Projective Identification and Psychotherapeutic Technique* (New York: Jason Aronson, 1982). Reprinted by permission of the author.

feeling-states corresponding to the unconscious fantasies of one person (the projector) are engendered in and processed by another person (the recipient)—that is, the way in which one person makes use of another person to experience and contain an aspect of himself. The projector has the primarily unconscious fantasy of getting rid of an unwanted or endangered part of himself (including internal objects) and of depositing that part in another person in a powerfully controlling way (Klein, 1946, 1955). The projected part of the self is felt to be partially lost and to be inhabiting the other person. In association with this unconscious projective fantasy there is an interpersonal interaction by means of which the recipient is pressured to think, feel, and behave in a manner congruent with the ejected feelings and the self—and object—representations embodied in the projective fantasy (Bion, 1959; Ogden, 1979). In other words, the recipient is pressured to engage in an identification with a specific, disowned aspect of the projector.

The recipient may be able to live with such induced feelings and manage them within the context of his own larger personality system—for example, by mastery through understanding or integration with more reality-based self-representations. In such a case, the projector may constructively reinternalize by introjection and identification aspects of the recipient's handling of the induced feelings. On the other hand, the recipient may be unable to live with the induced feelings and may handle such feelings by means of denial, projection, omnipotent idealization, further projective identification, or actions aimed at tension relief, such as violence, sexual activity, or distancing behaviour. In these cases the projector would be confirmed in his belief that his feelings and fantasies were indeed dangerous and unbearable. Through identification with the recipient's pathological handling of the feelings involved, the original pathology of the projector would be further consolidated or expanded (Langs, 1976a).

The concept of projective identification by no means constitutes an entire theory of therapy, nor does it involve a departure from the main body of psychoanalytic theory and technique. It does go significantly beyond what is ordinarily referred to as transference, wherein the patient distorts his view of the therapist while directing toward the therapist the same feelings that he held towards an earlier person in his life (Freud, 1912b, 1914g, 1915a). In projective identification, not only does the patient view the therapist in a distorted way that is determined by the patient's past object relations; in addition, pressure is exerted on the therapist to experience himself in a way that is congruent with the patient's unconscious fantasy.

Projective identification provides a clinical-level theory that may be of value to therapists in their efforts to organize and render meaningful the relationship between their own experience (feelings, thoughts, perceptions) and the transference. It will be seen in the discussion of clinical material that from the perspective of projective identification many of the stalemates and dead-ends of therapy become data for the study of the transference and a medium through which the makeup of the patient's internal object world is communicated.

The concept of projective identification integrates statements about unconscious fantasy, interpersonal pressure, and the response of a separate personality system to a set of engendered feelings. Projective identification is in part a statement about an interpersonal interaction (the pressure of one person on another to comply with a projective fantasy) and in part a statement about individual mental activity (projective fantasies, introjective fantasies, psychological processing). Most fundamentally, however, it is a statement about the dynamic interplay of the two—the intrapsychic and the interpersonal. The usefulness of many existing psychoanalytic propositions is limited because they address the intrapsychic sphere exclusively and fail to afford a bridge between that sphere and the interpersonal interactions that provide the principal data of the therapy.

The schizophrenic patient—and, to a lesser extent and intensity, all patients in an interpersonal setting—are almost continually involved in the unconscious process of enlisting others to enact with them scenes from their internal object world (Rosenfeld, 1965; Searles, 1963). The role assigned to the therapist may be the role of the self or the object, in a particular relationship to one another (Racker, 1957, 1968). The internal object relationship from which these roles are derived is a psychological construct of the patient's generated on the basis of realistic perceptions and understandings of present and past object relationships, misunderstandings of interpersonal reality inherent in the infant's or child's primitive, immature perception of himself and others, distortions determined by predominant fantasies; and distortions determined by the nature of the patient's present modes of organizing experience and thinking, for example, by splitting and fragmentation.

If we imagine for a moment that the patient is both the director and one of the principal actors in the interpersonal enactment of an internal object relationship, and that the therapist is an unwitting actor in the same drama, then projective identification is the process whereby the therapist is given stage directions for a particular role. In this analogy it must be borne in mind that the therapist has not volunteered to play a part and only retrospectively comes to understand that he has been playing a role in the patient's enactment of an aspect of his inner world.

The therapist who has to some extent allowed himself to be moulded by this interpersonal pressure and is able to observe these changes in himself has access to a very rich source of data about the patient's internal world—the induced set of thoughts and feelings that are experientially alive, vivid, and immediate. Yet, they are also extremely elusive and difficult to formulate verbally because the information is in the form of an enactment in which the therapist is participating, and not in the form of words and images upon which the therapist can readily reflect.

The concept of projective identification offers the therapist a way of integrating his understanding of his own internal experience with that which he is perceiving in the patient. Such an integrated perspective is particularly necessary in work with schizophrenic patients because it safeguards the therapist's psychological equilibrium in the face of what sometimes feels like a barrage of chaotic psychological debris emanating from the patient. The schizophrenic's talk is often a mockery of communication, serving purposes quite foreign to ordinary talk and often completely antithetical to thought itself.

Terrific psychological strain is entailed in the therapist's efforts to resist the temptation to denigrate and dismiss his own thoughts while the schizophrenic patient is attacking his and the therapist's capacity to think. Problems involving im-

pairment of the capacity to think are far from abstract philosophical questions for the therapist sitting for long periods of
time with the schizophrenic patient. The therapist finds that
his own ability to think, perceive, and understand even the
most basic therapeutic matters becomes worn down and stag-
nant in the course of his work. Not infrequently the therapist
recognizes that he is unable to bring a single fresh thought or
feeling to his work with the patient.

When such therapeutic impasses continue unaltered, the
strain within the therapist often mounts to an intolerable level
and can culminate in the therapist's fleeing from the patient by
shortening the sessions (because "thirty minutes is all the
patient can make use of"), or terminating the therapy (because
"the patient is not sufficiently psychologically minded to profit
from psychotherapy"), or offering "supportive therapy" that
consists of an exclusively administrative task-oriented interaction with the patient. Alternatively, the therapist may retaliate
against the patient directly (for example, in the form of intrusive "deep interpretations") or indirectly (for example, by means
of emotional withdrawal, breaches of confidentiality, "accidental" lateness to sessions, increases of medication, and so on).

It is easy to be scornful of such behaviour on the part of the
therapist, but defensive counter-therapeutic activity in one
form or another is inevitable in any sustained intensive therapeutic work with a schizophrenic patient. If these forms of
countertransference acting out are scrutinized by the therapist
and prevented from becoming established as accepted aspects
of therapy, they usually do not result in irreparable damage to
the therapy. This is not to condone countertransference acting
out on the part of the therapist. But it should be acknowledged
that in the course of intensive psychotherapy with disturbed
patients the therapist will find himself saying things that he
regrets. Such errors are rarely talked about with colleagues
and almost never reported in the literature. [Clearly, I am not
referring here to actual sexual or aggressive activity on the part
of the therapist. These represent extremes that indicate that
the therapy is entirely out of control. In such circumstances the
patient should be referred to another professional, and it is
hoped that the therapist will recognize the need to obtain treatment for himself.] However, from the perspective of projective

identification, a given error also represents a specific construction that could only have been generated in precisely the way that it was by means of an interaction between this therapist and this patient at this moment in the therapy. The task of the therapist is not simply to eliminate errors or deviations, but to formulate the nature of the specific psychological and interpersonal meanings that have led the therapist to feel and behave in this particular fashion. As will be seen, much of the clinical material presented in this paper involves analysis of facets of the therapist's behaviour and feelings that reflect confusion, anger, frustration, fear, jealousy, self-protectiveness, and so forth, and that no doubt at times constitute therapeutic errors. These feelings, thoughts, and actions are analysed from the perspective of projective identification in such a way as to allow the therapist not only to acknowledge his own contribution to the interpersonal field but also to understand the ways in which his own feelings and behaviour (including his errors) may reflect a specific facet of the transference.

## Projective identification and analytic technique

As with the concept of transference, projective identification provides a context for understanding clinical phenomena but does not dictate a specific technique with which the therapist communicates his understanding. Kleinian, the British Middle Group, and classical analysts are in agreement on the centrality of the concept of transference to psychoanalytic work; nevertheless, the technique employed by each of these groups in the analysis of the transference varies significantly. Similarly, the concept of projective identification provides a framework for thinking about the clinical phenomena occurring in psychotherapy and psychoanalysis, but the therapist's mode of intervention will be determined by an additional set of principles constituting this theory of technique: the clinical material that should be addressed first (conscious, preconscious, or unconscious, defence or wish, surface or depth, early or late developmental level, etc.); the timing of the intervention; the form of the intervention (verbal interpretation, confrontation, clarification, questions, silent interpretation, alteration in management of the framework of the therapy, etc.).

Despite the fact that a specific therapeutic technique is not intrinsic to the concept of projective identification, an understanding of the therapeutic process is inherent in the concept. The idea that there is something therapeutic about the therapist's containment of the patient's projective identifications is based upon an interpersonal conception of individual psychological growth: one learns from (in fantasy, "takes in qualities of") another person on the basis of interactions in which the projector ultimately takes back (reinternalizes) an aspect of himself that has been integrated and slightly modified by the recipient. The patient learns from that which was his to begin with. In discussing psychoanalytic technique, Freud (1913c) proposed a similar idea about that which the patient can take in from the analyst's interpretations. He stated that the analyst should not offer an interpretation until the patient "is already too close to it that he has only one short step more to make in order to get hold of the explanation himself" (p. 140).

The therapeutic technique for the handling of projective identification discussed in this chapter is designed to make available to the patient in a slightly modified form that which was already his but had been formerly unusable for purposes of integration and psychological growth. At certain junctures in a psychotherapy this goal is best achieved by means of verbal interpretation. Some of the factors that determine when one is at such a point in therapy will be discussed in this paper, as well as some of the forms such interpretation may take. However, verbal interpretation is not the only way in which the therapeutic goal outlined above is achieved, even in work with relatively healthy patients. For parts of our work with more disturbed patients, verbal interpretation will play a relatively small role. [It should be kept in mind that even if a non-interpretive approach is taken for portions of a therapy, the work may still be psychoanalytic: in discussing the history of the psychoanalytic movement, Freud (1914d), stated that in his view a therapy is psychoanalytic if it takes as its starting point an understanding of transference and resistance.]

In work with patients who are dealing predominantly with whole-object-related forms of transference, the therapist's well-timed verbal interpretation will frequently constitute the needed modification of that which was already an aspect of the patient. [The term "whole object" refers to one's experience of another person as separate from oneself (i.e. having life as well as feelings and thoughts that are independent of oneself) and continuing to be that same person despite shifts in one's feelings about the other person. The term "part object" refers to a more primitive perception of another person. Aspects of the object are experienced as existing autonomously. For example, the frustrating aspect of the mother is experienced as constituting a person that is distinct from the nurturing aspect of the mother. The object is not experienced as entirely separate from oneself and is usually felt to be within one's omnipotent control—e.g., the object can be magically destroyed and re-created.] However, when the patient is dealing with preverbal part-object-related forms of transference, verbal interpretations are often experienced as alien and having little to do with the patient. This is true not only of incorrect or poorly timed interpretations, but of any and all attempts to use language for the purpose of understanding meanings. That endeavour (to understand personal meanings) in itself is taken as the hallmark of the therapist and therefore not a reflection of the patient. Under such circumstances, the patient is faced with the dilemma of either (1) attempting to retain a sense of connectedness with the therapist by introjecting the interpretation, even though he does not feel as if it is his own, or (2) rejecting the interpretation, at the risk of feeling utterly alone and disconnected from the therapist. Usually when the patient internalizes the interpretation in an undigested form, he will feel that he has been forced to, or has chosen to, give up his own individual existence and instead has become the therapist in a literal way. Often the patient will at some point (frequently after termination or disruption of therapy) renounce the therapist as dangerous, self-serving, annihilating, and so forth.

Patients who have responded to verbal interpretation by having to ward off the therapist even at the price of feeling completely detached from him often seem to the therapist so walled-off and thickly defended that the therapist experiences corresponding feelings of isolation, frustration, and futility.

Even the most accurate, well-dosed, and well-timed interventions seem to make no difference to the patient. Other patients gratefully accept the therapist's interpretations and seem not only to understand them but to build upon them; it is thus all the more disappointing for the therapist to admit to himself after years of work that the patient has not changed (Khan, 1969; Winnicott, 1963).

It must be borne in mind that the perspective of projective identification neither requires nor excludes the use of verbal interpretation; the therapist attempts to find a way of talking with and being with the patient that will constitute a medium through which the therapist may accept unintegrable aspects of the patient's internal object world and return them to the patient in a form that the patient can accept and learn from.

The comments that follow about psychotherapeutic technique are in no sense meant as prescriptions; instead, they are intended to illustrate ways of working within the framework delineated by the understanding of the relationship between projective identification and psychological change that has just been discussed. [In this chapter I address only patient-initiated projective identifications; I have elsewhere discussed the management of therapist-initiated projective identifications (Ogden, 1982, ch. 6).]

## Clinical recognition of projective identification

In the clinical application of the concept of projective identification, one question that arises is: How does the therapist know when he has become the recipient of the patient's projective identification? It should certainly be considered as a possibility when the therapist begins to suspect that he has developed an intensely held but highly limited view of himself and the patient that is in an important sense shared by the patient. In other words, the therapist discovers that he has been playing a role in one of the patient's unconscious fantasies (Bion, 1959). This "discovery" is necessarily to some extent a retrospective judgement, since the therapist's unconscious participation in this interpersonal construction must precede its recognition.

Because of the therapist's unconscious participation in projective identification, the meaning of this type of intrapsychic–interpersonal event is usually not easy to discern and is more easily perceived and understood by those outside it (for example, by consultants and colleagues). The therapist's task of disentangling himself from a patient's projective identification can at times involve the pain of acknowledging to himself that he has been "drawn into" an enactment of aspects of the patient's pathology.

An experienced therapist had been treating an adolescent patient on a long-term inpatient unit for about 18 months when he presented his work at a case conference. He concluded from his experience with the patient that she could not be helped because of her intense need to defeat and punish herself. This need was enacted in an endless series of suicidal gestures and extended elopements from the hospital, as well as bizarre and potentially dangerous sexual exhibitionism and promiscuity. The therapist emphasized the "reality" that persistence in treating this patient would be a misuse of a hospital bed, which could be better utilized by another patient. Furthermore, the hospital itself might suffer if treatment of the patient were continued because of the risk of adverse publicity from the patient's sexual and self-destructive behaviour. The therapist stated this to the conference with conviction and with a feeling of having resigned himself to the inevitable transfer of the patient to a state hospital. There was visible dismay and considerable impatience displayed by the therapist when the inevitability of the patient's transfer was questioned by fellow staff members.

Much of the first 18 months of therapy had consisted of a powerful communication by means of evocation of feelings in the therapist. In order to feel any degree of connectedness with the therapist, this patient felt it necessary that the therapist feel her feelings, have her "knowledge" that the deepest truth (in reality, a partial truth) about the patient was that she could never be helped because her insanity would consume and defeat anyone who dared to come within its range. The therapist had become the receptacle for these feelings and experienced them not only as his own, but as indelible and absolute truth.

In the course of the discussion, the therapist was gradually able to understand the therapeutic impasse as an externalization by the patient of a powerfully influential set of internalized early object relations, in which the patient's mother had viewed the patient as the embodiment of her own primitive insane self and as an immediate threat to her own fragilely held sanity.

An ongoing dialogue with a supervisor, consultant, or colleague is often an indispensable adjunct to work with very disturbed patients because of the difficulty of the psychological work entailed in the process of recognizing one's unconscious participation in a patient's projective identification. The development of this type of unconsciously shared, inflexible, largely unquestioned view of oneself in relation to the patient is one of the hallmarks of projective identification.

The therapist's experience while serving as an object of a borderline or schizophrenic patient's projective identification may be contrasted with the experience of treating relatively well integrated patients. In the treatment of relatively healthy patients, the therapist is frequently able to maintain a flexible and relatively detached psychological state of "evenly suspended attention" (Freud, 1912e), although I feel that it is a myth that even quite healthy neurotic patients routinely allow the therapist such freedom. The therapist of the neurotic patient does at times experience an emotional distance from the patient that allows him to listen with the secure knowledge that he does not share in the patient's feelings, ideas, and problems. The therapist has the freedom to try out one identification and then another—for example, identifying for a time with the patient as he recounts an incident in which he has been subtly sadistic to his child and then, moments later, with the child's attempts to deny and defuse the hostility of the parent. Having tried on for size successive aspects of what the neurotic patient is feeling and thinking, the therapist is free to focus his attention (and at times the patient's attention) upon one facet or another of the clinical material.

The following segment from the psychotherapy of a successful businessman in his late thirties demonstrates qualities of a therapeutic relationship in which the therapist is able to view the patient from a secure and reliable psychological distance, that is, from a vantage point of clear self-object differentiation.

The patient, Mr B, suffering from a neurotic fear of death as well as other obsessional thoughts, had several days earlier been informed that the advertising agency where he had worked for over 11 years would be folding. After receiving the news, the patient cried during much of each session and said that he did not know what he would do or how he would support himself and his family. "Certainly I won't be able to continue to pay for therapy." In addition to the reality-based components of the patient's thoughts and feelings, the therapist recognized irrational transference elements in what was occurring.

During his childhood, Mr B had elicited anxious concern from his ordinarily very busy mother, an internist, by means of psychosomatic illnesses, phobias, and other forms of distress. The therapist understood the present situation in part as a transference re-enactment in which the patient was attempting to elicit a display of concern from the therapist whom the patient now viewed as cold and self-absorbed. The therapist, although not unmoved by the patient, did not feel any urgent need to comfort him. It was not difficult for the therapist to direct his attention to the task of interpreting the patient's need to repeat with the therapist an infantile form of relatedness that the patient, through previous work in the therapy, had already come some distance in understanding and relinquishing.

The distortion of the patient's view of the therapist represented a projection of aspects of his unconscious conception of his mother onto his current perception of the therapist. Had this been a projective identification, the patient would have unconsciously attempted to change not only his view of the therapist but also the therapist himself. There would have been considerable interpersonal pressure exerted on the therapist to engage in a less well differentiated form of relatedness and to share in the patient's distress (as his mother had), as if the loss of the job were as much the therapist's problem as the patient's. The therapist might have begun to feel moved to give advice or consider lowering the fee in order to "save the therapy". In the therapy of the neurotic patient being described, the therapist could rely on the patient's ability to observe and understand the wishes underlying his plaintive form of relatedness to the therapist. The patient himself was eventually able to point out the way he had preconsciously kept information from the therapist that would have made it clear that the patient's prospects were not nearly as bleak as he made them seem.

The following vignette, from the psychotherapy of a borderline patient, focuses on the therapist's task of recognizing his participation as the recipient of the patient's projective identification, as well as on his efforts to make use of this awareness in determining the content and timing of his interventions.

Mr C, an unmarried 29-year-old man, had been in psychotherapy three times per week for about a month. At that time he was functioning well as a stockbroker, although he had had two psychotic episodes during college, both requiring brief hospitalizations.

The patient had struggled for most of his life with feelings of "losing himself" in his father. The father would take intense interest in many of the patient's activities (Little League, science projects, homework, girl-friends, etc.), to the point that the patient lost the feeling of the activity being in any sense his own. For a period of four years following his second psychotic break, it had been necessary for Mr C to sever all ties with his father in order to maintain a sense of his own separate identity. The patient's mother was described in sparse detail and referred to simply as "a shadow" of her husband.

At the beginning of the second month of therapy, a senior member of the brokerage house where the patient was working, a man who had been a mentor for the patient, rather suddenly left the firm to accept a position in another city. The patient began to fill each session with talk that sounded like free association, but had the effect of forcibly crowding the therapist out. Mr C's speech was pressured and did not invite, or leave a moment's pause for, any kind of comment by the therapist. After several weeks the patient told the therapist that he had seen him on the street in front of his office talking with someone whom he believed to be a colleague of the therapist. Mr C said that the therapist looked awkward, self-conscious, and weak. Mr C imagined that the colleague was more competent and successful than the therapist, and that the therapist was getting advice of some sort from the colleague. The patient said he felt guilty for saying this to the therapist and did not want to hurt him, but that was the way he felt.

The therapist, although not usually rattled by insults from his patients, began to feel increasingly uneasy as time went on. He began to feel that his voice sounded thin when the patient allowed him an opportunity to speak. Mr C reported that he felt "very macho" during the sessions and felt guilty about the "fact" that he was more athletic and handsome than the therapist and could probably beat him at any sport. This denigration of the therapist as weak, unattractive, and emasculated continued over the succeeding weeks. These ideas were no longer labelled as feelings and came to be treated as objective facts. The subtle process of twisting reality was a more potent interpersonal force than the overt insults. The therapist was aware that feelings of weakness vis-à-vis his own father had been rekindled by this interaction with the patient. As the therapist experienced these feelings, he had the fantasy that the patient would eventually find him so ineffectual that he would leave in search of a new therapist. At this point the therapist attributed this fantasy to his conflicts related to his own father and explored with himself where things stood at present in that regard. The therapist decided not to intervene until he had a better grasp of the transference meaning of what was occurring.

About three months into the therapy, the therapist began to become aware of something that he had formerly only been preconsciously aware of: the patient had made no reference to his former mentor at work since he had initially spoken about the man's sudden departure. Mr C had not made a great deal of the event when first presenting it. However, as the therapist thought more about the changes that had taken place in the patient over the previous two months, and the powerful countertransference feelings of inadequacy and emasculation, he began to consider the possibility that his own feelings had been to a large extent evoked by the patient as a component of a projective identification that involved the patient's feelings of inadequacy in relation to a paternal transference figure. Although the details of this projective identification were still to be elucidated, the therapist found that the perspective of projective identification had already begun to release him from the previous countertransference pressure that he had been experiencing and allowed him to create psychological room within which he could now think about what was occurring in the transference.

It is apparent in the foregoing account that it was not possible for the therapist to observe comfortably the unfolding of the patient's conflicted paternal transference in the therapy, which was being expressed in part via a projection onto the mentor and in part through the transference. Instead, the therapist found himself in the midst of a stressful and confusing development wherein he felt intensely inadequate and ashamed of the sound of his own voice. When a therapist finds himself shaken in this way, he is very probably serving as the recipient of a projective identification. The therapist was aware that feelings of weakness had an important history in his own life and was able to consider the developments in his current life that might have contributed to an intensification of this conflict. However, the perspective of projective identification allowed the therapist to make use of his feeling-state to inform his understanding of the transference and not simply to further his understanding of himself or to prevent his own conflicts from interfering with the therapy.

Once one has begun to formulate an interaction in terms of projective identification, it is often useful to refrain from interpreting or intervening until one has lived with the evoked feelings for some time. For example, the therapist did not attempt to alleviate the discomfort arising from feelings of inadequacy by immediately interpreting the hostility (which was clearly present) in the patient's denigrating comments about the therapist. It was only by containing these feelings in the therapeutic situation that the therapist was able to allow associative linkages to emerge in his own mind clearly enough to be recognized and thought about. Frequently, the psychological strain from the evoked feelings diminishes, and the therapist is able to gain psychological distance when these feelings are recognized as components of a projective identification.

Before this distance has been achieved, however, the therapist's interventions are likely to be motivated by conscious and unconscious efforts to get the patient to stop doing whatever it is that he is doing that is leading to the therapist's feelings of being controlled or attacked or strangulated or imprisoned or paralysed. These countertransference feelings represent only a few of the more common unconscious fantasies evoked in the therapist while he is serving as the recipient of a projective identification.

## Interpretation of projective identification

Mr C's psychotherapy illustrates certain technical principles that come into play once the therapist has successfully begun to formulate an interaction in terms of projective identification.

When the therapist felt he understood at least one level of the patient's current defensive activity, he commented that Mr C had said very little about his mentor, Mr J, and that this had been particularly true since Mr J had left the firm. The patient described how Mr J had taken great interest in him and at one point had sided with the patient on a major protocol dispute at considerable risk to his own position in the firm. Mr C felt that Mr J had been able to see something in him that no one else had been able to recognize. The patient added that he had hardly noticed Mr J's absence and that a colleague at work had accurately pointed out that Mr J had had more charm than brains.

Mr C then returned to talking in a pressured, hypermasculine way with continued indirect reference to the now-accepted perception of the therapist as weak and inadequate. It was becoming clear to the therapist that the patient was having great difficulty accepting the loss of Mr J and that projective identification involving fantasized extrusion of the weak and abandoned self was being used in part as a defence against feelings of loss and disappointment.

The therapist listened for several more sessions in order to be sure that subsequent material supported this hypothesis. The therapist then made use of one of many available opportunities to comment on the way in which the patient had accepted as fact the therapist's physical and professional inadequacy. Mr C was at first somewhat surprised to have such a basic aspect of reality called into question. As he thought further about it, though, he was somewhat surprised by the way he had been thinking and acting. He reiterated that during the past weeks he had been feeling "very macho" and that it had felt so good to feel that way that he hated to talk about the subject because it might interfere with that feeling.

The therapist said that he thought that when Mr J left the agency, the patient had felt as if a valuable part of himself had been lost, the part that only Mr J had been able to appreciate. The patient confirmed this and said that he had felt empty in a very literal way. He said that when he heard the news, the first thing he did was to go to the candy machine in the basement of the building and buy several candy bars and eat them "almost in one mouthful". He said that, oddly enough, this failed to make him feel full, but he had decided not to eat any more because he began to feel nauseated. Later in the session the therapist said that he thought that Mr C now felt left with the dregs of himself and was trying to rid himself of these feelings by viewing the therapist as the weak, ineffectual person that the patient now felt himself to be. Mr C said that he felt embarrassed to say this because it sounded so childish, but he had wished to be Mr J's son and that he had frequently daydreamed about being a member of his family. For the first time in two months there were reflective silences in the session.

During the succeeding session, the patient reported a dream. In that dream Mr C was in a barber-shop having his hair cut when suddenly he noticed that too much had been taken off, and he sobbed as he stared at the hair on the floor. Mr C associated the hair with Mr J's greying hair. This had been of concern to the patient, since it reflected Mr J's age and the danger of his dying. Also, the hair was associated with the story of Samson, "who lost his strength when his hair was cut off". The relation of the dream to the projective identification that had been interpreted was clear to the patient: in fantasy, a part of himself that was mixed up with Mr J had been lost, and only now was the sadness being felt. (Hair is a particularly apt symbol, in that it is simultaneously a part of self and not-self. This ambiguity was utilized in the dream to express a similar relation to Mr J and to the therapist.) Clearly, still another level of the dream involved the idea of having been emasculated by castration as represented by the haircut, the Samson legend, and so forth. This level of meaning bore directly on the feeling of emasculation evoked in the therapist in the course of the projective identification under discussion.

The therapist had laid the groundwork for an interpretation of the projective identification by calling into question the "fact" of the therapist's weakness. Without this initial differentiation of the fantasy component of projective identification from reality, the patient's understanding of the interaction would probably not have been possible. As long as the therapist is the weak self, the patient cannot consider the way in which the idea of the weak therapist serves as a defence against feelings of inadequacy. The distortion of a specific aspect of reality is an important interpersonal means by which pressure is exerted on the object to see himself in a way that conforms with the patient's unconscious projective fantasy. Focusing upon this alteration of reality is often a crucial preparatory step for the interpretation of a projective identification.

The interpretation that was eventually offered involved explicit reference to: the patient's unconscious conception of a loss of a valued part of himself that had resulted from Mr J's departure; the defensive fantasy of locating the weak self in the therapist; and the reality of the interpersonal interaction by means of which these fantasies were enacted.

The patient's enhanced capacity to experience feelings of loss as represented in the dream, served as a partial validation for the interpretation. Equally important was the change in the relationship to the therapist that followed the intervention. The patient's increased capacity to tolerate thoughtful silences afforded the therapist the opportunity to formulate his own thoughts and to intervene at times. It meant that the therapist no longer had to be so tightly controlled and so urgently kept at arm's length by means of the patient's verbal flooding of the sessions. The projective identification described served as a defence not only against feelings of loss in relation to Mr J, but also (and perhaps even more difficult for the patient) the anxiety of beginning therapy. He was particularly fearful of a type of involvement with the therapist that could potentially lead to painful and conflicted paternal transferences, including feelings of melting into the father and intense castration anxiety.

## Technical problems of containment

I would now like to focus on the psychological work involved in serving therapeutically as a recipient of the patient's projective identifications. Processing the projective identification without acting upon the engendered feelings is an essential aspect of the therapeutic process (Heimann, 1950; Malin & Grotstein, 1966). Acceptance of the projected aspects of the patient as a communication to be understood—as opposed to proddings or assaults to be acted upon or fled from—constitutes the background of the therapeutic situation. The importance of an accepting therapeutic environment cannot be over-emphasized. When the containment process fails, the therapist forces back into the patient those aspects of self that the patient was attempting to project into the therapist. In such cases, the therapist's interventions overtly or covertly state: "You are trying to make me feel your pain (or experience your insanity) for you." Of course, this is one aspect of all projective identifications, but if this aspect alone is addressed, the patient will simply feel chastized for attempting to do something selfish and destructive.

Establishing in a given situation what it means to "live with" the feelings engendered in the course of projective identification can be a complex task. As can be seen in the following vignette, the idea of containment can become distorted at times, serving as a rationalization for "therapeutic" masochism.

Dr S, a European psychiatrist in her late forties who had worked extensively with young adults on an outpatient basis, began working on a long-term adolescent inpatient service staffed almost exclusively by psychiatrists and nurses in their late twenties and early thirties. Not long after Dr S joined the staff of this ward, a number of patients began using her in the service of splitting—that is, they villainized her and contrasted her with the "good" staff members. She also served as an object of projective identification in such a way that she was relentlessly treated by the patients (and to a much lesser extent by portions of the staff) as an object of derision and contempt. Dr S had read about projective identification and felt that it was her job to serve as a container for the bitter, negative maternal-transference feelings that she recognized as a basic component of the behaviour of the patients. Within a few months, the job became so painful and undermining of her self-esteem that Dr S did not know how she could continue to work on the ward. Before finalizing her plans to transfer to another section of the department, she sought consultation with an outside psychiatrist in an effort to determine whether she was unconsciously contributing to or perpetuating the painful situation.

In the course of the consultation, Dr S talked about feeling like a failure for not being able to "take it" from the patients. She knew from experience that working with adolescents was difficult, but she felt totally demoralized by their manner of looking through her and treating her as if the idea of being in the same room with her were repugnant. She talked about her wish to demonstrate to herself that she could contain their bitterness and disdain, which she understood in terms of splitting and projective identification.

Despite the accuracy of her understanding of the transference meaning of the patients' contempt, Dr S was not fully aware of the way she had masochistically interpreted her own role as "container" for these feelings. She was confusing the active psychological work of processing feelings evoked in the course of projective identification with the act of endlessly enduring punishment. As a result, Dr S had failed to integrate the induced feelings with other aspects of her personality. If such integration had taken place, she might have been able to mobilize more reality-based self- and object-representations, which would have included views of herself as a highly skilled clinician who had chosen to make herself available to this particular group of patients for the purpose of engaging in psychological work. This does not constitute a blank check for the exercise of the patients' sadism. Simple enactment of anger and contempt can be done anywhere and does not require the services of a therapist or a psychiatric hospital staff. Since Dr S had not felt able to reassert the reality of the therapeutic context for her interactions with the patients, she raised the matter in clinical meetings of the ward's staff.

Dr S's previous self-understanding gained in her personal analysis made it possible for her in the course of the consultation to recognize and loosen her hold upon long-standing unconscious wishes to serve as a martyr in a parent–child relationship. She raised her concerns in clinical meetings with fellow staff members, and these discussions led to a rectification of the therapeutic framework. Dr S began to see and present herself as a member of the ward staff and not as an appendage to it. Her feelings of discomfort were now discussed by her at ward meetings as data emanating from therapeutic interaction and not as admissions of failure.

It is essential that inpatient psychiatric services conduct clinical meetings in such a way that issues of this type can be discussed without fear of further attack by fellow staff members. When the leadership of a ward fails to provide a safe forum of this type, staff members are forced to attempt to manage emotional strain in isolation. In my experience, this results in a virtual shut-down of therapeutic work on the ward (even in individual psychotherapy), since staff members are no longer able to risk making themselves sufficiently emotionally available (and vulnerable) to deal with feelings that inevitably arise in the course of genuine therapeutic work.

In the above discussion, the focus was on the masochistic misuse of the concept of containment. A related problem regularly arises in the psychotherapy of potentially violent or suicidal patients. With such patients there is often intense pressure on a therapist to allow the patient to dictate the terms of the therapeutic relationship. The following material from the treatment of a suicidal patient highlights the special difficulties entailed in the containment process when there is a self-destructive threat looming over the therapeutic work. The clinical data are from a consultation involving a therapist who had reached an impasse in his work with a chronically suicidal, intermittently psychotic patient whom he had been seeing three times a week for two years.

The therapist sought consultation because he felt physically assaulted ("like I was getting punched in the stomach") by the patient's intense dependency and the constant threat of suicide, both of which had reached a crescendo after about a year of therapy. The patient, Mrs N, had been depressed but not suicidal until shortly before the therapist's vacation during the eleventh month of therapy. Shortly after the therapist returned, the patient took a moderately serious overdose of antidepressant medication and then called the therapist, who arranged for emergency treatment at a crisis clinic. Mrs N, now 28 years old, had made a serious suicide attempt in her early twenties and had been hospitalized at that time. She told the therapist that during her hospitalization eight years earlier, she had been unfairly held in the hospital on an involuntary commitment order. She was adamant that she would never consent to hospitalization again.

The therapist retrospectively viewed the patient's overdose as marking a turning point in the treatment. He felt that at that point he had been forced either to discontinue treatment or to treat Mrs N as an outpatient, knowing that he had to be prepared to accept the considerable risk of her suicide. He had decided on the latter course. In the consultation, the therapist reported that over the past several months the patient had looked increasingly pale and wasted, "like a dying patient". She would report "howling in pain like an animal" for hours at a time in her room. For months the therapist had expected that each phone call he received would bring news of Mrs N's suicide. More recently, he had become aware of intense wishes that she would die and get it over with.

The patient was the eldest of three children. Her father was an alcoholic, and her mother a chronically depressed woman who spent large parts of each day alone in her room, crying. There was such difficulty in getting the mother's attention that the patient would write notes to her in the hope of eventually having her mother read them.

Mrs N remembers that when she was 10 years old, her mother came into her room in the middle of the night to give her a kiss, which the patient refused by turning away. The next thing the patient recalls is hearing a loud blast from the next room. Her mother had shot herself in the head. Mrs N reports that she was told at the funeral not to upset her younger brothers by crying, and also that she was the one who caused the suicide.

The therapist indicated that in the week prior to the consultation he had said something to the patient that had made him feel better, but he did not know if it had done the patient any good. He had told her that it was impossible for him to think clearly and work effectively with her as long as suicide was a constant and immediate threat, as it had been for the past year. He went on to say to her that he knew that she was terribly depressed, but somehow the threat of suicide had to be put on the back burner.

The consultant pointed out that even though the therapist had not been thinking in terms of projective identification, his intervention concerning his unwillingness to accept the threat of suicide as the constant background for the therapy represented a clear statement of the successful elements of his own containment of a projective identification. The problem was that the therapist, not having the perspective of projective identification in mind, had been unable to formulate for himself the rationale for his intervention and consequently did not know how to follow up.

From the perspective of the concept of projective identification, the second year of the therapy could be seen as an interpersonal enactment of a specific internal object relationship, wherein the therapist was being forced to experience the unbearable responsibility felt by a 10-year-old girl for the life and death of her depressed, chronically suicidal mother. Mrs N could tolerate neither the continual dread of her mother's suicide (now an internalized mother representation) nor her hatred of and murderous wishes towards her mother for being so depressed and distant.

The therapist's intervention pointed out that an identical burden of responsibility for the life of a suicidally depressed woman was being forced upon him. Moreover, he was implying that, unlike the patient, he did not feel limited to the range of emotions and alternatives that the patient had had available to her at age 10 in her relationship with her mother. The therapist was implicitly stating that, despite the feelings of responsibility engendered in him, in reality he was not a 10-year-old girl with a depressed mother; he was a therapist with a depressed patient, and there is a world of difference between the two. The feeling of relief that the therapist had experienced after making this intervention reflected the fact that he had begun to free himself from the unconscious feeling that there was no choice but to play a specific role in the patient's unconscious fantasy. However, the therapist was in danger of simply forcing back into the patient that aspect of herself (the little girl with the hated responsibility for her mother) which she was attempting to communicate to the therapist by means of projective identification.

What was missing in the intervention was the therapist's statement of understanding of Mrs N's unconscious reasons for feeling and behaving as she was toward the therapist. As with all interpretations, the therapist should begin with whatever the patient can accept and, over time, following the lead of the patient, gradually address the more disowned and threatening material. In interpreting projective identifications, it is important to acknowledge the patient's attempt to communicate something important about himself rather than simply addressing the hostile, controlling, and escapist motivations that are almost always present as elements of projective identification. These latter motivations are usually far more unacceptable to the patient than his wish to communicate and, if prematurely interpreted, will be heard as accusatory and strenuously warded off.

The consultant suggested that the therapist's intervention might be supplemented by an interpretation of the following type: "I think you'd like me to know what it was like to feel fully responsible for your mother and yet totally unable to help her." If the clinical material that followed validated this partial interpretation, then, over time, as the opportunity arose, it would be important to address the patient's unconscious fantasy of turning the therapist into the helpless 10-year-old girl that the patient still felt herself to be. In the course of the analysis of this unconscious projective fantasy, the therapist would be likely to encounter the full intensity of the patient's transference hatred of the mother therapist, as well as the omnipotent wish to eject painful aspects of herself and her internalized

objects while simultaneously maintaining the internalized object relationship (the tie to the depressed mother).

The therapist viewed succeeding sessions with the consultant's comments in mind and confirmed for himself that the
therapy had in an important sense become an enactment of an
internal drama, in which he had become limited to playing the
role of the patient as a 10-year-old girl vis-à-vis her suicidal
mother. The interpretation of the transference (in this case, a
projective identification) was initiated along the lines discussed
above.

As this work was being done, Mrs N began to talk in therapy
more than previously, reported a dream (which was an unusual
event in this therapy), and noticed similarities between the way
she was treating her daughter and the way she felt her mother
had treated her. There was a marked diminution of suicidal
threats, with an accompanying reduction of pressure on the
therapist continually to imagine himself receiving news of the
patient's suicide.

Over the next several months, the therapist noted that the
patient seemed sexually attractive to him for the first time. The
patient had made only fleeting references to sex during the first
two years of the therapy but now began to complain that she
hated the way her husband acted, as if sex with her were his
right. A new level of transference and countertransference was
now unfolding that had been defended against by means of the
projective identification (transference resistance) described
above.

## Concluding comments

Unlike many of the "beliefs" of the different schools of psychoanalytic thought, projective identification is not a construct
that one accepts or rejects on the basis of an attraction to a
metaphor (such as the notion of psychic energy), a piece of
imagery (such as the idea of psychological structure), or the
compatibility of an idea with other theoretical or philosophical
views (such as the death instinct).

Projective identification is a clinical-level conceptualization with three phenomenological references, all of which lie entirely within the realm of observable psychological and interpersonal experience: (1) the projector's unconscious fantasies (observable through their derivatives, such as associations, dreams, parapraxes, and so forth; (2) forms of interpersonal pressure that are often subtle but verifiable; and (3) countertransference experience (a real, yet under-utilized source of analysable data).

# CHAPTER THREE

# Countertransference and the concept of projective counteridentification

*León Grinberg*

I have made a fairly thorough study of the disturbances caused in analytical technique by the excessive intervention of projective identification on the part of the analysand, which gives rise in the analyst to a specific reaction for which I suggested the term "projective counteridentification", and these have been published in various articles (Grinberg, 1956, 1957, 1958, 1962, 1979).

It is known that the psychoanalytical process is conditioned by a series of factors of different types. Among them it is important to single out the continual interplay of projections and introjections which develops during the analysis, on the part of both the analysand and the analyst. Starting from the approach of the latter, we can consider two co-existing processes: in one, the analyst is the active subject of those mechanisms of introjection and projection; in the other, he becomes the passive object of the projections and introjections of the analysand.

---

Reprinted and expanded from León Grinberg, *The Goals of Psychoanalysis* (London: Karnac Books). By permission of the author.

In the first, Process A, we can describe schematically three important phases or moments: (1) when the analyst introjects, actively and selectively, the different aspects of the verbalized and non-verbalized material, with its corresponding emotional charges, presented by the patient; (2) when he works out and metabolizes the identifications resulting from these introjections that arise from the patient's inner world; (3) when he (re)-projects the results of metabolization by means of interpretations (Fliess, 1942).

In each of these phases dangerous situations may occur, mainly determined by neurotic residues that will give a special tinge to his countertransference reactions, and the inevitable consequence of which will be a disturbance in interpretation, unless the analyst becomes aware of it in time and succeeds in avoiding it. On the other hand, if the countertransference is successfully sublimated, it will be the most useful instrument for detecting, building up, and formulating whatever is capable of interpretation.

The second, Process B, is of special interest for the problem I am posing in this chapter. In one of its phases it is the analysand who, actively though unconsciously, projects his internal situations into the analyst, who acts as a passive receptacle. But in this case two situations may occur: (1) the emotional echo that arises in the analyst may be due to his own conflicts or anxieties, intensified or reactivated by the patient's conflicting material; (2) the affective response may be largely independent of his own emotions and mainly or exclusively a response to what the analysand projects into him.

What happens then? The analyst reacts to these identifications as though he had taken in and assimilated *really and concretely* the aspects that were being projected.

It is as though he ceases to be himself and turns unavoidably into what the patient unconsciously wants him to be. For this special state I propose the term "projective counteridentification" as a specific response to the patient's projective identification, which is not consciously perceived by the analyst, who is consequently "led" passively to carry out the role that, actively though unconsciously, the analysand has forced upon him. When this happens—although it may only be for a short space of time, but sometimes dangerously prolonged—the analyst will resort to every kind of rationalization to justify his attitude or his disturbance.

Sometimes the analyst cannot tolerate this situation and reacts in various different ways: (1) with an immediate recoil, as violent as the material the patient is trying to project into him; (2) by ignoring or denying this recoil through strict control or some other defensive mechanism; nevertheless, at any moment the reaction may become obvious in some way; (3) by postponing or displacing his reaction, which will then become manifest with some other patient; (4) by suffering the effects of this intense projective identification and "counter-identifying" in his turn.

Actually, the analyst's response will depend on his level of tolerance.

Once this counteridentification has taken place, it is obvious that normal communication between the analysand's unconscious and that of the analyst will be interrupted. [A number of different analysts in the last few years have incorporated these ideas about "projective counteridentification" into their work; we may mention Langs (1979), Segal (1977), Kernberg (1984a), and Sandler (1960).]

I should like to point out in passing that it was a moment of particular satisfaction for me to find confirmation of my ideas on projective counteridentification in Bion's *Learning from Experience* (1962), in which he says explicitly that:

> . . . the theory of countertransference offers only a partially satisfactory explanation because it deals with manifestation only as a symptom of the unconscious motives of the analyst and therefore *it leaves the patient's contribution without explanation* . . . thanks to the beta-screen *the psychotic patient is able to provoke emotions in the analyst.* [italics added]

Bion also accepts the emergence in the object–analyst of emotions provoked by the patient (through his projective identifications) which are independent, up to a point, of the analyst's countertransference. He adds that "the use these patients make of words is more an action directed towards freeing the psyche from an increase of stimuli than a language". To understand this last statement it would be as well to say a few words first about the theory of the alpha function, as Bion calls the function that allows the transformation of sensorial experiences into alpha elements that can be stored and used to form dreams, memories, and so on. They are those that enable us to dream, think, and keep the distinction between the conscious and the unconscious. On the other hand, if the alpha function fails, beta elements then arise, which cannot be used to form thoughts but contain undigested facts, which can only be evacuated through projective identification and appear in the process of acting out. These theories offer a new contribution to the understanding of thought processes.

When, for various reasons, the thinking function fails, we can accept that it is replaced by projective identification as a means of freeing the psychic apparatus from increasing tension.

Racker (1960) is one of the authors who have paid most attention to the problem of countertransference; he has succeeded in explaining the complexities arising from the different meanings attached to the term.

On the basis of Freud's complementary series, he accurately describes a countertransferential disposition on the one hand and current analytical experiences on the other, with countertransference as a result. He adds that this fusion of the present and the past, of reality and phantasy, of external and internal, and so forth, gives rise to the need for a concept embracing the whole of the analyst's psychological response, and he recommends that the term "countertransference" should be kept for this concept. He explains, however, that it is sometimes possible to speak of "total countertransference" and differentiate between, or separate, one aspect or another within that term.

On the other hand, Racker emphasizes the existence of a "countertransference neurosis" in which "oedipal and pre-oedipal conflicts, along with pathological processes (paranoid, depressive, manic, masochistic, etc.), interfere with the analyst's understanding, interpretation and conduct".

At this point Racker, who has had the great merit of exhaustively studying the dynamics of countertransference in its various aspects, refers with particular emphasis to two types of identification of the analyst with parts of the analysand. On the basis of some ideas of Helene Deutsch, he points out that the analyst, with his empathic tendency to understand everything that is going on in the analysand, can reach the point of identifying "each aspect of his personality with the corresponding psychological part of his analysand; his id with the id, his ego with the ego, his superego with the superego of the analysand, *consciously accepting these identifications*" (my italics). These are *concordant or homologous identifications* based, according to Racker, on introjection and projection, on the echo of the external in the internal, on the recognition of what is alien as one's own—"this (you) is I"—and the association of one's own with what is alien—"that (I) is you". Concordant identifications would be a reproduction of the analyst's own past processes that are being relived in response to the stimulus from the patient, giving rise to a sublimated positive countertransference that determines a higher degree of empathy.

The second type of identification, called *complementary identification*, results from the analyst's identification with internal objects of the patient; he feels treated like these internal objects and experiences them as his own.

Racker also describes a *concordant countertransference* in which there is an approximate identity between parts of the subject and parts of the object (experiences, impulses, defences) and a *complementary countertransference* in which there may exist "an object–relation" very similar to others, a true transference in which the analyst "repeats" earlier experiences, the analysand representing internal objects of the analyst.

Here I should like to outline the difference between these countertransferential terms and my concept of "projective counteridentification".

To begin with, confusion arises only with regard to the distinction between "projective counteridentification" and "complementary countertransference", since "concordant countertransference" is related to the empathic link towards the analysand, the longing to understand him; and these are identifications *that are accepted by the analyst's conscience*, as Racker describes it. This means that they depend almost completely on an active attitude towards them on the part of the analyst.

We then see what the essential difference is between complementary countertransference and projective counteridentification. As I explained above, it follows that complementary countertransference arises when the analyst identifies with internal objects of the patient and experiences them as his own internal objects. In another paragraph, Racker stresses that the analyst *"repeats" earlier experiences in which the analysand represents the analyst's internal objects*; the combination of these latter experiences (which always and continuously exist) can be called "complementary countertransference".

In my opinion, this countertransference reaction is based on an emotional attitude due to the analyst's neurotic residues *reactivated by the conflicts introduced by the patient*. This means that it takes shape within the first situation of Process B, which I have described above, in which the analyst is a passive object of the analysand's projections, for example his internal objects, but he reacts with countertransference because of *his own anxieties and the reactivation of his own conflicts with his internal objects*.

"Projective counteridentification", on the other hand, corresponds to the second situation of Process B—that is, the analyst's reaction is largely *independent of his own conflicts and corresponds predominantly or exclusively with the intensity and quality of the analysand's projective identification*. In this case the accent of the process is placed on *the patient* and not on the analyst. It is the patient who, in one particular moment of regression, and because of the functional modality of his projective identification, will actively provoke in the analyst a fixed emotional response, which he will experience in a passive way (Grinberg, 1963).

In "complementary countertransference" a reaction always arises which corresponds to the analyst's own conflicts. In "projective counteridentification" the analyst *takes upon himself* a reaction or mechanism that *comes from* the patient.

To clarify the point, we can take one of the examples quoted by Racker (1960). This is the case of the analysand who threatens the analyst with suicide. The anxiety which such a threat sparks off in the analyst can lead to various reactions or defence mechanisms within him, for example a dislike of the patient. This anxiety and loathing would be the contents of the "complementary countertransference". His awareness of dislike may give rise in its turn to guilt-feelings in the analyst which may lead to desires for reparation and to the intensification of concordant identification and countertransference.

Now if we analyse this extract, we may find both processes superimposed on each other or co-existing simultaneously. (This usually happens.) The analyst experiences anxiety in the face of the threat of suicide. But this anxiety has two components; one corresponds to the analyst's own anxiety due to his feelings of responsibility when faced with the possible risk of the death of his patient, who, at the same time, represents one of his internal objects. (It may also be an internal object of his analysand which is felt as an internal object of his own.) This type of anxiety corresponds to a "complementary countertransference". On the other hand, the analyst takes upon himself the specific anxiety of the analysand who, by projective identification, has placed this in him with the idea of the analyst controlling and resolving it. This anxiety response now forms part of "projective counteridentification". The analyst then reacts with dislike (a mechanism actually belonging to "complementary countertransference") and guilt. If we go more deeply into the analysis of this guilt, we find that part of it has a persecutory characteristic, which determined the feeling of annoyance at having incorporated, even though only partially, the impotence and desperation of the analysand and his fear of not being able to make reparation. Another part corresponds to the "depressive guilt" (Grinberg, 1963) that the patient cannot yet perceive nor manage, and which, projected into the analyst as depository, makes him feel capable of making reparation. These latter considerations, with regard to projection on the patient's part, of the two types of guilt and the analyst's response demonstrate how projective counteridentification works. It does not exclude the two types of guilt, which the analyst may experience through his own conflicts, reactivated or unleashed by the patient's material (complementary countertransference).

Naturally, these processes are never pure nor isolated but generally co-exist in different proportions.

When, mentioning other examples, Racker maintains that a "depressive–paranoid" transference situation of the analysand has its counterpart—from the point of view of complementary identification—in a "manic" countertransference situation of the analyst, he is implying, in my opinion, the co-existence of the two mechanisms. Since the analyst can react manically through his own conflicts, which make him feel strong or dominant towards a depressed object, or because he has taken on the manic and triumphant attitude of the analysand, he has been "placed" in this situation due to the special use of projective identification.

In other words, through *complementary countertransference* each analyst, identifying himself with his patient's internal objects, will react in a personal way, according to the type and nature of his own conflicts. Different analysts will react *in a different way* faced with the same patient material. On the other hand the same patient, using his projective identification in a particularly intense and specific way, could evoke the *same countertransferential response* (projective counteridentification) in different analysts. I had the opportunity to confirm this through the supervision of material of a patient who had been in analysis successively with various analysts.

This is one of the important reasons that explain why I prefer to keep the name "projective counteridentification" to refer to the process that takes place in the analyst in response to the analysand's projective identification. Just as a transferential attitude calls forth a countertransferential response, so projective identification will be responded to by a certain projective *counteridentification*. Although from this point the analyst introjects, albeit passively, this projective identification, the important thing is to make clear that the analyst's specific reaction is due to the form in which the analysand projects, places, or "forces" his projective identification into him.

Here I should like to add that projective counteridentification will have, in its turn, different modalities, according to what the respective modalities of projective identification have been. This mechanism will be coloured by qualitative nuances, which will give it a functional specificity. Normally, in all extra-verbal communication, the type of function (degree and quality) of the projective identification of the transmitter (analysand) does not go over the critical threshold of the receptor (analyst), and the extra-verbal message produces countertransferential resonance. It stimulates the response that can be grasped, controlled, and verbalized with relative ease by the analyst. But on certain occasions, when the degree and quality of the projective identification impregnate its functional modality in a special way, the result is that the extra-verbal communication will pass over the critical threshold, producing projective counter-identification. This threshold will depend in every case on the analyst's personality, on his previous analysis, and on the degree of knowledge or awareness he has of this phenomenon (Grinberg, 1976).

I also think that on some occasions the analyst, because of his fear of an excessive projective identification on the part of the patient, may respond with a paranoid attitude, thus determining a counterresistance, which will indubitably affect his work. Although he understands and justifies rationally the analysand's wish to project his parts into him, using him as a dynamic reservoir for his conflicts, another, unconscious part of him will be afraid of feeling invaded and annihilated and of losing, even temporarily, his personal aspects, which have been expropriated—magically—as a consequence of projective iden-tification.

A clinical example will illustrate this last point: a woman patient arrived for her first session fifteen minutes late, lay down on the couch and remained motionless, without saying a word. After a few minutes, she said the session felt like her oral identification, to which she reacted with considerable nervous-ness and anxiety, and which, on the other hand, she related to her wedding night, when she also felt very afraid but managed to hide this in such a way that her father-in-law said she was like a statue. I told her then that she was reproducing with me the experience of the oral examination and the wedding night, and that she was afraid I would deflower her so as to put myself inside her and search her out. I said that here, too, she had behaved like a statue with her initial rigidity and immobility, with the aim not only of hiding her anxiety, but of defending herself from the material possibility of being penetrated.

Although I saw that the interpretation of her paranoid anxi-ety was correct, I felt that there was something wrong, without being able to say exactly why. It occurred to me then that what

I had pointed out to her was very close to her consciousness, and that I should go more deeply into the reasons for her exaggerated fear of letting me into herself. On the other hand her initial rigid attitude had caught my attention, and I surprised myself with the phantasy of analysing a corpse. After that, something happened that found expression in a humorous form: "she surely wants to force a corpse into me". This showed me my own paranoid reaction to her wish to project her objects into me. Guided by this countertransferential experience, I then pointed out that her initial silence and immobility might mean something more than the simple representation of a statue, and that she might perhaps be expressing in this way some feeling of hers in relation to death.

Her immediate reaction was to burst into tears and tell me that when she was small, her older sister had committed suicide because of a disappointment in love, and that she felt responsible for her death because the failure to stop it was due to her delay. She had seen the preparations for suicide (her sister had already attempted it on other occasions), and deeply affected by them, had gone out and watched from outside for a long time, perhaps fifteen minutes, until it occurred to her to run and seek her father. By the time he arrived, it was too late.

I had felt that the patient, with her "corpse-like attitude" was not only attempting to show me one of her more serious conflicts in relation to the dead internal object that she still had inside her, but was also trying to free herself from it by means of projective identification. From this initial moment of her analysis, I was the one who was to bear the burden. This motivated my defensive reaction, as I must have unconsciously perceived in her a certain ritual attempt to imitate the attitude of a corpse, which would automatically determine, by a kind of "imitative magic", the projection of this object into me. [P. Greenacre, in *Trauma, Growth and Personality* (1953), considers that one of the determinant factors of acting out is the tendency to dramatize, based on imitative magic, which predominates in the first years of life. These patients unconsciously suppose that to do something in an imitative or dramatic form—to make it appear true—is really equivalent to making it come true. This is related to the wish to avoid or produce something by means of magical activity.] I think this was the essential reason for my interpretation with regard to her paranoid anxiety, because in this way I was concealing or denying my own unconscious fear of feeling invaded by a dead object. On becoming aware of my reaction I could then better understand the deepest roots of the patient's paranoia and re-alize that her immobility was in itself a magical gesture or action with which she intended not only to immobilize the per-secuting object that she had within herself, but also to identify with it in its dead state, while she projected into me her fear of persecution.

Let us look at another example. A young analyst came to his session after having, in his turn, analysed a "difficult" patient, who made him feel "utterly beaten" because he had been very active in his interpretations without achieving any appreciable result. Depressed by the feeling that this session had been a failure, he told his training analyst what had happened and described his state of mind, after which he remained silent. Hearing his analyst's interpretations, which for the moment did not alter his state of mind, the young analyst had the impres-sion that the situation he had been complaining of not long before was being repeated, but with the roles reversed; he real-ized that it was his analyst who was "beating his brains out" trying to achieve some change in him, while he was reacting in the same way as his patient had. When he told his analyst, with a certain surprise, what his impression had been, his analyst told him that his (the young analyst's) behaviour had "obliged" him (textual expression) to identify with him. He then com-pleted the interpretation by saying that the young analyst en-vied him because he had better patients than he had. An intense identification had then taken place, through which the young analyst unconsciously wished his analyst to experience the same difficulties, dissociating himself and projecting into him the disappointed and dissatisfied professional part of him-self, while he was left with the part identified with the patient "who gives him work and no gratification". The training analyst, in his turn, "succumbs" (if that is the right expression) to this projection and is unconsciously "obliged" to counteridentify with the part he has received. When this happens—and it hap-pens more often than is usually supposed—the analysand feels unconsciously that he has achieved by magic the fulfilment of his wish, thanks to the "placing" of his parts in the object; and the analyst feels that he has not been able to oppose with the "counter-magic" of his work the "magic", this time more effective, of his analysand.

The student may make the supervisor feel the same type of emotional reaction as the patient made him feel. If the supervisor can become aware of the genesis of his affective repercussions, then he can, having more capability, objectivity, and experience, show the candidate the origin of the emotional reaction that he had experienced in the session with his patient.

Other authors have referred to similar problems, though starting from different schemes of reference and therefore using different terminology for the conceptualization and description of the phenomenon. [From this paragraph to the end of the chapter is an addition based on my work "Beyond projective counteridentification" (Grinberg, 1982).]

The dynamic interaction that develops constantly between the two members of the analytical couple is a fact to which more and more importance is attached. A happy phrase of E. Balint eloquently expresses the quality and scope of this interaction: ". . . now we have a more three-dimensional vision of transference". The analyst is not only a "mirror" in which the internal objects of the analysand are reflected; the latter often projects his phantasies and feelings not only *onto* the analyst, but also *into* him. I suggest that this conception of a third dimension can also be applied to countertransference.

At present I think that projective counteridentification does not necessarily have to be the final link in the chain of complex events that occur in the exchange of unconscious communication by non-verbal means with patients who, in moments of regression, function with pathological projective identifications. I believe, on the contrary, that it may also be the starting point of the possibility of experiencing a spectrum of emotions that, well understood and sublimated, may be turned into very useful technical instruments for entering into contact with the deepest levels of analysands' material, in a way analogous to that described by Racker and by P. Heimann for countertransference. But in order to achieve this, it would be necessary to be more *disposed* to receive and contain the patient's projections for as long as necessary. We do not always succeed in this. Very often we are afraid of feeling invaded by the psychotic contents of such projections, because they may threaten our own psychic balance. We then try to defend ourselves by rejecting them in different ways.

We know that the special nature of our work exposes us to running such risks, since we are seeking to communicate with the unconscious of the analysand who, in his turn, often attempts this communication by non-verbal means. Although the situation varies from patient to patient, some of them—with the psychotic patient predominating—use pathological projective identifications so as to evacuate their painful and persecutory phantasies and emotions into the analyst's mind. Such moments especially test our degree of tolerance and our capacity for receiving and containing such phantasies and emotions.

Taken to its most extreme expression, such an attitude shows itself in *consenting* to be invaded by the projections of the analysand's psychotic anxieties and phantasies, and to contain them until their ultimate consequences are fulfilled, so as to be able to *share, feel, and think* with him, to be *consubstantial* with the emotions contained in such projections, whatever their nature may be (murderous hate, fear of death, catastrophic terror, etc.), as though they were part of his own self. It is to offer all the time and mental space one has at one's disposal, to provide all the mental space and time that the patient, with his different affective contents, is going to need. In this way the analyst will arrive successfully at "at-one-ment" with the patient's "O".

In other words, I would say that the analyst experiences, in his own personality, a transformation, which enables him to reach the state of *convergence* with the anxiety, pain, delirium, or hallucination experienced by the analysand. The term "convergence" was suggested to me by a seriously melancholic patient whose case I followed as supervisor; she used it to express her desperation when she felt that she was not understood by her family, nor her friends, nor, at times, by her analyst. She said that the "convergence" between them, which she needed and hoped for so much, was not coming to pass. At other times, referring to the same type of problems of lack of communication, she expressed her wish that the analyst might belong to the sort of people who "when they're with you, they *really* are". Both the term "convergence" and the phrase "being really with somebody" are close to the concept of "at-one-ment" with the psychic reality "O" of the analysand.

Another borderline patient insisted on his need for the analyst to "come down" to him so as to understand him although he recognized that this involved the risk of "becoming infected" (I would call it "counter-identifying"), and that in that case he would not be able to help him.

Joyce McDougall (1979) suggests that communication (from the Latin *communicare*, which means, etymologically, "keep contact with", "have a relationship with", or "be a part of"), in its primitive form is nearer to crying, screaming, and groaning. She adds that such communication would be a means not only of remaining in intimate contact with someone, but "to discharge emotions in a direct form with the intention of *affecting* the other and making affective reactions emerge". Fusion and communion are then the most primitive means of binding oneself to other people.

I should like to recall here Freud's phrase that "there is much more continuity between intrauterine life and early infancy than the impressive 'caesura' of the act of birth would lead us to believe" (1926d [1925]).

Projective counteridentification is a caesura. But it is in the sense of a link in continuous transit (as transference and countertransference are), since what characterizes the analytic process is the constantly changing situations that take place in the interaction between the analyst and the analysand.

Elsewhere (Grinberg, 1981) I have referred to a characteristic that I have been able to observe in regressive and borderline patients: the rapid and unexpected change from one emotional state (pain, for example) to another (persecution and hostility), giving rise to disturbance, irritation, and so forth in the analyst's countertransference. I was also able to show the sudden volte-face that usually takes place in such patients from the "neurotic part" of their personality to the "psychotic part" and vice versa. The lability of the limitrophic zone between the different types of emotion and between the two parts of the personality and the frequency and rapidity with which these kaleidoscopic reactions occur in clinical practice, suggest to me the name of "razor's edge" for these situations. I would say *now*

that these "razor's edge" phenomena are also caesuras in so far
as they imply changes or transitions from one emotional or
mental state to another, sometimes completely opposed, also
causing reactions of "projective counteridentification" in the
analyst. The transition to the "catastrophic change", which
leads to "convergence", understanding, and mental growth,
must perhaps pass *inevitably* through projective counteridentification, but this transition must somehow lead *beyond* projective counteridentification, avoiding the danger of remaining
blocked in it with the implication of a *mini-catastrophe*.

How are we to decipher the multiplicity of meanings enclosed
in silences, sounds, and gestures in a person's breathing, his
handshake, body postures, and facial expressions? This is one
of the most complex challenges we must confront in our daily
practice. I do not think that there is any specific answer to this
difficult and enigmatic technical question. Nevertheless, I hold
that the use of sublimated countertransference, intuition and,
in some cases, the reactions of projective counteridentification
are important instruments for perceiving and deciphering the
contents of non-verbal communication.

The following clinical case concerns an unmarried, twenty-
eight-year-old woman from a traditional Catholic Spanish family. She was a borderline case with strong depressive and
schizoid components. The eldest of three children, her brothers
were three and five years younger.

According to the patient, her relationship with her parents
was always very conflictive due to their lack of affection and the
strictness and demands they placed on her at a very early age.
When she was two she suffered a long separation from her
mother, who had to go to another city to take care of her own
mother who was ill. Her father, a lawyer for an important company, was almost always absent, and she felt that he was inaccessible to her demands for affection. As a small child she
tended to isolate herself and did not play with her friends or
brothers.

From childhood on she had suffered symptoms of depression, with marked splitting and spatial disorientation. She
used to get lost in the streets without knowing how to find her
destination. She was inept in her relationships with others; she
did not pay attention to what they were saying or to what she

was supposed to say, as if she were lacking the norms and rules that govern other people's lives. She often functioned by magical thought and frequently confused fact with fantasy.

As for her behaviour in analysis, her stubborn silence was markedly noticeable, and she would spend entire sessions without uttering a single word. Nevertheless, she never missed a session and always appeared punctually. At first I felt frustrated and annoyed during her silences because she did not speak and, in retaliation, I did not speak either. It was a projective counteridentification reaction because the patient had deposited in me her rage for the frustration she had suffered in her life. Sometimes I felt tenderness during her silence, as if I were looking after a tiny defenceless baby. At such times, I felt that I was the container for a receptive and protective maternal image that the patient had projected into me. I could sense and feel a continuous flux of different feelings in her body tensions and in her posture and facial expressions.

I shall now describe some fragments of her analysis. During one of those silent sessions she played a game with herself: she would remove a ring from her finger and then quickly put it back on again. She did this over and over again, as if she were re-enacting the movements of coitus. But she did it in such a way that the "ring–vagina" functioned as the active part that moved repeatedly so that the passive "finger–penis" would remain introduced into the ring. I thought that she wanted to play the active and dominant role in controlling the apparently sexual situation, but I did not interpret it to her. I was not convinced that this game merely represented a sexual fantasy stemming from her erotic transference. I let a few sessions go by without referring to her game. She continued to take off and put her ring on her finger, but after a few moments she would wait, as if expecting something; she would then repeat the movements and wait again. I seemed to intuit that she was waiting for me to intervene and talk. This time I was convinced. I told her that she wanted to stimulate me to introduce myself into her mind and establish affective contact, but that she was afraid I would discover her dangerous fantasies and for this reason she wavered between coming close and getting far away from me. She interrupted her game for a few minutes and then she finally said, "Yes, you're probably right". I did not mention her game explicitly in the interpretation in order to avoid in her a persecutory reaction of feeling watched.

In another session she told me of a dream she had had in which she had been frightened by the appearance of a "zombie" who was like a "living dead" person. Having said this, she immediately stopped talking and became completely rigid. I noted, strangely, that for a long while I too did not feel like interpreting her dream, even though it did occur to me that it was she who was the "zombie", immobile in her silence, as if she were a "living-dead" person. Undoubtedly she felt apprehensive because a part of her functioned in that way, like a "zombie", but there must have been some compensatory counterpart in that image that guaranteed that she would not feel, think, or accept any responsibilities.

At that moment I had the fantasy of leaving her in silence until the end of the session without worrying about her or having the responsibility for understanding what happened to her. For some minutes my mind went blank. When I recovered from this projective counteridentification reaction and as a result of the feelings I had experienced, I told her that, paradoxical as it might seem, she sometimes preferred her "zombie" state so as not to have to think or feel; but as it always frightened her, she needed to place that aspect inside me, to have me take charge of it. She was making me experience what she was living through passively. Finally, after coming out of her silence, she admitted that, in effect, while she functioned as a "robot" she felt more sheltered and risked less. She added that if she lost the protection of her "robot" being, she might "lose her balance", become "distorted", "disoriented", and "mad".

Instead of making an effort to understand something that was difficult for her, she tried to avoid or deny the existence of whatever it was that she did not understand. When she could not see someone, she thought that the person had disappeared. Sometimes during her periods of silence she kept her eyes closed, but I had the impression that "her ears were also closed" because, after some remark of mine, she continued to remain silent, in a special state, as if she were in another world, neither seeing nor hearing me. I thought that her not wanting to "hear" or "see" was related to her not wanting to "understand". The fact that she did not listen to me was probably a defence against feeling that my interpretations were re-projections onto her.

It seemed to me that this lack of communication hid a non-verbal communication through which she asked me not to force her to understand because, in doing so, I would make her suffer. She confirmed my interpretation when I explained her attitude to her. She recounted a dream in which she saw herself with her head bandaged. She recalled having read somewhere of a Chinese or Japanese woman whose feet were bound as a small child, according to custom, so that they would stay small. Subsequently she married a European, and when he took off the bandages to free her feet, the pain she felt was more intense than ever. The patient was afraid, then, that if I took the bandage off her head so that her mind could grow and understand, the consequence would be an increase in psychic pain which she would not be able to tolerate.

Once, after a holiday break, she fantasized about terminating her analysis with the excuse of having found a better job in another city. This was her way of seeking revenge against the analyst who represented the mother who had abandoned her and the father who was distant and absent. This led her to a kind of narcissistic withdrawal (through her fusion with the analyst as an idealized internal object) by which she tried to get rid of her relationship with me (as an external object) and with others, by leaning on an omnipotent fantasy of being able to resolve everything by herself. In one dream she saw herself having a baby; she became pregnant alone and gave birth alone without experiencing any pain. Then she put the baby back inside her like a childish game. She did this several times until she heard a voice telling her, "It's not only yours, there must be a man too, and it hurts to give birth". While she was telling her dream, I associated the "baby game" with the "ring game". I knew that, on one level, the voice that she had heard represented her own adult voice. It was a voice that needed to keep the infantile part of her informed of the fact that reality was very different from the fantasies that participated in her game. She was also telling me that she needed to hear my voice in order to engender "word–babies" so as not to remain trapped in her narcissistic refuge of silence. She realized that this voice was the only one that would help her "to be born" into the external world and into her relationship with "the Other".

To sum up: I would include in the "psychoanalytic function of the personality" of the analyst the ability to regress, to let himself be invaded, and to "place himself" *within* the patient's productions, even psychotic, experiencing together with him the emotions contained in them, and being able to return to external reality in the same way as the poet who travels into the world of phantasy but finds the way back into reality, as Freud has shown us.

# PART TWO

# CLINICAL ILLUSTRATIONS OF COUNTERTRANSFERENCE: THEORETICAL AND TECHNICAL CONSIDERATIONS

CHAPTER FOUR

# A parallel voyage of mourning for patient and analyst within the transference–countertransference voyage

*Athina Alexandris*

## 1.   THE VOYAGE OF ARGO: OEDIPUS COMPLEX

Oedipus Rex is what is known as a tragedy of destiny.

His destiny moves us only because it might have been ours—because the oracle laid the same curse upon us before our birth as upon him.

Freud, 1900a, p. 262

This is the study of a father, our patient, who had a problem in choosing a name for his second son; he could not decide whether to call him Alexander or Jason. Neither of these names appeared in either his or his wife's family lines. He finally decided on the name Jason.

---

The first part of this case report, "Oedipus Complex", was written in 1984 and presented at an International Symposium; the second part, "A Process of Mourning", was written in 1991.

69

George, our patient, attempted to "resolve" the problems related to his oedipal situation—and change his destiny as a result—by the use of myths, songs, and fairy-tales. Of special relevance here is the myth that he employed, namely, "The Voyage of Argo" or "Argonautica", which was written by Apollonius of Rhodes some time in the middle of the third century B.C. [In the Argonautica of Apollonius of Rhodes, we have the only full account of Jason's voyage in quest of the Golden Fleece, a tale that seems to have stood, in the estimation of the Greeks, second only to the great cycle of legends that centred in the Trojan War. Apollonius' poem is thus unique. It has often been claimed that here we have the finest psychological study of love that the Greeks have left us (E. V. Rieu).]

From this myth, as well as from George's clinical material, elements that are relevant to the Oedipus complex are brought forward, and those corresponding to other areas are touched upon. Emphasis is placed on the defensive aspect of the usage of the myth. The psychopathology of this case is not dealt with, although it does come out indirectly. Lastly, the subject is discussed on the basis of Freud's theories.

I propose that we accompany this father on his personal psychoanalytic "voyage" and see what we can learn from it. To facilitate our own mission, we first have to keep in mind that Freud applies to myths and fairy tales the same technique that he applies to dreams in order to uncover their hidden, unconscious meaning, and second, that, myths and legends, "with all their confusion and contradictions, are bound to baffle every effort to bring to light the kernel of historical truth that lies behind them" (Freud, 1939a, p. 16). Third, we have to look into the patient's family heritage, which, according to Freud ". . . [is] the kind of fairy tale that someone produces . . . hints at the relations between the fairy tales and the history of the person's childhood and his neurosis" (Freud, 1912–13).

The patient was born and brought up in a rural area where he lived with his family until the time was right for him to leave home to pursue a university education. His grandfather, Spiros, who died of cancer at the age of sixty, had thrown his eldest son Peter (George's father) out of his house at the age of fourteen. This act was one that went against tradition. George's grandfather and father constitute the first oedipal situation.

Peter, the patient's father, had several siblings, some of whom had died at a young age. When he was thrown out of his father's home, he worked as a shepherd for the first two to three years in order to survive. He repeatedly stressed to his son, George (the patient), how unhappy and homesick he had felt during that period. He said that he never forgave his father for what he had done to him. In addition to his other problems, he had also been treated badly by his "boss", the owner of his flock.

After his unhappy job as a shepherd, Peter left that area and went to live in a small town, where he worked as a self-taught musician. What he had to do was to play an instrument during the local festivals. As the artist of the area, Peter became a marginal person. Music eventually turned into a vocation that seemed to suit him.

With his sudden departure from home, Peter was deprived not only of his father but of his mother as well. I believe that he was actually mourning for this loss when he played his musical instrument, like another Orpheus grieving for his lost Euridice. . . .

When Peter turned thirty, he met a woman a few years his senior in one of the local festivals and thought to himself that she was the right person for him to take as his wife. Indeed, after a brief engagement, they were married.

According to the material reported by George concerning his ancestors and the relationship between his parents, his mother was fixated to her idealized father, whom she had lost at the age of 15, but who, nevertheless, was very much alive in her mind, and with whom she kept an incestuous bond. I am inclined to think that when she met her husband, she made him believe that she would play the role of the parents he had lost. She offered herself as his parents. So, in the place of his cruel father, she offered him her own idealized father—i.e. a new oedipal father—and set her husband in competition with him. In the place of his mother she offered him herself. What she offered in fact was a new oedipal situation in the place of his own. This is the second oedipal situation in which incest is permitted.

Peter, the patient's father, submitted to his idealized father-in-law. By adopting the oedipal father of his wife, he castrated himself, and by doing so he also castrated his own father. He married a woman who was for him a maternal substitute, and who was still tied to her father by an incestuous relationship.

George, their firstborn, was named after his maternal grandfather, which was not in accordance with tradition. He became bound to his idealized, phallic—though unattainable—mother by an incestuous tie, while this mother was likewise bound to her own idealized father by a similar tie. Love for women is, therefore, to George an incestuous type of love: he became the accomplice of his mother, who turned him against his father.

The patient grew up in an environment where his mother belittled and constantly humiliated his father. This resulted in frequent fighting in the house. He shared his mother's "*myth*" about her idealized father. Mother and son spent hours together, whereby his mother would recount to him fairy tales and myths. George shared his mother's myths and feelings, especially her feelings about his father and other significant family members.

When George was nearly four years old, a new boy was born to his family. His little brother was named after his paternal grandfather Spiros. The paternal heritage was thus passed on from the paternal grandfather to the second son of the family, while the maternal heritage had passed to the first son, George, as it will be remembered.

George's brother Spiros died when he was only a few months old. His brother's death shocked George tremendously. His memories are very vivid, as he had to witness all the rituals connected to this death, such as the carrying of his brother's body outside the house in order to be buried, and so on.

The patient married a woman who accepted him and allowed him to continue idealizing his mother, as well as keeping an incestuous bond with her.

George's first son was named after his own father. His paternal line was thus passed on to his first son. This constitutes the third oedipal situation, and is in accord with tradition.

Approximately three years later, his second son was born. This boy had a special meaning for him. He wished to give him a name that would not be related to his paternal or maternal families, nor to those of his wife. He wanted to call him Alexander, after Alexander the Great, or Jason, after the hero of the voyage of Argo. When the boy was born, his father, Peter, insisted that he be named after his own father, Spiros, George's grandfather. This sent George into a panic, because the name of his grandfather signified for him a cruel person, potentially a killer—a man who had thrown his own son (the patient's father) out of his house at the tender age of fourteen. George remembered only too well how often his father had complained of the difficulties he had gone through because of this experience, as well as the fact that he had never forgiven his father for what he had done to him.

On the other hand, his grandfather's name (Spiros) had already been given to George's younger brother, who had died in the first year of his life, when George was nearly four. This meant to George that his little brother had been driven to death by his grandfather (whose name he carried), by his father (who had given his son this name), and by his mother (who had actually given birth to him). The patient feared that he could very well have been in his brother's place and suffered his fate.

For all of the above reasons, George rejected his father's proposition. However, his father came up with a new idea, which he tried to impose on him—that of naming the boy after the male version of his own wife's name (the patient's mother). This proposition was the cause of even greater anxiety for George, because his son's name would constantly remind him of his mother, the fact that she bore children who died, a mother who had incestuous relationships with her little boys and turned them against their father. Naturally enough, George rejected this proposal as well.

His father's pressing attitude in connection with the names was interpreted by George to mean that he was obliged to continue the family's oedipal destiny and that he was not allowed to escape from it. In other words, he had to repeat the inherited oedipal destiny, whereby fathers are cruel to their boys and can drive them to death, mothers bear children that die (George's maternal grandmother had given birth to a number of children, who had died shortly after birth), and/or develop an incestuous type of relationship with their boys, use them, and turn them against their fathers.

At the same time, the patient's wife's family demanded that their son be named after his wife's father. To George this meant that his son would have the same fate and experiences as he had had with his family, and he consequently rejected this new proposal, along with all of the others.

A great deal of arguing ensued among the two families for some time. George, however, had his own dreams for his son, long before this son had even been born. Nevertheless, he felt shaken and was under extreme pressure, because he did not know whether he should abide by his father's command or go through with his own plans. What he feared most was the cessation of all emotional ties with his family if he went against his father's wishes, which "for the individual (represents) a great danger, provoking great anxiety", as Freud puts it.

One day, in one of his sessions, the patient declared in a megalomanic and omnipotent manner: "I have finally made it! I resolved the problem and imposed my will upon them! I named my son Jason! This has been a great labour and an achievement for me."

His wife had been on his side during the period of fighting and gave her consent easily with regard to the name of their son. The grandparents, however, were so upset that they refused to attend the boy's christening. As for George, he celebrated the event with all the decorum dictated by tradition.

This achievement meant for George that he had managed to free himself of the two families and was now able to lead his own family undisturbed and in accordance with his wishes. Just like Jason, the hero, who had led his ship Argo on its perilous voyage successfully and had managed to pass through the Clashing Rocks unscathed.

All this he related to me in a triumphant manner and concluded by saying, "So, you see, I resolved the problem!" In this manner he attempted to gain control over the analytical situation by imposing the rules governing myths, magic, and so on on the analyst and by trying to make the analyst use George's technique in place of that of analysis (Freud, 1913c).

According to the myth, Jason in his voyage had to pass through a gate that was guarded by two huge rocks that opened and closed and crushed to death anyone who attempted to

cross them. Jason was the first to get through this with his ship
Argo and crew without being crushed.

It became obvious from George's narrative that "to free himself" meant freedom from the oedipal ties, i.e. giving up his
incestuous love for his mother, replacing it with affectionate
love, working through his ambivalence towards his father, and
eventually identifying with him (Freud, 1924d, pp. 173–79). As
for freeing himself of the two families, it is interesting to note
that, although he talked of his own family and of that of his
wife's as being two separate ones, it became evident at some
point that he had split his parental family into two—namely,
into a paternal and a maternal heritage, respectively, the latter
projected and displaced to his wife's family.

His fear of being crushed in passing through the Clashing
Rocks obviously represented his fear of castration, related to
coitus and the female genitals. In other words, he displaced his
fear of castration from men to women (mother–wife–analyst),
thus denying that men/fathers, like himself, are the castrators.
I also think that this expresses his feeling of danger of passing
through the Oedipal complex, as well as the fear of his personal
"voyage" through the analytical process; the inference to the
female analyst is quite clear.

Let me here remind you of Freud's (1912–13) definition of
the development of fear: the development of fear is fear of castration, fear of conscience, fear of death, and the anxiety lies
between the ego and the superego.

However, I would like to stress the fact that, at a deeper
level, things are a bit more complicated than that. George was
being threatened by the oedipal heritage of each one of his
parents, who, in turn, had inherited it from their own parental
families. He was afraid that this destiny would be passed on to
his son Jason through him, unless he did something about it.

As more material came to light in the course of analysis, it
became apparent that George had assigned a mission to his
son Jason: he wished that Jason restore his own father and,
through him, his grandfather on his behalf and thus ultimately
restore his whole paternal line for him. By restoring his father,
George also aimed at changing his mother's status within the
family—that is, have the mother submit to the potent father.

To George, Jason is a son outside the two families, who has escaped the death that stems from the paternal line as well as from the phallic mother. He is someone who is going to restore George's father, and through him his grandfather and himself (George), on account of George's oedipal deeds, which are to get rid of his father and have an incestuous relationship with his mother. This way the patient wishes to settle the pending problems (the debt he has towards his father) between himself and his father, with the hope that this would permit him to attain manhood through the restoration of his paternal line.

Jason is a hero whose fate is to change the oedipal destiny of three generations. George feels that only someone who is not related to the paternal and maternal families stands a chance of fulfilling this mission—someone, in other words, who has no oedipal ties whatsoever and further possesses special skills— for example, those of a hero.

In this context, it is as if Jason were George's appendix that had been detached from him and had become idealized, and who is ready to do everything that he himself could never have done; he is, therefore, his ego ideal, which George has taken as an object.

A similar mission had been assigned to the hero of Argo: Jason had to restore his own father from whom his paternal half-brother Pelias had deviously taken his kingdom away, and become king in his place.

Lastly, George also assigned a comparable mission to his analyst—namely to restore him and, through him, his paternal heritage.

Let us now consider another aspect of the myth. The name "Jason" comes from the Greek verb "ιαομαι–ιωμαι", meaning someone who applies therapy. What is a therapist, however? A therapist is someone who can resolve the problems of others and can pretend that he has resolved his own; a therapist is a neutral person, a sexless person—neither a man nor a woman, neither Laius nor Oedipus; it is someone who is detached from those he treats, who pretends to have no oedipal claims on them, and who does not permit them to get involved with him; a therapist possesses special skills—he is a magician who can perform tasks that other people cannot do.

Hence, the father projects on his son his own conception of the role of the therapist, and identifies with him.

It may now become much clearer why George assigned to his son this particular destiny, and also why he used this defensive manoeuvre to pretend that both he and his son were sexless, in an attempt to deny the whole oedipal situation. Of course, he conveyed the same message to his analyst. On another level, in the transference situation he presents the picture of an innocent and harmless four-year-old boy, who can only imagine things and has no oedipal claims on the analyst. The only thing that he needs is to be "loved and helped".

Let us now see whether Jason of the myth was in actuality a hero. If we read the myth ourselves, we will tend to agree with the experts of mythology (Kerenyi, 1966; Richepin, 1953; Rieu, 1971) who commented on Apollonius and his myth, who say that Apollonius set out to portray an epic hero but only managed to portray an ordinary man. During the Argo voyage, Jason does not really lead, and it is only through Medea's magic aid that he attains heroic stature. Jason himself achieved nothing outside the ordinary.

The patient, our own epic poet, also set out to portray a hero, Alexander the Great, but ended up by portraying Jason, a four-year-old boy. In this context, in order to achieve heroic stature, George chose a woman analyst, hoping that with her aid he would attain manhood.

The "Argo" experts continue by saying that Apollonius' identification with Jason prevented him from portraying a hero. We could definitely say that the same applies to George.

Another point of interest is that, although Jason of the myth had received all the necessary training by the Centaurs in the arts of war and was properly equipped to become a leader and a hero, he was nevertheless, unable to make use of his skills and assume the role of the leader. Likewise our own hero, George, had all the qualities of being a father–leader in his own family but could not make use of these qualities in order to attain his manhood and fatherhood, due to his unresolved oedipal problems. The patient's professional position is a leading one. Interestingly enough, the experts say the same of Apollonius.

"Jason, after all, had some of the makings of a leader: brains, abundant charm, and, above all, a most persuasive tongue. He was a man who knew how to make other people do things for him." George displayed the same characteristics, hoping at the same time that his analyst would do the work for him.

Apollonius and George employ the qualities they have attributed to Jason in a subtle way, to bring them both victory as well as defeat. Freud writes in this regard: "The hero claims to have acted alone in accomplishing the deed, but it is often found that this hero carries out tasks with the help of others" (Freud, 1921c, p. 136).

But what is a hero? According to Freud (1921c, p. 136), "The hero was a man who by himself has slain the Father." "Some individual [who], in the exigency of his longing, may have been moved to free himself from the group and take over the Father's part. He, who did this, was the first epic poet. This poet disguised the truth with lies, in accordance with his longings. He invented the heroic myth." "The poet who created the first ego ideal" (Freud, 1921c, p. 136). Jason, in our case, is the ego ideal of our poet George, whom he has taken as an object due to the inhibited aims of his oedipal impulses.

His ultimate feeling of triumph could be understood in the context of something in his ego coinciding with his ego ideal. Freud says, "the Hero was probably afforded by the youngest son, the mother's favourite, whom she had protected from paternal jealousy, and who . . . had been the father's successor" (1921c, p. 136). "The woman was probably turned into the active seducer and instigator to the crime" (1921c, p. 136). We must remember that George was the first son—and his mother's favourite. Jason in the myth was also an only son.

George, the poet–hero had in his imagination set himself apart from the family as a group. Freud writes (1921c, p. 136), "The myth then is the step by which the individual emerges from the group psychology." [It is interesting to note that in Ancient Greece, when Democracy flourished and the Greek tragedies were written (fifth century B.C.) by Aeschylus, Sophocles, and Euripides, if a member of the society (a citizen) set himself free from the group, it was considered as "hubris" (Gr: wanton insolence, L. *superbia*, transgression of all divine and human rights, exceeding of measure), which means stepping outside of the rules which the group has set for its members.

This act is according to ancient tragedy the first tragic guilt of the tragic hero, who in the end is always defeated. This is to remind you that the Greek roots are not only in mythology, but also in ancient tragedy.] "The poet who has taken this step, has in this way set himself free from the group in his imagination." The hero in our case is none other than George himself. The hero—longing for a father in his imagination—is seeking to revive the primal father and become the chief of the group. I believe that George does want men (grandfather, father, himself) to be the leaders of the family, as opposed to the women (mother, wife, analyst).

The very first time George came to see me, he complained about his wife to the effect that she was a very good mother, but that she would not let the boys become independent. In his opinion she needed treatment. The patient reported a few examples about this that are of no relevance to our case. It was obvious that what made him anxious was that he was passively submitting to his wife's controlling power over himself and his sons. I thought that here we were dealing with a mother who permitted incest, and who was perhaps pre-genitalizing it—a powerful mother who controlled father and son, and who played games with both of them.

George was not aware that the struggle with his father was an internal one. Neither was he aware of the fact that he was trying to settle an intrapsychic conflict by external means, such as the use of a name that seemed to possess magic powers. He actually believed that he had solved all of his problems.

In recapitulating, I would like to say that, when George was planning to have a family, he was progressively becoming more anxious as to whether he would be in a position to assume leadership within his own family, or whether he would eventually submit to his wife and thus repeat the same situation that had existed within his original family.

He feared fatherhood—that is, entering into a new oedipal situation, whereby he would have to become somebody like Laius, who was obliged to deal with his son Oedipus. His own oedipal situation was in this fashion being reactivated.

Then what he did was to project and displace his oedipal feelings onto his son and identify with him. This revived the situation when he was a child, and he longed for a father who would protect him from his mother. I believe that his wish to restore his father was a revival of this longing.

His wish not to repeat the same oedipal destiny and his fear that he might were sources of great anxiety for him. The strong, conflicting forces that were dominant within him, and their mutual inhibition, made him resort to this individual solution —that is, the usage of a myth in an attempt to resolve his problems; in his effort he chose the myth of "The Voyage of Argo" which psychologically seemed to suit him best. His difficulties in working through his problems, in other words, forced him to seek solutions that were illusionary and imaginary.

It is not surprising that he reported this version of his myth, and all of the above material, when his son was nearly four years of age and was expressing his oedipal intentions. In fact, he entered analysis at the time when his son's murderous desires towards him became too much for him to bear. We must here remember that the patient was of the same age (four) when his brother Spiros (who had been named after his grandfather) had died; this age stands, therefore, for him as a reminder of the fact that his brother Spiros had been the victim, not only of his parents, but also of George himself, due to the hostility he had shown towards him as the intruder of the existing binary situation with his mother.

During his analytical "voyage", his unconscious is progressively unfolding, in parallel with "The Voyage of Argo". We follow the history and the vicissitude of his wish and, in the transference situation, we can clearly discern his compulsion to repeat his childhood experience within the analytical process: he storms into the analysis like a hero wishing to alter his destiny, prepared to go through the necessary sacrifices and undergo the painful working through, and ends up in the image of a four-year-old boy who is asking his female analyst to apply "magic" and thus change his destiny. Which is exactly what happened to Jason in "The Voyage of Argo"; he started off as a hero, but ended up as a child at the mercy of Medea.

The whole regressive picture can now be understood, together with the reason for which George has to transmit his message to the analyst in such a disguised way, as well as the reason for his having sought treatment when his son is four years old.

The patient's feelings for his firstborn, Peter, are, in my contention, that Peter's destiny is not in danger because, by naming him after his father, he projected and displaced on him all the love he had for his father. To his second son, Jason, however, he was passing on all the hatred of the ambivalent feelings he had for his father.

I think it is clear that this myth was used by George as a defensive measure against his great oedipal anxiety, and against the return of the repressed. However, this defensive method does not meet with success; as Freud points out, "In the realm of fantasy repression remains all-powerful in myths" (Freud, 1913d, p. 223). It is also evident that by the use of myths he has resolved his oedipal problems only in his imagination.

I believe that this defensive measure was motivated not only by his anxiety, but also by his guilt towards his oedipal objects and his younger brother, as well as by the longing for his father, which was being mobilized with the reactivation of his oedipal situation. However, he also possessed what Freud calls "a creative sense of guilt": "They feel remorse for the deed and decide that it should never be repeated and that its performance should bring no advantage" (Freud, 1912–13, p. 159).

Another factor that should not be disregarded in considering the patient's choice of myths, songs, and so on is his apparent identification with his father, a musician, who, like Orpheus—a demigod of arts and healing—cannot fight but soothes the opposing parties with his lyre and settles arguments amongst people. Orpheus played a similar role in "The Voyage of Argo". There was also, his identification with his mother, who often told him stories about her father, and so on.

The function of George's myth is to transmit his message in a disguised way due to the transference situation, whereby he avoids exposing himself and waits to see whose side the analyst will take—his father's or his own. His disguised wish is expressed through and by the complicated content of the myth, as well as by the use of mechanisms such as denial, splitting, projecting, and displacement. This in itself portrays a very fearful person.

The use of myths as a means of resolving problems is a regression to primitive thinking—i.e. from logical and rational thinking (Freud, 1912–13); a regression to the first system of thought or the first picture of the universe, i.e. the animistic or mythological one. Magic and omnipotence of thought are part of the technique and strategy of the animistic phase. The world of magic "treats past situations as if they were present" (Freud, 1912–13, p. 85). "The animistic phase would correspond to narcissism, both chronologically and in its content" (Freud, 1912–13, p. 90).

We have seen how George's anxiety made him regress to the animistic or mythological–narcissistic phase, which is characterized by omnipotence of thought, magic, and narcissistic triumph (Freud, 1914). Another evidence of his narcissism is that he overvalues psychical acts as opposed to factual reality, and that he reacts to thought just as seriously as normal people would react to reality. The thought is a substitute for the deed.

The patient's mythology reflects to some extent his instinctual world. By the use of myths he "renounces his instinctual satisfaction" (Freud, 1912–13, pp. 93–98) to some degree, despite the fact that the pleasure principle is at work. He does not offer to himself substitute objects or substitute acts in the place of the prohibited ones (because everything is in his imagination), so I don't believe there is much compensation (Freud, 1912–13, pp. 28–50) for the lack of satisfaction in his wishes. In this way he does not facilitate the binding of his unsatisfied wishes; he remains bound to his original objects and perpetuates his conflictual psychological state.

What we learn while accompanying George on his personal, unconscious voyage is that he has not resolved his oedipal problems by the use of myths, as he was hoping to; that the use of this myth is a defensive measure against anxieties and the return of the repressed, which, of course, is unsuccessful, because the painful working-through process is bypassed.

People come to analysis to do something about their past, and about their destiny. George came to an analyst in the hope of receiving help to fulfil his wish, which is that of escaping his oedipal destiny. The fact that he transmits this message in a disguised fashion (through the myth) may only signify that, by projecting on the analyst his oedipal claims, he is afraid that she, too, like his mother, will trap him into an incestuous relationship and set him against his father. He is, therefore, afraid that he will suffer the same fate as Jason in "The Voyage of Argo", whereby Jason is finally defeated by Medea by submitting to her persuasion that his father-substitute, King Pelias, must die, so that the oracle proclaiming that Jason would kill Pelias may indeed come true.

It is hoped that the patient will be able to go through the painful process of working through, which will enable him to resolve his oedipal problems successfully and make his own oracle come true.

## 2.   THE VOYAGE OF ARGO: A PROCESS OF MOURNING

> We only wonder why a man has to be ill before he can be accessible to a truth of this kind.
>
> Freud, 1917e, p. 246
>
> George "*veut aller au ciel sans mourir*".
> [George wants to go to heaven without dying]
>
> Charles Baudelaire, 1821–1867

In my study for this work I was tempted to treat the subject by applying concepts such as projective identification, counter-projective identification, and so forth, as I had done in my recent papers. However, I preferred to adhere to the Freudian theory, as I did in 1984, when the first part of this chapter was first written.

I believe that the clinical material presented in the first part of this chapter is sufficient to illustrate the point I wish to make with reference to the parallel voyage of mourning for patient and analyst within the transference–countertransference voyage.

---

Since I began writing about countertransference, the need to write about this patient prompted me to revise this work within that context. This second part was written in May 1991, when the patient had long completed his analysis.

It becomes evident that the patient, instead of going through the process of mourning, attempts to resolve his problems through the use of magical thinking, omnipotence, megalomania, and illusions, as these are contained in fairy tales and myths; more specifically, by the use of the myth of Jason in the Voyage of Argo, which unconsciously suits him best. By employing a variety of defensive manoeuvres, he wishes to circumvent the voyage of mourning, which is related to his heritage of unresolved mourning (for losses, such as deaths, abrupt separation, idealization of objects, etc., in both his paternal and maternal families and transmitted to him from generation to generation through his parents), as well as his own unresolved mourning. Thus he proposes to restore his paternal line (i.e. his father, through him his grandfather, and ultimately himself) by using the myth of Jason (which is illusionary) but without having to mourn for his cruel grandfather, for his father who was thrown out of his family by his own father, for himself who was trapped in an incestuous relationship with his mother who set him against his father, and so forth.

Moreover, it was quite clear that the burden of his heritage became too much for him to bear and work through, so by projecting and displacing the myth of the voyage of Argo on his son Jason he charged him with his own debt—i. e. the role of doing what he felt he himself was obliged to do, which was to restore his paternal line. This would free him of his fate and allow him to lead a better life. To this end, he chose to spare himself the pain of suffering involved in going through the process of mourning, which was the only way for his goal to be achieved, and he bypassed it by using the magical and illusionary thinking contained in myths and tales.

Along with his family's heritage of unresolved mourning, the heritage of defensive measures used by George's ancestors against mourning was also passed to him through the parent-child relationship. These defensive measures—i.e. the use of myths—were meant for him to be "immortal". Myths, after all, are immortal. Let it be remembered, for example, that the myth of Jason was created in the third century B.C. Myths do not only fail to resolve mourning, but they also serve to perpetuate and prolong it. Freud says that "the existence of the lost object is psychically prolonged" (Freud, 1917e, p. 245). These defensive measures constitute therefore fruitless attempts on the part of the user to deny his losses, i.e. death and separation. Thus the dead ancestors are kept alive in fantasy.

The patient was an average-looking man in his late 30s. During the early phase of his analysis he presented himself as a small, innocent, and harmless child, wearing a childish, yet seductive smile. He had a pleading look on his face, demanding the mercy of his analyst for his "misdeeds". He displayed abundant charm, often asking minor favours of his analyst, e.g. to change his appointment for a more convenient time, and so forth. He usually exhibited his weak, impotent, and fearful side to his analyst, keeping out of the analysis that part of himself which was playing a leading role in society. During the analysis, this behaviour reappeared at moments of regression. By presenting himself in this fashion, what he really wanted of his analyst was to make her accept his method of resolving his problems (by magic, etc.) and, in return, have the analyst "love" him, use magic means, and thus save him from going through the process of mourning. He wished to "seduce" her and repeat with her the relationship that he had had with his mother.

He often succeeded in making the analyst feel sorry for him for having to go through so much pain. She would tell herself, "Poor George, why couldn't life have been easier for him. . . . What bad luck he had to grow up in a family beset with such problems . . .", etc. Up to this point it did not take long, nor was it difficult for the analyst to be aware of her own projection of sadness to the patient and her identification with him, to deal with these feelings adequately and to continue the analytical process.

At other times the patient would try to gain control over the analytical situation by imposing his own technique (i.e. the rules governing myths, magic, etc.) on the analyst in place of those of analysis—just like his unconsciously "witchy" mother had imposed on him her own rules of dealing with mourning, had shared with him her own myths about her dead and idealized father (who was, nevertheless, very much alive in her mind), had set him against his father, and had kept him in an incestuous relationship with her. She was a mother who overprotected him and excited him at the same time. Thus it may be

said that the patient's earliest reality was his mother's unconscious.

The function of the tales and myths lies in the fact that the
teller and the listener share omnipotence, magical thinking,
identifications with heroes and their achievements; further,
they provide acoustic satisfaction (acoustic holding), satisfaction of libidinal and aggressive impulses (through the heroic
acts), temporary relief from conflicts and catharsis to a certain
extent. Freud (1913d) says that myths are seeking a compensation for the lack of satisfaction of human wishes and that the
function of the myth is to prevent the return of the repressed.
Some myths, such as the one we are dealing with (the Voyage of
Argo), circumvent the mourning process and offer illusionary
solutions.

During his analytical "voyage", the patient's unconscious
was progressively unfolding, in parallel with "the Voyage of
Argo". In doing so, he proved to be a very gifted story-teller. It
is precisely this element that turned out to be the difficult part
in the analyst's countertransference. She often caught herself
being amused and getting satisfaction from the patient's extraordinary narrative of the adventures of Argo's voyage.

My childhood experience as a listener to myths and tales is
quite pertinent at this point. As no television existed at the time
and the households consisted of many relatives living together,
Greek children were brought up and nourished by the adults
who used to narrate to them all sorts of myths and tales, which
lasted for several hours at a time. This happened as a rule
when the children were being put to bed or had been naughty.
In this fashion they would relax and go peacefully to sleep or to
school.

I was personally over-indulged as a child and tremendously
amused (as a listener) by the stories of a certain gifted relative
who lived with us and who was around for several years during
my childhood. He was an untiring story-teller who drew a great
deal of joy out of his narrations to us children. His tales made
me travel many an adventurous journey and identify with several heroes and their achievements. I went on the voyage of
Argo many a time with him and enjoyed it tremendously. I am
often nostalgic about the experience of sharing with this story-
teller the tales, the heroes and their exploits, the magic means,

the omnipotence of the myths, etc. Though we both knew there was not much truth in them, we never confessed it to one another, because it would have meant the end of our relationship and of our enjoyment.

In fact, between story-teller and listener a certain complicity always seems to exist, which aims at maintaining this special relationship that is so enjoyable and significant to both. This relationship can be of vital importance, when it is the substitute for a parental one.

Back to the "hero" of our paper, the patient proved to be most skilful in detecting my countertransference feelings and in making use of this knowledge for his own benefit. He had acquired these skills mainly from the interaction with his mother, becoming an expert in detecting her feelings and often making use of them. If I had let myself be carried away on this "Voyage of Argo", I would have repeated with the patient my own past experience. I would have put him in the place of the story-teller (past important figure) and kept the position of passive listener. At the same time, he would have repeated with me his experience with his mother by reversing the roles. Thus, patient and analyst would have travelled within their transferential–countertransferential voyage in such a way that the psychoanalytic voyage would have missed its objective entirely.

Much to her distress, the analyst became aware of her countertransferential feelings of sadness for having to frustrate "poor George" and for having to play the unpleasant role of the person who would have to lead him through the painful voyage of mourning. Because of her identification with him, her feelings were projected onto the patient. The analyst had to accept and suffer the loss of the mythical aspect of her significant family figure—the story-teller—as well as the mythical aspect of herself. She also had to suffer the loss of the mythical aspect of their relationship (story-teller and analyst–listener). She had, in other words, to demythologize this important experience, in order to gain a more realistic understanding of it (mythological vs. realistic)—i.e. the magical (paranoid–schizoid) dimension of this relationship was contextualized in a new way by a depressive form of experience.

This realization and its inevitable outcome were for her quite painful. It was like finding herself at a cross-roads. Her countertransference was put to the test: she either had to accept the patient's appointed role or to renounce her satisfaction and go on with the psychoanalytical voyage. She was fortunately willing to go through her own voyage of mourning, step by step and bit by bit, before she could help the patient and lead the way for him to get on with his own—similar—voyage of mourning. In parallel and within the transference–countertransference voyage, both parties—patient and analyst—had to go through a specific voyage of mourning with reference to their similar experience. From there on it became possible—despite several set-backs—for the psychoanalytic voyage to achieve its objective in an atmosphere of empathy, due to concordant identification, rather than in an atmosphere of sympathy caused by the analyst's complementary identification (Racker, 1957; Kernberg, 1987).

Obviously, this patient was the only one in my psychoanalytic career who obliged me to come face to face with this part of my past, which I had preciously protected from analytical scrutiny. He further forced me to work through my own countertransference, without which his analysis would have totally failed.

## Summary and discussion

The patient came to a female analyst and entered analysis like an innocent, helpless—yet seductive—child asking for help. He felt he was at the mercy of his wife (a mother substitute), who did not let her male children grow and become independent. In his opinion, she was in urgent need of treatment.

During analysis it became obvious that when he was planning on having a family, he began to question his ability to assume leadership within his own family and feared that he would eventually submit to his wife and repeat with her the same situation that had existed within his original family.

The patient wished to free himself of his oedipal ties and assume manhood. He longed for the restoration of his paternal line, which included his father, his grandfather, and, finally, himself. Through this restoration he also aimed at changing his mother's status within his family by having her submit to the potent father.

However, the way he proposed to achieve this goal was by avoiding going through the process of mourning. "We only wonder why a man has to be ill before he can be accessible to a truth of this kind" (Freud, 1917e, p. 246). George "wanted to go to heaven without dying," as Baudelaire put it. Instead, he attempted to resolve his oedipal heritage by means of magic, fairy tales, and especially by employing the myth of Jason and the Voyage of Argo. He named his son Jason after the hero of the myth and charged him with the mission of fulfilling his own wishes.

In the course of analysis, it became apparent that his unresolved oedipal problems, as well as his unresolved mourning—i.e. his inability to mourn—had been transmitted to him from generation to generation, both from his paternal and maternal families, through the parent–child relationship. At the same time his ancestors' defensive measures against mourning (use of fairy tales, myths, magical thinking, omnipotence, illusionary solutions, etc.) were transmitted to him in the same way. As a result, the mourning was prolonged and perpetuated, instead of becoming completed and terminated by the acceptance of the losses.

> They must then have persisted from generation to generation, perhaps merely as a result of tradition transmitted through parental and social authority. Possibly, however, in later generations they have become "organised" as an inherited psychical endowment. [Freud, 1912–13, p. 31]

During his analytical voyage, the patient's unconscious was progressively unfolding in parallel with the "Voyage of Argo". While this was taking place, he was trying, by reversing the roles, to seduce his analyst and thus repeat with her the relation he had had with his mother.

The analyst caught herself to be gaining amusement and satisfaction from the patient's narrative of the adventures of Argo's voyage. This was due to a similar experience she had had in her own childhood, where she was often entertained by the myths and stories narrated to her by a significant family member. Her countertransference was thus put to the test: she would either have to repeat with the patient her own past experience, or give up her enjoyment and go through her own process of mourning, which consisted of demythologizing her experience and accepting her losses. In this fashion she would be able to help the patient go through his own process of mourning, i.e. demythologizing of his own experience and acceptance of his losses. Hence in parallel and within the transference–countertransference voyage, both parties—patient and analyst—had to go through a specific voyage of mourning with reference to their similar experiences. From there on it became possible for the psychoanalytic voyage to achieve its objectives.

It is understood that the mourning related to the patient's oedipal resolution also took place, enabling him to assume manhood and to get on with his life. Obviously the patient's transmitted heritage of unresolved oedipal problems of his paternal and maternal families acted as an accomplice to his little boy's fantasy life at a time when he was struggling with his own libidinal and hostile oedipal desires. This rendered the solution of his oedipal conflict more difficult than usual.

These superimposed experiences—which had a traumatic element in them—were used by the patient as resistance against further exploration of his unconscious. However, during the process of his analysis it became possible to interpret these traumatic events as though they were his own projections and the result of omnipotent childlike thinking, e.g. that the patient had caused his father impotence and submission to his mother, etc. From that point on the mourning and identification processes, which had been blocked by the patient's repressed infantile fantasies, were able to resume their course.

## Postscript

I had already completed this work when I came across Dr Vamik Volkan's views on the "Chosen Trauma" and the "Chosen Glory" (Volkan, 1991), which, I found, related well to the subject. Dr. Volkan writes:

The "chosen trauma" refers to an event that causes a large group to feel helpless and victimized by another group. What is "chosen" is the psychologizing and mythologizing of the event. By this I mean that the group draws the mental representation of the traumatic event into its identity. This mental representation is passed from generation to generation as a psychological marker. This intergenerational transmission occurs because the chosen trauma . . . is activated in the parent–child relationship; and every child, regardless of the differences in his or her developing personality, identifies with the effects of the chosen trauma. Chosen traumas are not mourned. Sometimes a group is too humiliated, too angry, and, at the same time, too helpless to mourn over the chosen trauma. The "inability to mourn" is also passed from one generation to the next generation. The new generations share a conscious and unconscious wish to repair what is done to their ancestors and to unburden themselves from the humiliation which is now part of their identity. Alongside the "chosen trauma" the leader may also evoke from his followers an identification with the group's "chosen glory"—with the mental representations of successful past generations, past leaders, etc. The activation of both the "chosen trauma" and the "chosen glory" are psychological efforts to maintain the group's identity and the leader–follower relationship at times of regression.

Although Dr Volkan's conclusions are drawn from his observations of large social groups, I believe that they may well apply to smaller groups, such as families. In our case, the patient is the victim of his paternal family's "chosen trauma", namely the psychologizing and mythologizing of his father's traumatic experience of being thrown out of his family by his own father. At the same time he is the victim of his maternal family's "chosen trauma", i.e. the death of his mother's father when she was fifteen. Both parental "chosen traumas" are mixed with "chosen glory" elements, more so in the case of the patient's mother who glorified her trauma—the death of her father, whom she over-idealized and mythologized, keeping him thus immortal.

From these observations I find myself in agreement with Dr Volkan's views with regard to (1) the concepts of "chosen trauma" and "chosen glory", which I find extremely useful; (2)

the ways in which these "chosen traumas" and "chosen glories" are transmitted from one generation to the other; (3) the fact that these traumas cannot be mourned and that this inability is also passed from one generation to the other; and (4) the fact that individuals, such as our patient, have a strong wish to repair whatever has been done to their ancestors in order to free themselves and have a better life.

What I would here venture to add is (1) that there are "chosen traumas" that are the vehicles of "chosen glory" elements, as may be seen in our case (allowing us to speak, in extreme cases of "glorified traumas"); and (2) that along with the "chosen traumas" and the "chosen glories" come the "chosen defensive measures" which, at least in some cases, are also transmitted from one generation to the other. In our case, in order for the patient to resolve the effects of the chosen traumas passed to him by his parents, he makes use—by identification with his mother and his ancestors—of their "chosen defensive reactions"—i.e. of the fairy tales and myths and, more specifically, of the myth of Jason, in which he involves his own son, in the same way that his mother had involved him in hers. Freud (1939a) writes: "The effects of traumas are of two kinds, positive and negative" and "the negative reactions follow the opposite aim: that nothing of the forgotten traumas shall be remembered and nothing repeated. We can summarize them as 'Defensive Reactions'" (p. 76).

## Conclusions

From the study of this case it becomes evident that it is quite important during the working-through process for the analyst to pay special attention to the analysis of the patient's "chosen" traumatic events and "chosen" defensive measures. To this effect Freud writes, "Such an event as an external trauma is bound . . . to set in motion every possible defensive measure" (1920g, p. 29). The patient can thus be better understood and helped to go through his particular voyage, as it became possible in our case.

It should be kept in mind that the "chosen" traumatic events serve the function of resistance to the unfolding of the analytical process. They can be used as an alibi; as a resistance to further exploration of these traumas.

Let it be remembered that patients par excellence project their feelings and fantasies to the "chosen" traumatic events.

The analytical process progresses if the "chosen" traumatic events can be interpreted as though they were a projection, the result of omnipotent childlike thinking. From this point on (in our case) the mourning and identification processes, blocked by the patient's repressed infantile fantasies, are able to resume their course. Thus I am in full agreement with Joyce McDougall (1980) regarding the handling of these traumas in the psychoanalytic situation.

In some cases, like the one presented in this paper, the affect aroused in the analyst by the patient during the analytic session—i.e. the countertransference affect—is the first signal that informs the analyst that his countertransference feelings should be further examined; in my case, these were "feeling sorry for poor George", being amused by the patient's extraordinary narratives of the adventures of Argo's voyage, and so forth. Thus this investigation will lead the way to further exploration of the analyst's total countertransference reactions (Beres & Arlow, 1974; McDougall, 1980; Schafer, 1959; Tansey & Burke, 1989). It is understood that this first signal (the countertransference affect) will at the same time alert the analyst of the inner experience of his patient and help him in formulating his interpretation in the psychoanalytic situation.

Our study further shows—as this has been demonstrated time and time again—that we, analysts, in searching for the truth in the unconscious of our patients, come face to face (through our countertransference) with our own truth in our own unconscious. How we deal with this truth will be the decisive factor that will determine the outcome of the analysis. In our case the analyst's discovery of the truth put her countertransference to the test. Thus she was obliged to go through a specific voyage of mourning, parallel and similar to that of her patient. In this way the psychoanalytic process eventually achieved its objectives.

When the analyst feels the need to write about a particular case, this reflects his or her need further to work through
and understand the relationship between transference and
countertransference, with the emphasis on the countertransference. Let it be reminded that writing is, after all, a working-
through process in itself.

# CHAPTER FIVE

# Countertransference
# and primitive communication

*Joyce McDougall*

C ertain patients recount or reconstruct in analysis traumatic events that have occurred in their childhood. The question has sometimes been raised as to whether we treat this type of material differently from other analytic associations furnished by the patient. And if so, what are the differences? Ever since Freud's discovery that the traumatic sexual seductions of his hysterical patients revealed themselves to be fantasies based on infantile sexual wishes, analysts have been wary of mistaking fantasy for reality. Nevertheless there are many "real" events that leave a traumatic scar on our patients—such as the early death of a father, having a psychotic mother, or a childhood handicapped by illness. When these events are within conscious recall, they inevitably present us with special problems because of the varied use the patient will make of them, and in particular because he will so frequently

First published under the title, "Le Contre-transfert et la Communication Primitive", *Topique* (1975), No. 16; translated into English by the author.

advance the argument that there is nothing to analyse in this material since the events "really happened". They have, however, become part of the patient's psychic reality and must therefore be listened to with particular attention.

With regard to traumatic events stemming from even earlier periods, before the acquisition of *verbal* communication, the detection of their existence becomes considerably more complicated—to the point that we may only become aware of the traumatic dimension through the unconscious pressure it exerts on the analysand's way of being and speaking, and thus may eventually only be accessible if captured through our *countertransference reactions*.

Before proceeding further, it is necessary to define what constitutes a psychic trauma for any given individual, since it is evident that events that may have exercised a deleterious effect on one patient appear to have left another unscathed. The appreciation of "traumatic" sequelae is further complicated by the need to distinguish these from the universal "traumas" inherent to the human psyche, namely the drama of separating oneself off from the Other, the traumatic implications of sexual difference with the interdictions and frustrations it engenders, and finally, the inexorable reality of death. Human beings must come to terms with each of these traumatic realities, or they will fall psychically ill. My contention is that a catastrophic event may in general be considered traumatic to the extent that it has impeded the confrontation and resolution of these ineluctable catastrophes that structure man's psychic reality.

Before coming to the question of *early* psychic trauma in adult patients, it is pertinent to the aim of this chapter to consider briefly the role played in analysis by catastrophic events that have occurred after the acquisition of language and the capacity for verbal thought. Such events when recounted in the course of the analysis often present themselves as unshakeable facts, rather than as thoughts and free associations that can be explored psychically, and as such they serve the function of resistance to the unfolding of the analytic process.

Such was the case with a male patient whose mother had been killed in a road accident while driving her car, when he was only six years old. The father, warm-hearted and attentive to his little boy, was also represented as being somewhat alcoholic and, at such times, irresponsible. In the early months of his analysis the analysand attributed the totality of his neurotic character problems to his mother's premature death, thus using the tragedy as an alibi, which became a resistance to further questioning. Later his associations revealed the fantasy that the accident was in fact a suicide. In the mind of the bereaved child his father's drinking problem and irresponsibility (representing, in the unconscious, a form of sadistic primal scene) had pushed his mother to this act of despair; the father was therefore responsible for the loss of his mother. However, under the impact of the ongoing analytic process, yet another fantasy came to light: it was he himself who was responsible for this crime. He wished to take his mother's place with his father and be the only one to share in his warm sensuous way of relating. By dint of magical thinking he had caused the death of his mother. Whatever the facts of her accidental death may have been, the only reality with which our analytic work was concerned was this inner reality, a childhood fantasy based on a repressed homosexual wish and a repressed death wish towards the mother. These unconscious wishes weighed heavily upon the psychic functioning and the libidinal economy of the patient. An external event had accidentally become an accomplice to the little boy's fantasy life at a time when he was already struggling with homosexual and heterosexual oedipal desires, thus presenting him with a doubly traumatic experience that was to render the solution to his oedipal conflict more than usually difficult. In the process of the analysis it became possible to interpret the tragic happening *as though it were a projection*, the result of omnipotent childlike thinking. From this point onward the mourning and identification processes, blocked by the patient's repressed infantile fantasies, were able to resume their course. In place of a constant feeling of living fraudulently, of inner deadness, of terror in the face of any fantasy wishes, the patient was now able to construct an inner world peopled with living events and objects, and thus confront the world of others on a more adequate basis.

Although it is important to distinguish between real and fantasy events, it is nevertheless true on the whole that psychoanalysis can do nothing to modify the effects of catastrophic events if they cannot also be experienced as omnipotent fantasies; only then can the analysand truly possess these events as an integral part of his *psychic capital*, a treasure trove that he alone can control and render fruitful. In other words, no one can be held responsible for the tragedies or traumatic relationships that the external objects and the world have brought into the small child's ken, but every individual is uniquely responsible for his *internal objects* and his *inner world*. The important thing is to discover to what use he puts this inner treasury with its full quota of pain and loss.

It is admissible on this basis to hold that traumatic events often function as screen memories and as such may yield much valuable analytic material. Neurotic symptoms may be conceived of in general as springing from parental words and attitudes, more precisely, from the child's *interpretation* of his parents' silent and verbal communications; they may likewise arise from his interpretation and psychic elaboration of traumatic happenings, as in the case cited above. In the long run, the analyst's way of handling material stemming from traumatic events, although more complicated, is not markedly different from his way of dealing with neurotic intrapsychic conflict. From the point of view of countertransference, he has only to be aware of the danger of complaisant confusion with the patient, since the tragic event, or crippling accident, did actually take place.

Can the same be true for traumatic experiences that have occurred before the acquisition of verbal thought and communication through the symbolic use of speech? In the first years of life the child communicates through signs, chiefly cries and gestures, rather than through language. And in fact he can only be said to *communicate* by means of these signs to the extent that they are understood by another who treats them as communications. From this point of view it may be said that *a baby's earliest reality is in his mother's unconscious*. The traces of this early relationship are not inscribed in the preconscious, as are those elements that have become part of the symbolic verbal chain; they have a different psychic position from representations contained in the form of *repressed* fantasies, and thus have little chance of seeking partial expression through neurotic symptoms. The traumatic phenomena of infancy (*in-fans* = non-speaking) belong to the area of primal repression.

When subjected to mental pain, the baby can only re-establish his narcissistic equilibrium through primitive defences such as projection–introjection and splitting mechanisms, hallucination and repudiation, and these are only effective to the extent that the relationship with the mother allows them to operate through her attempts to understand her infant and her capacity for introjective identification with him. It should be noted in passing that psychic suffering at this pre-symbolic phase is indistinguishable from physical suffering, a fact that is evident in psychotic communications as well as in many psychosomatic manifestations. If the verbal child may be said to *interpret* his parents' communications in his own way, the infant makes, so to speak, a *simultaneous translation* of the parents' conscious and unconscious messages. Since the capacity to capture another's affect precedes the acquisition of language, the nursling cannot but *react* to his mother's emotional experience and her unconscious transmission of it in her way of relating to her baby. The mother's ability to capture and respond to her infant's needs will depend on her willingness *to give meaning* to his cries and movements, allowing him eventually to introject this meaning and be in communication with his own needs. Outside of what he represents for his mother, the baby has no psychic existence. Not only is she the assurance of his biological and psychological continuity, she is also his *thinking apparatus* (Bion, 1970).

This digression concerning the mother–baby relationship may serve to elucidate two of the main themes of this chapter —namely, the nature of our analytic approach to those analysands who would seem to be marked by a breakdown in communication with the mother in babyhood, and second the way in which such breakdown may express itself in the analytic relationship. The burden of this lack may then fall to the analyst, who will find himself in the position of the mother, obliged to decode or to give meaning to his patient's baby-like, inarticulate messages. It is of course true that this primitive form of communication and archaic link is always present in the relation between analyst and analysand. We might call it the original, or *fundamental transference*. But this basic dimension does not require particular emphasis when the analytic discourse is freely associative, and when its manifest aim is to communicate thoughts and feeling states to the analyst. We are then listening to a manifest communication that contains rich latent meaning to the analytic ear. The patients I have in mind use speech in a way that has little in common with the language of free association. In listening to them the analyst may have a feeling that it is a meaningless communication at all levels, or he may be aware of being invaded with affect that does not seem directly attributable to the content of the patient's communication. The question is how to understand and use such countertransference affect. I hope to show that these analysands frequently use language as an *act* rather than a symbolic means of communication of ideas or affect. At such times, unknown to analyst and patient alike, the latter is revealing the effect of a catastrophic failure in communication that has occurred at a time when he was unable to contain or to work through, psychically, what he was experiencing. The traces of these early failures are either confined to somatic expression, which may be considered as an archaic mode of thought, or may give a hint of their presence by the incoherences and blanks they produce in the patient's way of thinking and feeling about what happens to him or concerns him. Such experiences may leave some verbal traces or find symbolic expression, but the attempt to elaborate or interpret these stops short. One may discover that with such patients any feeling or fleeting thought that risks re-animating the original catastrophic situation is immediately stifled, or ejected from the mind, with such force that the individual will suffer from authentic disturbance in his thinking processes or may appear to function like a robot. He is unable to allow sufficient psychic space or sufficient time for the unconscious remnants to become available to conscious processes. Once the nascent thought or feeling has been ejected, he will frequently plunge into action of some kind in an attempt to ward off the return of the unwelcome representation and mask the void left by the ejected material. Economically speaking such action assures a certain discharge of tension, and might thus be termed an "action-symptom". In this way talking itself may be a symptomatic *act* and therefore an "anti-communication". The analyst might thus capture in negative what has been up till then an inexpressible drama. The lost material behind such action-symptoms will often reach symbolic expression, for example, in dreams, but then fail to stimulate associations or mobilize affect.

Here is an example of one such dream from a patient whose problems led one to suspect that his inner world contained many areas of desolation and destruction of meaning:

> "I dreamed I was back in the town where I was born. It's a small village, but in my dream it was vast. And empty. There wasn't a living soul. Empty houses, empty streets. Even the trees were dead. . . . I woke up suddenly. There was more to the dream, but I can't remember what. And all because of my wife! We had a violent dispute at that moment over some silly thing. And I don't remember that either."

No associations were given, and the patient's interest in his dream seemed to vanish with the telling of it. The dream theme, which awakened in the analyst a feeling of desolation and of something uncanny, gave rise to no such sentiments in the analysand. On the other hand, his quarrel with his wife, a familiar theme with this patient, continued to fill him with rage, even though he had forgotten what the quarrel was about. His intensity over the incident was in marked contrast to the deadness of the dream theme and mood. An unconscious link between the two "forgotten" items clearly provides a clue to the dynamics of the patient's psychic situation. We had already discovered that he only felt "fully alive" when he was engaged in hostile exchanges with those around him. The quarrel was a form of "manic defence" against dead or depressing inner experiences, the latter having failed to find representation in either thought or feeling. There was little doubt in my mind and indeed in the mind of this patient that he had suffered early psychic catastrophe in his relation to those who cared for him, but there were no memory traces, and such remnants as were able to arise from unconscious sources led to no further associations. They appeared to seek expression solely in action. The repressed elements from which we might hope to reconstruct the infantile past are non-existent here. The "catastrophe" has affected the patient's capacity to think about himself and to contain painful affect, and can thus only be guessed at through his acts—acts not yet capable of translation into communicable thought.

For certain analysands, *speech itself becomes this act* in the analytic relationship. Rather than seeking to communicate ideas, moods, and free associations, the patient seems to aim at making the analyst *feel* something, or stimulating him to *do* something: this "something" is incapable of being named, and the patient himself is totally unaware of this aim. Such an analysand will often put questions to his analyst or say things like "Well, after all the things I've told you, isn't it time you said something? Can't you tell me what's wrong with my life?" Or: "How do I know there's someone there if you don't speak? I might as well talk to a wall!" Obviously, all patients are apt to express such feelings, but the usual neurotic patient will accept that his turning to the analyst and addressing him in this way has scme meaning and will try to co-operate with the analyst when he seeks to interpret the feelings that prompt such remarks. With luck he will recognize readily that a child-like part of him demands reassurance or feels frustrated by the rigors of the analytic relationship, and he may then use this insight to further his understanding of his personal history and his forgotten past. But the patients I have in mind are not able to maintain sufficient distance to observe these phenomena in themselves and so are unable to examine the underlying significance of their transference. They feel constantly angry or depressed with the analysis and yet desperate about the feeling of stagnation. The demand that the analyst interpret in a context in which there is no apparent interpretable material is a sign that the analysand is in the throes of an experience that cannot be expressed, giving way instead to a feeling of uneasiness. This in turn makes him want to call upon the analyst to show signs of his existence in order to stifle the rising tide of emotion, or to put a stop to the continuation of the analytic process. One discovers later that at such moments the patient is inundated by feelings of rage, or anxiety, to a degree that prevents him from *thinking further* in this context. In his distress he is no longer sure that he is accompanied by a live person who is listening and following him, in his difficult analytic adventure.

The analyst, who tends to feel constantly questioned or pushed to take action, will at the same time find himself blocked whenever he attempts to interpret. That is, he will become aware *that he is no longer functioning adequately as an analyst*. In fact, he is receiving what I am calling a *primitive communication*—in the same way in which we may conceive of an infant who is gesticulating wildly, or screaming, as *communicating* something to someone.

I am making two propositions here:

1. In these cases it is permissible to deduce the existence of sequelae to early psychic trauma, which will require specific handling in the analytic situation.

2. This "screen discourse", impregnated with messages that have never been elaborated verbally, can in the first instance only be captured by the arousal of countertransference affect.

To better illustrate what I am describing, I shall take a clinical example. This analytic fragment, which dates back over fifteen years, is not one of the most incisive to throw light on this type of analytic problem, but it is the only case on which I took lengthy notes at the time, and indeed was prompted to do so because I did not understand what was happening between my patient and myself. Since that time I have often been able to capture such oblique communications, and this has enabled me to establish better contact with an archaic dimension of the patient's psychic structure—thanks to what I was able to learn from the analysand about whom I am going to tell you.

\* \* \*

Annabelle Borne was 44 years old and had 11 years of analysis behind her when she was first sent to me by a male colleague. After a single interview with this colleague, she asked him for the name of a woman analyst. In our initial interview she told me she had already had three analysts. The first analysis had been terminated on her own initiative because the analyst became pregnant during the third year of the analysis, and this fact was intolerable to her. She continued for five more years with a male analyst, a valuable experience in her opinion since she was able for the first time in her life to have a sexual relationship, after many years of painful solitude, and to get married at the age of forty to a man with whom she shared many intellectual interests. Although not frigid, she was uninterested in the sexual side of their relationship. Partly because of this loss of sexual interest, but also because of a persistent feeling of dissatisfaction with all her relationships, a feeling of not understanding people, of being an outsider, badly treated by others, decided her to continue with a third analyst. The latter, after three yeas, advised her to discontinue on the grounds that she was "unanalysable".

Perhaps because I showed surprise at this apparently forthright prognosis, Mrs. Borne asked the analyst to write to me, which he did, saying that he did not advocate analysis but that the patient might benefit from a modified form of psychotherapy. In spite of this gloomy verdict, Annabelle Borne wanted to continue with analysis. Life seemed so hard, and she had already been greatly helped by her former analytic experience. At our second meeting she told me something of her initial reasons for seeking help. She did not feel "real" and had little contact with people of her own sex and none whatever with men. At the age of nine she had been sexually attacked by a brother six years older than she. For many years she believed that this event had permanently damaged her and was responsible for most of the painful aspects of her life. She no longer felt this to be a sufficient explanation of her difficulties, but that the answer to her problems probably lay within herself, although she could not see why. She added that she had little hope of finding an analyst who would suit her. She had not cared for Dr X who sent her to me, and she didn't care for me much either. Nevertheless, she had decided to ask me to accept her as a patient in spite of this mistrust. I, on the other hand, found her likeable. Her story intrigued me, and her frankness also. Several months later we began our work together, and this continued for four years.

Our first year together was trying for both of us. Nothing about me suited my patient. My silence exasperated her, and my interpretations even more so. My consulting room, my clothes, my furniture, my flowers incited constant criticism. As for her life outside analysis, it seemed that everyone in her entourage lacked tact, thoughtfulness, and understanding in their dealings with her. At the nursery school attended by her little boy, no one gave her the co-operation she expected. We searched in vain for some insight into this endless repetition, both within and without the analytic situation. Interpretations that one day seemed fruitful proved the day after to be sterile, or would give rise to a flood of denigrating remarks from my unhappy analysand. She considered me indifferent to her painful experiences or, if not, incompetent to understand and help her. When, one day, I remarked that she felt me to be a disastrous mother who would not, or could not, help her child to understand what life and living was all about, she replied that I was exactly like one of Harlowe's cloth monkeys—a reference to H. Harlowe's famous research experiments on infant rhesus monkeys brought up by a surrogate cloth mother. (These monkeys, incidentally, were noted for their incapacity for contact with other monkeys, and for their inappropriate expressions of rage.)

Annabelle also accused me of ridiculous optimism in continuing my persistent efforts to understand her distress. I myself began to feel that I was about as useful as a cloth monkey for all the good she was able to get out of our analytic work together. A couple of days later this pessimistic opinion became a certitude. On this occasion Annabelle Borne found yet another metaphor apt for expressing her discontent and irritation with her analyst. She had recently read of Konrad Lorenz's experiments with ducklings who have lost their mother in the first days of life. If presented with an old boot, they will follow it just as readily, and will show to this grotesque maternal substitute the same attachment as they would have shown towards a real mother. I was this old boot—and she, presumably, was the bereaved duckling. I suggested she was waiting for me to become a *real* mother to her. "Not at all", she replied. "I've never expected anything from anybody. But you're worse than nothing! This analysis is making no progress . . . if anything, my problems are getting worse . . . it costs money, so that all the family must suffer because of you. Otherwise we could have long holidays in the sun. But I keep coming here, no matter how bad the weather. . . . Impossible to park my car in this wretched Latin Quarter. I'm sick of analysts . . . sick of you . . . your blond hair, your consulting room, your flowers! You don't care about me—and you haven't the guts to tell me that this analysis is a waste of time!" And so on, till the end of the session. As she was leaving, Annabelle cast a withering glance at a pot of flowers on my desk and spat out one last furious remark: "People who like flowers should be florists—not analysts!"

This session was not markedly different from many that had preceded it, yet on this occasion I felt discouraged and depressed. Up to this point my patient's negativism, although fatiguing, had given me food for thought and led me to question the efficacy of a classical analytic approach with an analysand so devoid of insight and of willingness to examine anything at all. Yet she obviously suffered greatly, so I was prepared to carry on in the hope that one day we would discover the true object of her immense rage and frustration. But it now seemed to me that what little therapeutic alliance existed had finally fallen apart. She was clearly unwilling to continue in analysis, so why should I bother to encourage her in such a fruitless endeavour? The more I thought about it, the more I became convinced that she was right, though I was aware of stifling an uneasy feeling that I was simply slipping out of a disagreeable task and letting down a patient in distress. To get rid of this uneasiness, I decided to take notes on the session, and to make a summary of our year's work together—a final attempt to see more clearly into her impalpable psychic world.

Her parents as she presented them were a typical middle-class couple: father much admired but very involved with his professional activities, mother represented as somewhat vague, artistic, narcissistic. Then there was the brother at whose hands she had suffered sexual assault when she was nine. She had never dared tell her mother about it because he was the mother's favourite child; nor could she tell her father, because she felt too guilty about the whole incident. Her many years of analysis had led her to understand that she had experienced the sexual relation as an incestuous one with her father. In spite of its traumatizing quality, it had also repressed the fulfilment of an infantile oedipal desire. From her earlier analyses there had been many interpretations relating to penis envy as the basic reason for her bitterness and dissatisfaction with her life. She had complained often of her mother's preference for the older brother, and of the supposed facility of his life as compared with her "hard" existence, but other than this had furnished little material that warranted further interpretations of her envious attitude to her brother or his penis. Her associations tended to be centred on the feeling that her mother was more gifted, more feminine, more loved by the father and that she herself could never equal her mother. There was a recurring screen memory relating to her mother, which dated from the time when she was four or five years old. She had a clear vision of gazing at her mother's breasts, which were overflowing with "green sap". This fantasy–memory filled her with anguish. My attempts to link this green sap—sap of life? cadaverous death?—with other associations such as her feelings about the analysis and all she hoped or feared from her mother, or from me as an analytic nursing mother, had led us nowhere. My attempts to uncover the underlying significance of her manifest thoughts and feelings were rebuffed as a refusal to admit the daily injustices from which she suffered.

Apart from the vivid screen memory, there was little other evidence of fantasy activity and a paucity of dreams. My interventions had failed to set in motion that interplay of primary and secondary processes that is the hallmark of a functioning analysis. As for the transference, all attempts to find a meaning in it were given short shrift. I had little doubt that she experienced me as a bad, almost a dead mother, and that I and the whole environment that treated her so badly also occupied the place of the envied brother, nourished with the green sap of maternal love—of which Annabelle so clearly felt herself deprived. But a year's work had shown me that Annabelle wanted nothing of this, rather as though she clung to feeling angry and ill-treated and wanted to prove that nothing could be done about it.

Having thus collated and reflected on the many harassing questions this analysis raised in me, I took the decision—not without a twinge of guilt—to tell Annabelle that she was right to wish to terminate her analysis with me. After all, I said to myself, I would not be the first analyst to find her "unanalysable".

Right on time, as always, Annabelle arrived with an expression almost of gaiety on her face. She began speaking the moment she stretched out on the divan.

"I don't remember a thing about yesterday's session—I only know it was a *good* one. I did lots of things afterwards."

I heard myself reply, "You don't remember anything about yesterday's session?"

"Absolutely nothing!"

"What makes you feel it was a 'good' session?"

"Well . . . I remember that I was humming a song as I went down the stairs, straight after I left here. And goodness knows I don't often feel that happy!"

Still acutely aware of my distinctly *unhappy* feeling and anxious searching after this same session, I asked her, thinking it might provide a clue, if she remembered the song she was humming.

"Let's see . . . umm . . . oh, yes, that children's song, '*Auprès de ma blonde, qu'il fait bon, fait bon . . . dormir*' [How good it is to sleep beside my blond girl]."

Her angry vituperation of the previous day in marked contrast with the euphoric aftermath, her irritated reference to my blond hair, in equally marked contrast with the revelation of a libidinal wish in the song, and other incongruities, decided me to tell her that I remembered yesterday's session very clearly; she had expressed strong feelings of anger, disappointment, and irritation with me and the analysis. There had been no trace of feeling that it could be "good to sleep" beside a blond analyst. Annabelle was very struck by this recall of the material of her session and began to wonder herself what all these contradictory expressions might mean. I suggested—following my own countertransference affect of the day before—that perhaps she went off so light-heartedly with the hope that *I* would feel disappointed, irritated, and angry in her place.

"How strange! I think you're right. I've often thought to myself that I'd like to see you cry."

"Would they be *your* tears that I am to weep?"

For the rest of the session Annabelle gave much thought to this new idea—in striking contrast to her familiar attitude of disdain or dissatisfaction. At the same time I began to realize that she rarely ever expressed any *depressive affect*. Indeed, in thinking back I was also aware, for the first time, that in spite of the virulent content of her analytic discourse, I had the impression that much of what she said was *devoid* of affect. Her apparent anger was perhaps hiding inexpressible sadness.

The following night she brought a dream:

> "They were taking me to the police station in a sort of tumbrel. A huge poster announced that 'Mrs Moon was wanted for murder.' I am wheeled down a long corridor, like a big hospital. I'm very small and the tumbrel has turned into a cot. As we go along I throw pieces of cotton in a furious way onto the floor."

In her associations to the dream, "Mrs. Moon" suggests the analyst, "who is supposed to throw light on what is dark and murky". Then she went on to realize that this dream name was also an anagram of her own mother's name. The cotton recalled something she had been told about her babyhood. She was a baby who "never cried"; her mother, who was often occupied for long periods of time, would give the baby pieces of cotton in her cot, and she would suck these frenetically until her mother returned. "But where was she?" cried Annabelle. "I never had a mother!" And she began to sob. The little "child who never cried" was to cry in her analysis for many months to come.

> "To survive is easy. The hard thing is to know how to live."
> [*Annabelle Borne*]

I shall leave aside all the associative links, forgotten images, and fantasies, which enabled us to reveal in Annabelle the small abandoned baby-self, catastrophically searching for an omnipotent yet absent mother. All she could find was a surrogate cloth mother with breasts of cotton, and for which, apparently, no true transitional object had ever been created. Any introjection of, or identification with a loving, care-taking mother stopped at this point, depriving Annabelle of any possibility of being in contact with her own needs, or in any way fulfilling a maternal role towards herself. As in the analytic situation, she made magic, megalomanic demands on people, at the same time treating them like cloth monkeys and punishing them accordingly. In moments of tension she could neither contain, nor psychically elaborate upon her distress.

The next three years were spent in recognizing this dilemma and in studying the moments when the lonely, rage-filled baby occupied the whole of her inner psychic world; then, in putting this traumatized infant into communication with Annabelle Borne the adult.

Although these two sessions allowed me considerable insight into the way in which my patient thought about herself and her relation to the world—or, rather, the way in which she *prevented* herself from being able to think and feel about her involvement with internal or external objects—she found no immediate relief in our analytic work. Later she was able to tell me that the two years that followed this phase of the analysis had brought her more suffering than she had ever known. Nevertheless, the working-through of this psychic pain wrought a profound change in her, which she herself called her "rebirth". I should add that she did not suffer alone. My own countertransference was sorely tried, but I was better able to put it to use. I had constantly to be on the lookout for her tendency to pulverize any nascent thoughts or feeling states of which she became aware; and she would frequently evacuate these by trying (unconsciously) to get me to feel them instead. Further, I was in no way free from feelings of exasperation when she would systematically decry or destroy the meaning of any interpretation that promised to modify her stony feeling of anger and incomprehensible solitude. It was through analysing my own perplexity that I discovered she felt *humiliated* by each discovery and each new turning in her analytic adventure. My compensation was that I no longer felt lost with her on this difficult journey. Even though my words often angered her, I knew she needed to hear them. For, without my realizing it, my somewhat silent and expectant attitude during our first year of work together had reproduced the original situation that she carried inside her, of an evanescent maternal imago that was out of reach and persecutory at the same time. Thus Annabelle did not treat me like a real person. She accorded me as much individual status as a voracious nursling might; she could not conceive of my having any independent thoughts or wishes that were not controlled by her; nor could she accept that I be occupied with any other person or thing than herself without feeling that this would be damaging to her. The painstaking exploration of her struggle allowed us to analyse her constant use of projective identification, and the inhibiting effect this exercised on her constantly painful existence. Instead of immediately getting rid of any hurtful thoughts or depressed feelings that came to consciousness during the sessions, she would now try to hold on to them and to put into words the unexpressed, at times inexpressible, fantasy and affect they aroused in her. Three years of patient work allowed us to (re-)construct and explore the contours of the empty desert of baby Annabelle's psychic world. The old-boot–analyst that one was unwillingly but compulsively bound to follow, the cloth-monkey–analyst with cotton breasts that one was obliged to accept as nourishment, slowly became a *transference object* whose existence was recognized, and towards whom infantile needs and primitive wishes could now be attached and talked about. Every object in my waiting room or consulting room, the slightest sign of the existence of any other people in my life (particularly other analysands), any change of clothing or furniture, my pots of flowers, all brought forth torrents of anger that seemed to Annabelle not only painful, but impossible to contain and to reflect upon. We needed many sessions to plumb the wells of hatred and despair that lay behind her earlier provocations. "You will never be able to imagine how much I hate you and envy you; how much I want to tear you apart and make you suffer."

Despite the fact that my existence as a separate person, having needs, wishes, and rights that did not necessarily coincide with hers, was a source of constant pain, and the fact that the idealized object she projected upon me engendered a continuing narcissistic wound, at least I was also now part of her analytic process, no longer a simple receptacle destined to contain all that was too heavy for her to carry alone, no longer a mummified mask for all the objects who had failed her in the past. We came to understand that she felt constantly persecuted by me, as she did by everyone in her entourage, but neither she nor I had been aware of this. Her despair, so long a part of her, had become virtually painless.

The most important conflictual material at this stage of her analysis could be summed up under all that is included in the Kleinian concept of *envy*. Instead of being caught in the toils of jealousy and in conflict with the desire to triumph over the rivals for her mother's or father's love, she sought total *destruction* of any object belonging to the Other. In the light of this understanding, her sexually traumatic relationship with her brother took on a new significance. Through the sexual act, she now possessed her mother's adored object—and in her fantasy she possessed it *in order to destroy it*. She had created an illusory solution that was not a psychotic but an erotic one, and thus could feel she had triumphed over the traumatic event. She was able for the first time to reveal the elements of her erotic scene, and this enabled us eventually to be able to analyse its significance. Her childhood and adult masturbation fantasies all turned around her brother. She would imagine him immobilized against a wall, while different kinds of "tortures" were carried out on his penis; these were fantasized as being orgastically satisfying to the brother, and were highly exciting to her. Thus she controlled, in imagination, her brother's sexual response. Under the guise of giving him pleasure, his image was also protected against feelings of destructive hatred. As with many sexual deviations, her sexual game served several contradictory purposes: she was able to show and deny at the same time her incestuous wish; and, more important, she was able to master actively what she had passively experienced, for she was not both author and actor of her fantasy film, and no longer the victim of the rape that had been lived as a castration. She was the all-powerful castrator. The disavowals included in her erotic fantasy also allowed her to triumph over the primal scene—by inventing a new one—and provided her with fantasied revenge for the mother–son relationship. But it gave her no adequate resolution of her oedipal conflicts and also left her with a damaged image of her own body and sexuality. One part of her had never assumed her feminine gender reality. When, for example, adolescent classmates talked about waiting to get their periods, she would mock them in her mind "because I was convinced that this would never happen to me. I was somehow different from all other girls in my imagination. When I finally discovered my own menstrual blood, I didn't recognize it. I thought it was something due to masturbation. I kept it a secret for two months."

With regard to this nexus of sexual fantasy and the torture game on her brother's penis, it is evident that "penis envy" is not an adequate explanation. The destructive elements of the fantasy went far beyond the traumatic experience and also had primitive roots that were concerned with more archaic sexuality than the discovery and understanding of sexual differences. These roots led us back to the green sap of the mother's inaccessible breasts. The manifest "game" of her brother's castration, rendered ego-syntonic through erotization, hid a deeper fantasy—namely that of controlling and destroying the breast–mother in order to possess for herself the magical green sap. Father and brother, symbolically represented as phallic appendages of the omnipotent mother, were regressively fantasied as being the contents of her breasts.

Without sex, without sap, without knowledge about how to live, Annabelle lived out defensively an unelaborated depression, poorly compensated by her particular form of relationship to others, more an act than an exchange, contact rather than communication, but nevertheless a living link.

In an effort to transmit her continuing experience that each day presented her with insurmountable problems, Annabelle would often talk of the "hardness" of life. The word recurred incessantly, attached at one time or another to each relationship, to all the part-objects . . . the mother's stony breast, the brother's dangerous penis, the analyst's rigorous timetable. "I have come to realize that I have never for one minute felt comfortable—either in my body or in the presence of others. It's so hard, hard to feel good, hard to do the simplest things. Eating, walking, defecating, making love. So hard, so complicated. Why do I not have the secret? Why don't you give it to me, you mean, hard creature?" The analyst–breast, omnipotent idealized image had survived as an inner object in spite of the three years of "hard" blows dealt out to it by the suffering analysand–child, who occupied most of Annabelle's inner psychic space. There was no doubt that I now existed as a separate person and also as an analyst, so that she could "use" me effectively to understand different aspects of the inter-systemic war within her (Winnicott, 1971). But she refused all approach to the idealized, hard, omnipotent being who was supposed to contain the secret of life and of *her* life. I had to be patient while waiting for the possibility of interpreting this idealization. I was able eventually to make an intervention born in part out of my exasperation at not being able to get further on this question. "Why are you so hard? Why do you not tell me *how to live*? You stand there mocking me, waiting for me to discover everything all by myself." I replied that she asked me for a secret to which she alone held the key, that I did not know the answer, nor why she stopped the sap of life from running through her veins. I understood how much she was suffering, but I too was discouraged by my own failure to be able to interpret better what she was experiencing. "I know you are trying to communicate this hard and terrible feeling", I said, "and it is a failure on my part somewhere to catch your message; I do realize that we are both going through a hard moment, and I feel I have let you down". This intervention produced an unexpected and explosive reaction—of joy. Could it be possible that an *analyst* did not understand? That an *analyst* could feel baffled, discouraged? That analysts were not *omniscient* had never once crossed Annabelle's mind in fifteen years of analysis. I was eventually able to show her that she needed to believe in this fetishlike magical "knowledge" in order that she too, at the end of her analysis, might come into possession of it. Her discovery that no one was endowed with this ineffable quality inaugurated the final phase of her analysis with me. The exploration of her idealizing projection enabled her to mourn for its loss and to relinquish her own omnipotent demands: the demand to be spared every frustration, to triumph effortlessly over every "hard" reality, whether internal or external.

Annabelle was at last able to take care of the confused and desperate child within her, and to understand that there were solutions other than destructive elimination whenever she was faced with envious rage and voracious wishes. Construction began to replace destruction in ways that she alone could discover. For the first time she began to care genuinely about her body, her health, her appearance, her love life, her work life, all of which had been left untended, as though growth and change were impossible. She confided these changes shyly to me. In one of our final sessions she said, significantly, that she had sown flower seeds in the spring without telling anyone, in case they died. To her astonishment they had all borne flowers.

Some years later Annabelle sent me a beautiful book dealing with the artistic domain she had made her own, and of which she was the author. In a hand-written dedication she attributed to analysis the discovery of the essence of creativity—that *living was creating*.

## Primitive communication

I have given the name of *primitive communication* to this kind of analytic discourse in order to emphasize its positive aspects, since in general we are much more aware of its negative effects. Patients who tell us many things as a way of not saying anything, of not revealing, even to themselves, what lies behind their communication, or who talk in order to keep the analyst at a distance, are of course maintaining strong resistance to the analytic relationship and mustering powerful forces against the analytic process itself. And they may even be quite conscious that this way of communicating with the analyst (and often with their whole entourage) is defensive, and in some way is eluding what they really would like to say. Nevertheless, to the extent that the analyst reacts to the patient's words, some form of communication is taking place. This latent communication is not a truly symbolic one and cannot be compared with the repressed thoughts that lie behind normal–neurotic analytic associations. Here, instead, we find words being used in place of action—as weapons, as camouflage, as a desperate cry for help, a cry of rage or of any other intense emotional state of which the patient is but dimly aware. These feeling states may have no connection with what the patient is recounting.

This kind of analytic material raises a number of questions. We might question the function of such "communication" and then compare it with the free-associative analytic monologue that ordinary neurotic patients produce in response to our invitation to do just that. We might also ask why certain patients are more apt to use verbal channels in this way and what may be inferred from such language "symptoms" with regard to traumatic childhood history and its ensuing effects on ego structure and defences. Although I shall deal briefly with these questions, my main interest is the exploration of the way in which the analyst receives this kind of analytic communication, and how he may best use it to further the analytic process. This process depends to a high degree on language communication, and the particular mode of communication that we call free association allows us to explore the interpenetration of primary and secondary processes. The "basic rule" relies on the verbal expression of thoughts and feelings, and it is hoped that, to the extent that the analysand can eventually allow ideas, fantasies, and emotional states free expression in ways in which he would not normally permit himself to function verbally, this interpenetration of conscious and unconscious knowledge of himself will set the analytic process in motion. The invitation to "say everything"—along with its implicit counterpart "and do nothing"—not only opens the way to transference affect but also enables the analysand in hearing his own words, to get to know his thoughts and feelings in an entirely new way. However, this expectation becomes questionable with people who use language in ways that alter its essential function, and more particularly in the analytic situation, with its intimate dependence on language and communication.

What indeed are the aims of what I am calling primitive communication, and in what major ways does it differ from other verbal communications? What role does it play in psychic economy? To what system of internal object relations is it entailed?

Although the efficacy of *words* in the communication of thoughts and emotions is considerably more limited than we like to admit, nevertheless the primary aim of verbal exchange among adults is the desire to communicate information to those to whom one chooses to address oneself. But this is far from being its only aim. Communication [from the Latin *communicare* = to render common, to be in relationship with, to be connected] reveals its underlying etymological and affective meaning. All people in certain situations and some people much of the time, use verbal communication literally as a way of maintaining a contact, being in relation with, or even being part of—"common to"—another person. This vital link with the Other may override in importance the symbolic function, which consists of the desire to *inform* someone of something. From such a viewpoint verbal communication might be considered an approximation to crying, calling out, screaming, growling, rather than to *telling* something. To this extent such communication would be a means not only of remaining in intimate contact but also a way of conveying and discharging emotion in direct fashion, with the intent to affect and arouse reactions in the Other.

The analytic situation, since it dispenses with the usual conventions of verbal exchange, is particularly apt to reveal unusual features in verbalization that might pass unnoticed in everyday conversation (Rosen, 1967). The austerity of the analytic protocol tends to highlight such differences. In Annabelle Borne's analytic associations it was noted that her words had partially lost their communicative aim. In addition, this use of verbalization impeded the free association of ideas. The fact that we were able to discover together the wide gap between what she *said* and what she *felt*, between the content and its accompanying affect, finally allowed her discourse to become meaningful to both of us, and the patient to recover many lost feelings. At the same time we were able to understand that she frequently spoke with the main intention of arousing feelings in the *analyst* without knowing why this was so important, or what this feeling represented to her. Her need to induce feeling states in others was in fact connected with early traumatic situations in which she had been unable to deal with intense emotion and did not know how to communicate her need for help; instead of containing and elaborating her emotional pain and using it to think further, she had effaced all knowledge of its existence or meaning. Thus past events and affective experience had been simply ejected from consciousness, as though they had never existed. For the first time many of these emotional states were able to achieve psychical representation. Communications like those of Annabelle Borne differ in an essential way from those found in an ordinary neurotic associative process, even when these are directed towards arousing feeling in the analyst. In the latter, the attempt to let one's thought and fantasy roam freely tends to reveal, behind the patent communication, a latent theme to which the analyst is "listening". The person, unknown to himself, is communicating another story, revealing himself as an actor upon another stage, but for which the script, once conscious, has been forgotten. Such secret scripts and dissimulated scenes are of course present in patients who use language to penetrate the listener and provoke reaction from him, but from the standpoint of analytic work vitiate the aim of laying bare this latent underlying meaning and render the capturing of repressed ideas and memories peculiarly difficult. Meanwhile the analyst is likely to feel bewildered and invaded by affects that hinder his analytic functioning—*unless he pays attention to them.*

The depressive and frustrating feelings that Annabelle Borne aroused in me had little to do with repressed ideas in her analytic material. The primary aim of her words might well have been described as an attempt to discharge, through the very act of talking, pent-up and painful tensions, whose content and causes were unknown to her. The secret aim of which she was able to become conscious was to *share* a pain that could not yet be expressed through the medium of language and was not capable of being thought about. It was a demand to be *heard rather than listened to*, a need for communion rather than communication. In the months to come we were able to pinpoint the moments at which such communication became imperative. Faced with the slightest hint of a painful thought or feeling, Annabelle would immediately manage to pulverize its psychic representation. As a consequence she had no true awareness of the existence of the idea or affect in question. But the debris of this psychic elimination had the effect of altering her perception of others, and in consequence her manner of feeling about them and communicating with them. The same thing occurred in the analytic transference.

Of course, the various themes that Annabelle Borne used to fill up the essential silence left in the wake of all that had been repudiated from consciousness were not devoid of significance in themselves, nor of any reference to repressed material. It was, for example, patent that lurking behind the persecutory images and ideas, the problem of *Envy* loomed large, but it remained out of interpretable reach as long as the ejected feelings of depression, abandonment, and deprivation—along with their inevitable corollary, intense feelings of hatred—remained blocked from access to psychic expression, blocked therefore to verbal reflection and expression. In a sense many of Annabelle's remarks and observations were devoid of interest for her; she was relatively unaware that they might have a potential effect on her analyst, her friends and family, or any others with whom she maintained communicative links. The unconscious benefit thus procured was the protection of her inner object world from destruction due to her envious rage and narcissistic mortification. At the same time it permitted her to maintain contact with the external object world in spite of the continual feeling of dissatisfaction that her relationships afforded her. Perhaps, too, her aggressive contact strengthened her feeling of identity. But all this was obtained at a high price. Not only did she feel overwhelmed by the "hardness" of existence in all its aspects, she suffered a veritable impairment of her capacity to *think*, in particular with regard to the causes of her mental suffering. With her defensive, almost brutal elimination of awareness of affective pain she was in fact hampered in dealing with her genuine *needs*, and not only with the fulfilment of wishes. At the beginning of our analytic work together she was relatively unaware of having any personal desires other than the wish to be "comfortable", and was equally unaware of what she demanded and expected from others.

\* \* \*

This way of experiencing raises the question of the space occupied in psychic life by the external objects. Implicitly the Other is called upon to capture and deal with an inexpressible appeal. In a sense it is a demand to be understood without passing by the normal verbal channels, to be understood by mere signs. *Infans*, the infant unable as yet to talk, must have his needs heard and dealt with in this way, since he has no other means of communication. When he is capable of *asking*, it is no longer a question of vital need, but until this time he is totally dependent on his mother's interpretation of his cries and gestures. To the extent that an infant can conceive of Another who will respond to his cry, he may be said to be "communicating" in this primitive way. At this point he has already reached a certain stage of psychic growth with regard to the object; he no longer feels that the Other is a hallucinatory part of himself (which might be equated with a psychotic form of object relation) but instead believes the Other to be *all-powerful,* in which case the response of the object to the signs emitted is interpreted as positive because the object wants the infant to be gratified, or, in the case of a negative response, as a refusal because he wants the infant to suffer. That is to say, this type of relationship is under the sway of primary-process thinking: if good things or bad things occur, in either case they are felt to derive from the omnipotent desire of the all-powerful Other. This Other automatically understands and responds as he wishes! (This type of thinking prevails in what we might call narcissistic character pathology.) With regard to this projected idealization and expectation of the external world we are sometimes inclined, as Bion (1970) has pointed out, to overlook the fact that, in spite of the satisfaction that symbolic communication eventually brings to the growing person, to be *obliged* to speak in order to be understood and to have wishes granted is a continuing narcissistic wound in everyone's unconscious. For certain people, fusion and communion, rather than separateness and communication, are the only authentic means of relating to another person. (One patient who regarded separateness as a calamity used to say that if she had to *tell* her husband what she needed or wished for in any field, then his complying with her wish no longer had any significance. It was, indeed, a proof that he did not love her).

Fusional communion, that archaic form of loving that is the nursling's right, is still implicitly awaited by certain adults. Any threat of separation or reminder of subjective difference such as having to convey one's wishes through verbalization can only spell punishment and rejection. We are dealing here with the "infant" inside the adult, who has never truly understood the role of verbal communication as a symbolic means of making one's desires known. No doubt these are the babies who were not sensitively "listened to" and "interpreted" by those who brought them up. My own clinical experience with patients who live out this inarticulate drama leads me to believe that their childhoods were marked by incoherent relationships with the earliest objects, and in a context in which the inevitable frustrations of human growing and development were not tempered with sufficient gratification to make them bearable, so that the supreme reward of individuation and subjective identity was not acquired with pleasure, but instead continues to be lived as a rejection and an insult. The fact that one's wishes can be both communicated and responded to is scarcely believed to be true. Such was the case with Annabelle.

One further factor: the demand to be understood without words implies also a terror of facing disappointment or refusal of any kind. This is felt not only as a narcissistic wound, but as an unbearable pain that cannot be contained and psychically elaborated, and which may destroy one. Thus the ineluctable factors that structure human reality—otherness, sexual difference, the impossibility of magic fulfilment of wishes, the inevitability of death—have not become meaningful. Otherness, with its reward of personal identity and privacy; sexual difference, with the reward of sexual desire; the refinding of magic fulfilments in creativity; the acceptance of death itself as the inevitable end, which gives urgent and important significance to life—all may be lacking for these patients. Life then runs the risk of being "meaningless" and "hard". Other people tend to be seen as vehicles for *externalizing* this painful inner drama of living. It is in fact the creation of a system of *survival.* At least contact with others is assured and something is communicated. Many people with this way of relating find themselves pushed to manipulate others, although unaware that this is what they are doing, in order to bring about the catastrophes they already anticipate. Thus relationships are often directed towards proving the inevitability of preconceived conclusions concerning them. This is another way of "communicating" one's distress and of combating one's feeling of utter impotence in the face of overwhelming forces. There are many ways in which such a system of interpersonal relations may be expressed theoretically: in terms of persecutory anxiety and projective identification (Klein, Grinberg); of the need of the subject to use others as containers (Bion); of the urgent necessity to recover lost parts of oneself, the "selfobjects" (Kohut); the tendency to deny the independent existence of others as a defence against pathological forms of object-relating (Kernberg); the "false-self" concept (Winnicott); the use of others as "transitional objects" (Modell).

Out of touch with important aspects of themselves, these patients have difficulty in accepting that others are also prone to anxiety, depression, frustration, and irritation. Thus the struggle against archaic fantasies and emotions is reinforced by the struggle against outer reality and the pain of others. Like nurslings forced to become autonomous before their time, they must be prepared to stave off all sources of conflict and psychic suffering, whether these come from inner or outer psychic space. Unknown to themselves, they are working with a model of human relations in which separate identity must be vigorously denied, since absence and difference have not been compensated by a well-constructed inner object-world; thus the patient's own feeling of identity is unstable. Nor is it easy then to grasp what others are trying to communicate, and assumptions about human motives run the risk of being erroneous. Separateness is rejected as a postulate, and in its stead we find the constant externalization of conflict in an attempt to keep everything in its place, and in this way exercise an illusory control over other people's reactions. These are the "wise babies" described by Ferenczi, who must control everything with the baby-like means at their disposal. We must of course admit that such an imperious nursling slumbers inside all of us, but he is usually confined to the omnipotent world of dreams. Neurotic patients discover this megalomanic child within themselves, with astonishment; others, like Annabelle, discover that throughout their lives they have been striving to reinstate the rights of this demanding infant and, most of all, his right to be heard and his need to be in meaningful communication with others. Although the adult ego is unaware of his existence, the angry and desperate child is screaming to be allowed to breathe. Only thus is there any hope that this inarticulate infant may have access to a more elaborated form of self-expression.

It is evident that the analyst who receives such communications in analysis finds himself listening to a discourse that will not make sense if he consistently treated it as a normal–neurotic transmission of ideas and affects under the sway of free association. He will seek in vain for repressed ideas pushing their way into consciousness, and will be forced to realize that he is observing a part of the personality dominated by primitive mechanisms of defence: disavowal, splitting, foreclosure, all of which serve to exclude psychic events from the symbolic chain, particularly those that are apt to produce psychic pain. We might well ask ourselves to what extent it is possible to penetrate the barriers of primal repression and explore the basic layers of the personality structure. Can we hope to "hear" that which has never been formulated in ways in which it might form part of preconscious ideas, that which has never been encoded as thought and thus not preserved in a form accessible to recall and to symbolic elaboration? Here the limits of the analytic process must be called into question.

I would suggest, however, that to the extent that areas of experience have been repudiated from the psychic world to be projected into the external world, these ejected fragments of experiencing are expressed in behaviour, or constantly enacted in the form of primitive exchange. In certain privileged situations and moments we can "hear", at least, the distress signals; we come to know that these signs are an indication of profound pain, which cannot yet be fully recognized by the individual as personal suffering. He feels blocked, hampered, hamstrung, and furious with the world. This is the basic message.

## The role of countertransference

How does this message strike the analyst? In the first place the analytic ear may be rapidly alerted by the particular *use of words*. In the case of Annabelle Borne, there was a notable discordance between content and affect, so that much angry and discontented feeling was in fact hiding inexpressible depression; with other patients, in a similar inner drama, we find ourselves listening to an interminable monologue recounting daily facts that seem to have no further echo beyond the mere words, either for the analysand or the analyst; others again use words in ways that make us feel confused—that is to say, the ordinary associative links such as we find in everyday conversation and everyday analytic communications may be lacking. Rosen speaks of subtle disturbances in the encoding of thought processes that emerge in the analytic situation, and of the fact that the analyst must sometimes become aware of the latent content through media other than words—signal systems such as gestures, posture, facial expression, intonation, pictograms, etc. I think that we are often attuned to such subliminal messages well in advance of being able ourselves to encode and verbalize what we have understood. Modell (1973) suggests that the capturing of affect may well precede the acquisition of language. On the basis of personal experience with very young babies (who often react in striking fashion to the affective states of those who are looking after them) and also deductions drawn from my analytic observations, I would go further and say that the transmission of affect unquestionably takes place earlier than symbolic communication. Modell's further observation, that an analytic discourse that lacks affect is a sign that the analytic process has come to a halt, seems to me highly pertinent to analytic research into the nature of communication.

A further observation concerning "primitive communication" is that veritable "free association" (with all the limitations and filtering systems that normally accompany it) is lacking. There is no *Einfall* (which means, literally, a sudden upsurge or breakthrough of a thought, fantasy, or image from some inner but hitherto unrecognized source). This interpretation of primary and secondary processes, hallmark of a functioning psychoanalytic process, is not taking place, and thus tends to give a featureless aspect to the analytic monologue. Although it may seem like an "empty" communication, it will often produce a feeling of "fullness" in the analyst, a frustrating feeling to which he must turn his attention. In the analysand's desire to be intimately "linked" with the analyst through his verbalization, he may take little heed of the fact that the analyst is apt to respond emotionally to the content, especially if it is depressive, aggressive, or anxiety-arousing, and there is correspondingly little questioning of the supposition that the analyst will be equally pleased to be linked through this verbal stream—even though it be, for example, a vituperative monologue that takes the analyst as its target, or a confused discourse that takes no account of the difficulty in seizing its meaning. In their efforts to remain plugged in, as it were, to the analyst's mind, these patients are appealing for help and pushing the analyst away at the same time. The patient may be said to be under the sway of a condensation—not of thought, but of aim. He seeks to obtain love and attention, which will reassure him that he is being heard and being held, that he exists, and at the same time must punish the Other for all the bad and hard things he has had to endure. It could be conceived of as a demand upon an idealized breast, the maternal function, such as a nursling might experience it were he able to express it.

If these patients do not talk about what really concerns them—their contradictory seeking, their pain in living, their difficulty in feeling understood or truly alive—it is because *they do not know it*. Unaware of the impact of their words, they are equally unaware that they, too, occupy a psychic space in the minds of others. The others are considered to be alive, existent, and therefore need little else, whereas the subject of this distress is screaming out his right to become alive too, with the underlying assumption that the world owes him this. For many patients the discovery of this dilemma may be an inaugural experience encountered in the analytic situation. The analysand may for the first time make a conscious distinction between himself and Another, with the recognition that both exist, each with his individual and separate psychic reality. People with no clear representation of their own psychic space and their own identity tend otherwise to relate to others in ways that elude *their* psychic reality too—that is, they tend to perceive only what accords with their preconceived notion of the Other, and of the world in general, and to eliminate perceptions and observations that do not fit in with the existing idea.

This way of relating has a marked effect on the transference relationship. Much of the force of transference comes from the interplay between the analyst as a figure of imagination and projection and the analyst as a real being. As an imaginary object, he becomes the eventual target for all the investments attached to the original inner objects, whereas his qualities as a real person remain largely unknown to the analysand. Patients who operate within the relational framework described in this chapter maintain only a minimal distance between the imaginary and the real analyst, so that transference projections are rarely perceived as such. Neither partner to the analytic tandem will be endowed with any clearly delineated identity. This sort of analytic relationship might be included in the concept of an idealized narcissistic transference as described by Kohut, or as an attempt at fusional denial of separateness, or again as an attempt to establish a pathological form of archaic object relations as envisaged by Kernberg.

Such patients will tend to use a model of human relationships based on the postulates that belong to primary-process thinking—that is to say, all things bad or good that happen to the subject are due to another person's wish and, indeed, his good or bad will. There is little questioning of the important events in his life as far as his own participation is concerned. In analysis, if the patient feels bad, he is quite likely to believe that the analyst is indifferent because deep down he *wishes his analysand to suffer*. If and when these analysands become conscious of their own projected aggressive and destructive wishes, they are more than likely to stifle such feelings and rapidly eject their associated ideas from consciousness. Thus they often do not know when they are angry, frightened, or unhappy.

As already emphasized, we are not dealing with mechanisms of repression or isolation, but of repudiation from the psychic world, splitting, and projective identification. In consequence the principal anxieties to be faced are more concerned with the self and the maintenance of identity than with sexuality and the fulfilment of desire; "psychotic" anxiety mobilized by fear of disintegration and dedifferentiation takes a larger place than "neurotic" anxiety attached to all that is included in the classical concept of the castration complex. If the latter runs the risk of producing sexual and work inhibitions or symptoms, the former disturbs the whole pattern of relationship with others. There will be a tendency to use others as parts of oneself, or in the place of transitional objects where they are destined to play a protective role and to be used to filter hostile impulses. Within the analytic relationship this tends to create the type of fundamental transference to which Stone (1961) referred in his classic work on the analytic situation—that is, transference affect that is more concerned with Otherness and the fear of (wish for) fusion than with the transferences typical of the neurotic structure.

The symptomatic kind of analytic discourse that ensues may be a manifestation of a number of psychic ills. In a sense the "signs" discerned here as being the unformulated but true communication might be regarded as minimal elements of psychotic thought and expression; nevertheless there is no contamination of thought, nor do we find the surrealistic use of words so markedly present in psychotic verbalization. Annabelle Borne had not created a personal grammar; there was no confusion between the signifier and the thing signified. But she had a similar fragility in her idea of herself and her relations to others in which the limits were ill-defined, suggesting a lack of early structurization of a stable self-image and consequently an unclear picture of others. This kind of relationship may well give rise to a form of personal Esperanto whose communicative aim might have psychotic overtones. The idiosyncratic use of language that may pass unnoticed as such in the everyday world, since it respects syntax and symbolic reference, seeks nevertheless, in the way that psychotic communications do, to restore the primary mother–child unity, to be understood through and in spite of one's way of communicating. The distinction may be said to lie here: patients like Annabelle Borne do not use words in accordance with primary-process functioning, but their way of relating to others follows the primary-process model, namely, of total dependence on the omnipotent will of the Other. Thus language is used in the service of this form of relationship. Perhaps in this way psychotic disorganization is prevented, for these patients are not detached from outer reality; they do not dream up situations, causes, and perceptions that exist only in their inner world. Instead, they utilize others, in accordance with what they find, who are apt to take in and give back to the subject something that is offered and something else that is demanded. Nevertheless the patient may be said to be "creating" the meaning that the other person has for him without taking too much account of the Other's reality, while at the same time submitting himself to this Other and suffering accordingly. I would add that such relationships are by no means rare in the world at large, and that relatively few such people seek analytic help.

My contention is that when we find this way of communicating and relating reproduced in the analytic setting, we have indications of early psychic suffering, presumably rooted in the period when the small child tries to use the mother as a sub-

sidiary part of himself and so deals with vital needs and conflicts through the "language" at his disposal. We might say that
part of the patient is "outside himself", in analysis as in everyday life, and he therefore treats others, or the analyst, as va-
grant segments of himself, which he naturally attempts to
control.

It is evident that this will give rise to countertransference
phenomena that are different from those that arise with the
normal–neurotic analysand. For the latter, equipped as he is
with the familiar neurotic forms of defence against psychic pain
and conflict, the analyst becomes a figure of projection for his
own inner objects, since his mental conflict stems in large part
from intrapsychic struggles. Such a patient introjects a representation of the analyst, who thus becomes an object of
the analysand's ego, although constituted differently from the
genuine inhabitants of his inner universe. The analyst is, so to
speak, an immigrant with a temporary visa, who draws upon
himself forbidden desires, idealized representations, threats,
fear, anger, etc., belonging to the original objects. The analyst's
unique position in this psychic world provides the transference
relationship with considerable force, and as already emphasized, permits the patient to measure and explore the distance
that separates the analyst as an imaginary person from the
analyst as a real being with an individual identity. It is in this
space between the visions of the analyst that the most fruitful
interpretative and reconstructive work is accomplished. Countertransference interference, if present, stems mainly from unresolved personal problems of the analyst—and it is not an
uncommon occurrence for a "good neurotic analysand" to become aware of these, see clearly that they are not a matter of
his own projections, and point them out!

But in the case where the distinction between transference
projection and reality observation is blurred, the way in which
the analyst receives the patient's transference expression is
likely to differ. Hidden in the shape of "pseudo communication"
that seeks less to inform (literally: to give form to) the analyst
of his thoughts and feelings than to get rid of painful intrapsychic conflict and arouse reaction in the analyst, we must
wonder how the latter may best capture and interpret this "lan-

guage". In the beginning he does not "hear" the message, nor does he immediately become aware of its emotional impact. It is difficult to detect what is missing, particularly since its ejection leaves no unconscious trace, and no neo-reality has been invented to take its place, as with psychotic patients. Gradually affect is mobilized and indeed accumulates in the analyst; while the analysand flattens or distorts his affective experience, the analyst becomes literally "affected". The patient's associations have a penetrating or impregnating effect, which is missing in the usual neurotic transference and analytic monologue. What has been foreclosed from the world of psychic representation cannot be "heard" as a latent communication. It is the emotional infiltration that contains the seeds of future interpretations, but in order to be able to formulate these the analyst must first understand why his patient's discourse affects him in the way it does. I would agree fully with Giovacchini (1977) when he points out with regard to delusional patients that to view them as unanalysable on the basis of an insufficiently self-observing ego is too glib a dismissal of a complex problem. With the kind of patients I am describing the analyst is apt to feel in the first instance that he has somewhere along the line *ceased functioning adequately as an analyst* with this particular analysand.

Although the analogy cannot be carried too far, the analyst is at these moments in the situation of the mother who is trying to understand why her baby is crying in an angry or distressed fashion. At this stage it is evident that the baby can have no identity over and beyond what he represents for his mother, and it is she who must *interpret* his signs and give them meaning—that is, convert them into communication. In Bion's terminology she must fulfil the role of being her child's thinking apparatus until such time as he is able to think for himself. The analyst, of course, has more modest aims than those that would imply becoming his patient's thinking apparatus! It is not his role to teach his analysand how to perceive the world and how to react to it. At most he hopes to lead his patient to discover who he is—and for whom. But to do so he must be prepared to decode the sounds of distress that lie behind the angry or confused associations.

One is tempted to surmise that these analysands had mothers who were unable to "listen" to their infants and to give meaning to their primitive communications. Perhaps the mother herself reacted with resentment and rejection to her baby's unformulated demands, as though they were a personal attack on her or reflected a narcissistic failure on her own part; in such cases she would fail in her role of "interpreter", who must teach her baby to express his needs, to discover his desires, finally to be able to *think* for himself. But then this also requires a mother who grants her child the *right to independent thoughts*, even if these run counter to her own at many points. We have here another seed to the creating of communication disorders.

Whatever the reasons may have been, the analyst who inherits this psychic puzzle will feel himself "manipulated" by his analysand in the latter's attempt to protect himself from psychic pain and avoid, forever after, becoming the plaything of another's desire. By writing the script in advance, he lays out the scene in such a way that little is left to chance—other than the capacity of the chosen actors to fulfil their roles. Traumatic thoughts and feelings are in this manner controlled through immediate evacuation from the subject's own psyche, to be played out in the external world—an attempt at magic fulfilment and narcissistic reparation.

The analyst must be prepared to capture the patient's difficulty in thinking about himself through the blockage he experiences in his own thinking, in order eventually to recover the expelled representations and the stifled affects. These may then be rendered into archaic fantasy, capable of being expressed verbally, and the associated feelings contained and explored within the analytic relationship. The durability of this relationship functions as a guarantee that such powerful affects may be safely experienced and expressed, without damage to either analyst or patient. I think this is what Winnicott means when he says that

> the reliability of the analyst is the most important factor (or more important than the interpretations) because the patient did not experience such reliability in the maternal care of infancy, and if the patient is to make use of such

reliability he will need to find it for the first time in the analyst's behaviour. [Winnicott, 1960, p. 38]

It is probable that what has been submitted to primal repression cannot be communicated except through "signs" such as those described here, and that these signs will be registered through countertransference feelings. The inadequate functioning of the analyst at these times will manifest itself in many subtle ways. In addition to feeling manipulated, he may find himself reacting to the sessions with boredom or irritation, or catch himself giving aggressive interpretations, maintaining a stubborn silence, or wandering in his mind along paths that have no relation to the patient's associations. In spite of all the well-known pitfalls of countertransference affect, I am obliged to suppose here that these "signs" in the analyst are more than the unique reflection of his own inner emotional state or his unconscious reactions to the patient's monologue, and that we are dealing not with a repressed, but with a primitive communication, not decodable in the usual way. If at such times the analyst persists in seeking repressed content, in giving interpretations as though to neurotic material, in replying aggressively, or turning away in silence, then the *analyst is acting out*. He is now obstructing the analytic process by his *countertransference resistance*. Like all other human beings, we as analysts have difficulty in hearing or perceiving what does not fit into our pre-established codes. Our own unresolved transference feelings play a role here, since the garnering of analytic knowledge has been accomplished through and deeply impregnated with transference affect and thus tends to carry a built-in resistance of its own, making it difficult for us to "hear" all that is being transmitted. We tend to resent the patient who does not progress in accordance with our expectations, or who reacts to our efforts to understand as though they were hostile attacks. These problems, added to our personal weaknesses, provide us with a delicate task.

Annabelle Borne's analysis had come to a standstill due to my own inability to catch the meaning of and to examine my countertransference expectations and irritations—up until the moment when I told her she sought not so much to communicate her ideas and emotions as to make me feel sad and helpless. When she was, so to speak, able to take back and possess her own tears, we could then listen together to the paralysed, unhappy child entrapped within her. From that time forward we could permit this child to grow and to express herself for the first time.

The way in which we normally listen to our analysands, a free-floating attention similar to that asked of them, might better be described as free-floating theorization, and it is notable that with the patients under consideration here it is difficult to utilize our various "floating theories" about the patient and the nature of his analytic tie to us. Such floating hypotheses take much longer to organize themselves. This is due in part to the analysand's particular way of communicating and in part to the difficult roles he implicitly needs us to assume on his behalf. The attitude of "expectant silence" that to the neurotic spells hope and opens a psychic space wherein long-buried desires may once more come to light offers little but desolation and death to patients like Annabelle. Their need to feel they exist in other people's eyes, to feel truly alive, to a large extent dominates all other wishes and invades almost totally the territory of desire. The unsure limits between one and the other makes the analysis of the relationship between the two partners hazardous and the mourning of lost objects difficult. It is impossible to mourn the loss of an object one has never possessed, or whose existence has never been truly recognized as distinct from one's own, or as an integral part of one's inner world. On this shifting sand, "transference" interpretations are not constructive, and indeed run the risk of perpetuating the misunderstandings and mutual distortions of the first communications between mother and child. Silence, or the so-called "good analytic interpretation", instead of creating a potentially vital space for feelings and thoughts to come into being or stimulating further associations and memories through which a new way of experiencing may come to life, runs the risk of opening instead onto the silence of the primal unconscious, psychic death, nothingness.

Nevertheless all that has been stifled by the force of primal repression remains potentially active, and indeed actual, since it is inevitably ejected into the outer world. All that has been silenced becomes a message in-action, and it is this action-communication language that may install itself within the analytic situation, there to express itself through signs and secret codes. It is then possible for the analyst to aid his patients to stop the psychic haemorrhage created through continual acting out and direct discharge of tension, pain, and confusion; to render the action-symptoms expressible through language, and to enable the patient to undertake his analytic adventure.

# CHAPTER SIX

# Countertransferential bodily feelings and the containing function of the analyst

*Athina Alexandris*
*Grigoris Vaslamatzis*

> Ah, this terrible pain before prophecy
>
> Aeschylus, *Oresteia*

## Introduction

Psychoanalytic psychotherapy to persons exhibiting borderline personality or, broadly speaking, primitive personality—brought to our attention phenomena taking place during treatment, that are beyond the verbal interchange of patient–analyst. Kernberg (1987) describes these channels of communication and considers that during the analytic therapy of borderline patients, "The emergence of dominant unconscious object relations in the transference typically occurs by means of non-verbal communication" (p. 205). Also, McDougall (1980) refers to primitive models of communication by the patient, which indicate that the patient has suffered pre-verbal, severe traumas or deficiencies during the early maternal relationship.

It is generally accepted that in the treatment of this kind of patients with primitive personalities and/or severe traumas, the understanding and use of countertransference is of special value. In these cases the analyst often faces bizarre and intense phenomena in the primitive transference of the patient. Also, the analyst has to handle his own intense feelings, which these patients usually provoke.

To this effect Segal (1985) writes, "There is a constant pressure on the analyst to act out his appointed role in the patient defensive system" (p. 40).

The redefinition of countertransference as a concept, in the broader sense, by including everything the therapist feels in relation to his patient, its re-evaluation as a research tool, as opposed to an obstacle, for the better understanding of the patient, and the introduction of projective identification—introduced by Melanie Klein (1946)—which has become the hallmark of the Klein–Bion model of theory and technique—have contributed to the fuller understanding of transference-countertransference. The concept of projective identification and its use in clinical practice was enriched and expanded by Segal (1981), Rosenfeld (1983), Kernberg (1988), and Betty Joseph (1988), and discussed from other viewpoints by Ogden (1979) and Joseph Sandler (1988). Thus, the primitive modes of communication between mother–child and analyst–patient, as well as the mode of relatedness that the patient establishes by means of primitive object relation in the clinical psychoanalytic situation, have become more understandable.

Further discussion of these views would be beyond the scope of this chapter. However, they do constitute a frame of reference.

In our present study, the focus is on the discussion of:

1. the meaning of intense bodily feelings—such as physical discomfort, agonizing bodily tension, cold sweats, bodily nervousness, restlessness—accompanied by mixed feelings of agony, fright, frustration, self-pity, and a sense of incompetence, which the analyst frequently experienced during sessions for a whole year before he became aware of their unconscious meaning;
2. the analyst's handling of these feelings;

3. the role of these feelings in the analytic situation;

4. the way in which these feelings relate to the containing function of the analyst.

A synthesis of theoretical and clinical considerations is also attempted, although the full analysis of the case presented, as well as the psychoanalytic process involved, are beyond the scope of our study.

## Case presentation

Sophia, a 40-year-old married woman, the mother of one son, was referred for psychoanalytic therapy shortly after the initiation of her son's psychotherapy. Sophia is a tall, sturdy, and physically fit woman, haughty in countenance, with an ironical half-smile fixed on her lips. From the very first session she described her childhood—a terrible experience, full of frustration and pain. Her father was violent and explosive, screaming and yelling at the slightest provocation. Her parents would constantly fight, and she was the witness of their exchanges. At the peak of these battles her father would often leave home, and he returned whenever he felt like it. When she was 8, her parents separated, and, without warning, she was temporarily placed in a boarding school. She changed schools several times after that.

In the session she was exigent, demanding answers to the difficulties she was having with her son and becoming furious when the analyst avoided a direct reply.

Frequently during sessions, the analyst felt under pressure and experienced great tension in his body, discomfort, cold sweats and the need to fidget in his chair. These agonizing bodily feelings were accompanied by a mixture of fright, frustration, self-pity, and a sense of incompetence.

The patient spoke disparagingly of her son's therapist as well as of other therapists. To her analyst she sometimes commented, "today you were fine", or "today nothing came of it", etc. She accepted the analyst's acknowledgement of her suffering, running on the lines of, "I understand how much you were traumatized as a child and how fearful you must be lest these traumas be repeated in your life or in your psychotherapy". However, all the analyst's attempts to use interpretation at the transference and countertransference level, were rejected by the patient, who commented in a scornful manner, "All you psychoanalysts say the same things, because you are referring to yourselves. I came here to get well!"

In transference, the patient oscillated between moments of intense *"menos"* (a word that she often used to express her emotional state, which in itself means being subject to great internal pressure from intensive, often uncontrollable psychical impetus) in which she attacked the analyst, and moments of acting like a frightened, terrified and hopeless child. We have here, in other words, the activation of the emotionally opposite relations towards the therapist, as an alternative enactment of the two aspects of her relationship with her father.

This more or less is how analysis proceeded during the first year. It is important to stress here that the analyst was not aware of the meaning of his bodily feelings during the entire year.

We shall present here an excerpt taken from a session at the beginning of the second year of therapy:

Sophia comes to session as usual, with her haughty face and her half-smile. She says that of late her *menos* towards her son has subsided, that she has stopped beating him (something she used to do mercilessly) and that she feels indifferent towards him. She remembers that when her son had started school, he had severe eating problems, and she used to spoon-feed him like an infant.

At this point the analyst intervenes and says, "With your over-protection then [i.e. by spoon-feeding him] and your indifference now [at the present time] you avoid your *'menos'*." The patient accepts the analyst's interpretation, and she goes on to say, "I know that he [her son] is aware of my feelings when I address him: I generate great anxiety in him. I look at him and I know he sweats. He becomes terrified that I will beat him. These days I talk to him nicely and yet the memory [of her severe beatings and similar abuse] is enough to cause him great agony."

It is at this precise moment that the analyst suddenly remembers his own hard times that the patient has been giving him, i.e. his agonizing bodily feelings (cold sweats, nervousness, physical discomfort).

Sophia continues by saying that she and her husband had a big fight at home and she threw him out. He left without saying a word. "It is the others", she says, "who instigate me to play the role of the bogy. . . . I don't understand how all of a sudden I find myself fighting; I never intended for the other person to take it that way".

The balance of the session is of no interest to our study.

From this clinical material it becomes quite evident that the analyst began to understand the meaning of his countertrans-ferential bodily feelings only in the second year of his patient's therapy, and, more precisely, during the session presented above. This happened at a moment when:

1. his patient's *menos* has considerably subsided, and the intensity of the massive violent projective identification processes have been lessened;

2. when the therapist's anxiety has also subsided, as indicated in the session;

3. when the frequency and intensity of the analyst's bodily feelings has decreased;

4. when the non-verbal / pre-verbal means of communication had gradually given way to verbal communication and symbolization; and

5. when the interaction between analyst–patient and vice versa took place via the patient's son (path led down by the patient and accepted by the analyst), as evidenced by the quotation, "With your over-protection then and your indifference now you avoid your *'menos'*."

By leaving aside direct interpretations on the transference–countertransference level, the analyst avoids the provocation of the patient's *menos*; consequently, he avoids his own counter-transference responses to it and, above all, the re-experience of his strenuous bodily feelings, whose repetition have by now taken on a traumatic-like flavour.

It seems that the manner with which the analyst was handling the patient's *'menos'* was by storing it in his body and keeping it (split off and repressed) unconscious and apart (dissociated) from the rest of his personality. At this level, the therapist's bodily feelings were the expression of his ultimate effort to bear the patient's *'menos'*, on the one hand, while keeping himself under control, on the other, from acting out his own counter-*'menos'* in the analytic situation.

It is important to mention here that when the patient spared her analyst from her *menos*, she created positive feelings in him due to his concordant identification with her.

It is also obvious that the communication between therapist–patient and vice versa via the patient's son was suitable and agreeable to both. It was the way they adopted in order to save their relationship, i.e. by leaving the *menos* out (at least for the moment) and going on with the therapy. This is confirmed by the response of the patient to her therapist's interpretation (mentioned above), manifested by the patient sustaining her calmness, and by the fact that she went on to reveal further and deeper feelings about him, as well as her relationship towards him, when she said, "I know that he is aware of my feelings when I address him: I generate great anxiety in him. I look at him and I know he sweats. He becomes terrified that I will beat him"—which is her usual way of handling her son. "These days I talk to him nicely, and yet the memory [of her severe beatings and similar abuse] is enough to cause him great agony."

And while the patient was talking about the role that the memory of the beatings played on her son, the therapist remembered his own bodily experiences during their sessions. Indeed, the memory of his bodily feelings was enough to cause him "agony", as his patient said. He also became aware of how the omnipotent power of projective identification used massively [and violently] by his patient had affected him. However, he felt relieved and more relaxed at the end of the session because of the light thrown on their interaction, and from understanding his patient's regressive and primitive transference and his own countertransference, especially that of his bodily experiences.

The therapist's realizations could be summed up as follows:

1. The patient was actually referring to him and to their relationship via her son.

2. She was using her *menos* and intensive massive projective identifications with the intention of placing him in the frightened, abused, hopeless, terrified part of herself, and pushing him to live it out. This caused the therapist to feel cornered under the intense and continuous pressure, fidgeting in his chair, feeling extreme physical discomfort, and bathing in cold sweat. Another motive of the patient was to take over the therapist's role in order to control him and keep him, lest she lose him, as she had lost the previous therapist. Here projective identification is used as a defence mechanism against separation;

3. The patient was actually perceiving the therapist's bodily feelings all along, mainly by means of non-verbal / pre-verbal communication, and that she was unconsciously aware of provoking those feelings;

4. She unconsciously felt that, if she pressed her therapist further, she might lead their relationship to the same outcome as with her son—i.e. drive him mad—or with her husband—i.e. throw him out, or force the therapist to throw her out, as the previous therapist had done.

5. Their main channel of interaction was by means of nonverbal / pre-verbal communication, which suggests that the patient had suffered from violent, massive, intensive projective identification processes used by the parental figures since her early life, i.e. at the pre-verbal phase, when the child thinks with its body, feels with its body, and experiences everything with its body (Kernberg, 1988; Segal, 1981). Here projective identification processes were also used by the patient as a means of communicating to her therapist her early traumatic experiences, in order to be understood by him. The patient aimed, as it were, at inserting those undigested parts of her experience and inner world into the analyst, as a way of having them understood and returned to her in a more manageable form (as demonstrated by Bion). Let us here recall that the patient had from

the very first interview related her history, which was summed up in the fact that she had suffered great *menos* and massive violent projective identification and abuse since she could remember, which was associated with her traumatic infantile experience (Grinberg, 1962, Hanna Segal; quoted by Grinberg).

We feel that her regressive emotional state right from the beginning of her treatment, related to the fact that her son had been urgently referred for treatment and that the first psychotherapist she had gone to did not take her on but referred her to the present therapist. She felt unwanted and rejected by the first therapist.

It seems that of the various motives for the patient's projective identification, the most frightening one for the therapist was her intention to force the therapist to live out her early traumatic experience in the unique way she did—i.e. by forcing into him the frightened, abused, and mistreated part of herself. She was, in other words, activating the relationship she had had with her father, only their roles were reversed.

In this case, projective identification was employed at an almost psychotic level. The therapist's attempts to interpret projective identifications at the transference level were futile.

By means of complementary identification (Racker, 1968; Kernberg, 1988), the therapist took temporarily the place of the frightened, terrified, and abused self-representation of the patient. The therapist's acceptance of this complementary identification (representing a regressive phenomenon) in his countertransference could be seen as a realistic reaction to the transference (Kernberg, 1988), which might have helped the persecutory nature of what was projected in projective identification.

At another level, the patient activated a specific object representation on the therapist; the physical feelings the latter experienced during the sessions can be seen as what Grinberg (1979) designated as projective counteridentification, in which the therapist ". . . reacted as if he had acquired and assimilated the parts projected onto him in a real and concrete way" (Grinberg, 1962, p. 437). Projective counteridentification is of course a more regressive phenomenon than complementary identification. However, during the first year of therapy the therapist was not aware of the meaning of his strenuous bodily experiences. Nevertheless, he felt that the therapy was threatened by these experiences, because he could barely tolerate them. At that point he stopped interpreting and tried to absorb the patient's projective identifications (Rosenfeld, 1965, 1978) because he felt that contrary action would lead them both to a "mad" situation (Kernberg, 1988).

However, each time the patient left the consultation room, after having caused her therapist the feelings under discussion, he would be swept by anger against his patient and think, "She is crazy! She's abusing me!" Moreover, he was furious at the referring doctor: "He did not want her. He unloaded himself by getting rid of her and loaded her onto me."

The above meant that the therapist was unaware of what his body already knew:

1. that he was loaded with the patient's intensive, massive, violent projective identifications;

2. that he was angry and frustrated at his patient who put him through this ordeal, i.e. of living out what she had been through;

3. that he could barely tolerate her, and that he was at the end of his tether;

4. that he was somehow imprisoned in this relationship with his patient; and

5. that the bodily feelings he experienced during the sessions were the evidence of strain that this patient had caused him.

## Discussion and Conclusions

It seems that in the case of psychoanalytic therapy here presented, in order for the therapist to endure and contain his regressed patient, he made a regressive defensive detour within his countertransference, whereby by using regressive mechanisms, such as regressive identifications (complementary and projective counteridentification), splitting, dissociation, and denial, he repressed and postponed his awareness, by displacing in his body everything that was difficult for him to tolerate. He used his body as a place to store his patient's *menos*, the load of the massive violent projective identification, as well as his own counter-*menos* and countertransference responses. The therapist's body was the place where the potential "madness" was kept.

This use of his body was kept unconscious (part of the regressive and defensive detour) and apart (split off and dissociated) from the rest of his personality for a whole year. This time lag between unconscious and conscious awareness (Heimann, 1960) helped him to keep some distance and freedom in the therapeutic situation; to make use of his knowledge; and to maintain his own balance and empathy, which included elements of concordant and complementary identification. By displacing in his body the above-described unbearable feelings, he protected and defended his mental functions from the effects of his patient's *menos* and from her massive, violent projective identification processes.

This regressive detour also protected both participants from getting into a "mad" situation—i.e. the patient destroying the therapist with her attacks, and the therapist acting out his counter-responses. It was, however, betrayed by the conscious bodily feelings and their accompanying mixed affects. Nevertheless, their deeper symbolism remained unconscious within the regressive detour, that is, the bodily experiences were the witness, so to speak, of the unconscious use of the therapist's body.

In 1900, Freud (1900a) wrote, "Repression divides the psychic system into two distinct 'agencies', the Conscious–Preconscious (Cs–Pcs) and the dynamically unconscious". In our therapist's case, this "split" of the containing function, i.e. that part which remained unconscious for a whole year, troubling him as it did, and the other part, which was more or less conscious, constituted a specific type of containment (Melanie Klein, Bion, Rosenfeld, Kernberg), a specific type of holding (Winnicott), unique to this therapist. Equally unique is the patient who caused this specific type of containment to take place. To this effect Betty Joseph (1988) underlines that each patient is a unique patient. Winnicott, on the other hand, could have said that a good-enough mother is like a unique therapist who meets the particular needs of his patient.

However, the containing function was progressing hand-in-hand with the better understanding by therapist of the patient's primitive transference and his own countertransference. Eventually it developed into a more integral one.

As we have seen, the therapist's strenuous bodily feelings were a part of his countertransference, and it was thanks to them that he began to understand his own responses to the primitive transference of his patient. His bodily feelings were discharge phenomena to the internal potential "madness". Freud, in the Ego and the Id, (1923b) writes that, unpleasurable sensations "impel towards change, towards discharge" (p. 22). Also, to quote a popular saying, "Where there is smoke, there is fire". The therapist experienced not only mentally and psychologically, but also bodily, what had happened to his patient at the pre-verbal phase of her life at the hands of her paranoid father, who had abused her both physically and psychologically. The therapist understood that this was the only way the patient could communicate her early traumatic experiences to him. His tolerance of his painful bodily feelings reassured her that she would not repeat with him her traumatic past, because he was capable of understanding her and tolerating her.

By following the therapeutic process closely, we can see the progress made from primitive communication with the massive use of projective identification processes, to more mature processes—to projections, as Kernberg would have said (1988). Progress is also considered by Joseph Sandler (1988) the concept of projective identification based on the work of Bion (1962) for the containing function of mother–child or of therapist–patient. Thus, we might say that, as the patient's projective identifications have defensive and communicative functions, in the same way the countertransferential bodily experiences serve a similar function in the therapist, who succeeds in feeling and containing his patient and, therefore, in helping her to develop as she did. Primitive communication was achieved between therapist and patient, resulting in the progress and development of the means of communication and defence, as presented in the session above.

Furthermore, the bodily experiences are the witness of the therapist's capacity to endure the unknown, i.e. the unconscious meaning of his physical feelings. They are the witness of pain preceding the enlightenment of the unconscious—"Ah, this terrible pain before prophecy" (Aeschylus, 458 B.C., *Oresteia*). The increase in awareness of the meaning of his bodily feelings resulted in the decrease of both frequency and intensity of these experiences. Also, the bodily feelings were par excellence used as a tool for the further understanding of the patient (Heimann, 1950; Segal, 1981; Joseph, 1988; Kernberg, 1965; etc.).

In this presentation, emphasis was placed on the countertransferential bodily feelings, their comprehension, meaning and relation to the containing function; how they were provoked and how they affected the therapeutic relationship; also, as a mere source of information for the deeper understanding of the patient, as well as of the therapist's countertransference.

# CHAPTER SEVEN

# Countertransference reactions commonly present in the treatment of patients with borderline personality organization

*Vamik D. Volkan*

This chapter is concerned with countertransference reactions usually experienced by analysts during the course of treating borderline patients. These reactions are commonly shared, and they are more than just reflections of the analyst's own unresolved childhood conflicts. The type of countertransference about which I am writing here is very much a part of the psychoanalytic treatment of borderline patients.

Boyer (1961) stated that the analyst's unresolved countertransference is one of the major impediments to success in treating regressed individuals. As far as I know, Boyer was the first person to introduce this concept in the psychoanalytic literature of North America, although European writers, especially the English (Balint, 1968; Heimann, 1950; Khan, 1964), implied something similar, as did Racker (1968), writing from South America. Boyer's study of the analyst's countertransference during the treatment of regressed patients was supported by collaborative work with Giovacchini (1967), and by the independent work of Searles (1953, 1986). Their pioneering studies attracted considerable interest in this sub-

147

ject and, recently, a review of relevant literature has been compiled by Boyer (1990). Here I am simply acknowledging the influence of the writings of Boyer, Searles, and Giovacchini on the clinical technique I use with regressed patients, especially concerning the role of what I call "common" countertransference manifestations, as an aspect of my technique. I should point out, however, that my metapsychological understanding (Volkan, 1975, 1976, 1979, 1981, 1987) of the psychic organization of such patients has followed the object relations theory as described by Jacobson (1964) and Mahler (1968) and as systematized by Kernberg (1967, 1975a).

Schizophrenics, patients with borderline personality organization, and individuals with low-level narcissistic personality are all categorized as *regressed*. They come to psychoanalytic treatment already regressed or undeveloped, and no matter what the surface picture may be, their dominant conflicts concern self- and object relations rather than being structural in nature. I have noted (Volkan, 1981) that structural theory continues to be our most useful conceptualization in our attempts to understand the psychopathology of patients who are classified as *advanced*, and who have fully differentiated id, ego, and superego aspects, in dealing with transference–countertransference manifestations in their treatment. This approach is less useful, however, when applied to the treatment of regressed individuals whose dominant psychopathology reflects (re)activated internalized object relations and their interaction with self-representations. Regressed patients induce certain transference–countertransference phenomena that are best understood through an examination of their undeveloped or unintegrated self-concepts and object worlds.

I focus here *only* on regressed types who have borderline personality organization. In this context, four questions arise:

1. How do I identify the borderline personality organization?
2. What two preoccupations do such patients have that are reflected in "common" countertransference reactions?
3. What do I mean by countertransference?
4. What do I mean by "common" countertransference reactions in the treatment of individuals with borderline personality?

## Borderline personality organization

This diagnosis is made by assessing the nature of the patient's self- and object representations rather than by referring to symptoms or personality traits. Kernberg (1975a) focuses on the patient's ability to: (1) differentiate self- and object representations; and (2) integrate a "good" (libidinally invested) self-representation with a corresponding "bad" (aggressively invested) self-representation, as well as integrate a "good" object representation with a "bad" one. Advanced (neurotic) patients can do both, but if regressed they can do only one; schizophrenics can do neither; and borderline and narcissistic patients can do the first, but not the second.

As Jacobson (1964), Kernberg (1967, 1975a), and I (Volkan, 1976, 1987) have demonstrated, until a child is able to tolerate ambivalence, there is a "normal" developmental split between libidinally and aggressively invested self- and object representations. Such "normal" splitting persists, to a predominant degree, in individuals with borderline personality organization, but for them the splitting changes function and becomes the dominant defence mechanism. By using this *defensive* splitting—often along with denial, feelings of omnipotence, devaluation, and various projective mechanisms—the ego strives to maintain early opposing identifications: thus, the integration of ego identity is precluded and identity diffusion (Erikson, 1956) is likely to occur. Patients with borderline personality organization exhibit ego weaknesses such as poor tolerance of frustration and poor impulse control, although their reality testing remains relatively intact.

Katan (1973), Furman (1986), and Paulina Kernberg (1969) have confirmed that certain childhood traumas, such as the loss of a parent or the experience of incest, can lead to deficiencies in the integrative ability of the child's ego. I have identified (Volkan, 1987) types of early family environment and correlated these distinctions with the influence they have on the child's integrative functions. For example, multiple and contradictory parenting may lead to multiple and contradictory identifications that tax the child's integrative abilities. In this context, Searles (1986) has described the regressed patient's problems with dual and even multiple identity.

Certain constitutional biological factors may contribute further to the child's inability to integrate. According to Kernberg (1967), pathologically predominant pregenital aggression, especially oral aggression, may obstruct the integration of libidinally influenced "good" self-representations with the aggressively influenced "bad" self-representations, as well as the integration of "good" and "bad" object representations.

Organic biological potential, the environment, culture, and education all contribute to a child's development, and all colour the interaction with the mother, whereby the child forms his inner psychic structure. In some cases, biological factors may be dominant, and the analyst facing a regressed adult patient for the first time will most probably be unaware of just how much nature and nurture have contributed to the patient's regression. As Freud (1914c) noted, "disposition and experience . . . are linked up in an indissoluble etiological entity" (p. 18).

Much has been written about the metapsychological understanding of the borderline personality organization; here I am concentrating on common countertransferences that occur during the treatment of people in this category, taking note at the outset of two specific "preoccupations".

## Two preoccupations

Generally, there are two methods of psychoanalytic approach to patients with borderline personality organization (Volkan, 1987). The first technique aims to keep the patient at the level on which he is already functioning, but it strives to circumvent further regression as well, by providing new ego experiences through clarifications, suggestions, confrontations, and interpretations that can help the patient integrate opposing self as well as object representations. Analysts who endorse this style maintain that if their already undeveloped and regressed patients regress further, they will become psychotic and lose the ability to differentiate self- and object representations and thus be unable to test reality. These analysts deem psychotic patients to be beyond the help of analysis.

Proponents of the second approach maintain that patients with borderline personality organization must experience further regression in order truly to modify their inner structure: when this regression is controlled, it can become therapeutic. No attempt is made to interfere with the therapeutic regression, which is even deeper than the chaotic one previously demonstrated. The concept that ego regression gives way to a new psychic organization has been demonstrated in the developmental process and under certain clinical conditions. For example, in normal development, a new psychic organization is ushered in by the natural regression that takes place during adolescence; in normal mourning, after the loss of a love object, the mourner experiences regression before being able to reestablish an adaptation to his external reality and his inner world. In controlled, therapeutic regression the borderline patient is able to abandon the defensive use of splitting and reactivate "normal" developmental splitting. Once the patient is back on his normal developmental course, he can follow the path of psychic growth and gain integrative ability, just as a child would. Analysts who advocate this approach know that transference psychosis may accompany the therapeutic regression, and they are willing to continue analytic work if it does.

My experience with borderline patients follows this second mode. I have described elsewhere (Volkan, 1987) the phases these patients go through in preparing for and passing through therapeutic regression that is followed eventually by upward-evolving transference neurosis.

During the early years of analysis such patients activate their unintegrated self as well as unintegrated object representations within the transference–countertransference axis. Following their therapeutic regressions, there comes a time when they consolidate opposing self as well as object representations and their accompanying drive derivatives. At that point they resemble (advanced) neurotic patients. The common countertransference manifestations that materialize occur before this point, reflecting two preoccupations with which these patients are involved during the initial years of their treatment.

## The first preoccupation

The first concern relates to the development of an integrated self-representation and a cohesive sense of self, and the corresponding integration of object representations. The borderline patient uses defensive splitting rather effectively in everyday life, and initially in the analytic setting, so his preoccupation with the development of a more differentiated and integrated state is not evident on the surface. It must be remembered that with such people, splitting is a defence against tensions that arise from an attempt to bring together opposing self- as well as object representations that are associated with opposing affects. My clinical experience with such individuals persuaded me that all had a *psycho-biological push* towards rising to a higher level of psychic organization, and that this is activated by the analytic process.

At first, the psycho-biological push towards integration clashes with the expression of defensive splitting, but after therapeutic regression occurs, the patient can revert to using normal developmental splitting, which is the precursor of integration. Thus, we can conclude that borderline patients are preoccupied with integrating their self- as well as object representations and their accompanying affects. This first preoccupation accompanies a second one that helps the patient to respond effectively to his psycho-biological push, in the therapeutic setting.

## The second preoccupation

Borderline patients are preoccupied with relating to their environment within an *introjective–projective cycle*: when the patient is ensconced in a therapeutic setting, the analyst is included in this cycle. Such patients continuously project onto external objects aspects of their unintegrated self as well as object representations, and then reintroject and re-project them. Some projective and introjective identifications—temporary ones usually—are formed and dissolved in the process.

The use of *projective identification* by borderline patients has been rather wisely discussed in recent literature, but the definition of this term has led to some confusion, as Goldstein's (1991) review of this concept indicates. I prefer the term *introjective–projective cycle*, which refers in a general way to all inner and outer flow. In using this term, we must explain each process that is involved: what is introjected; what is projected; what is the level of differentiation between the outer and inner worlds as this process occurs; and what is the fate of the introjections and the projections.

Once the analyst is involved in his patient's introjective–projective cycle, his psychoanalytic stance and the psychoanalytic setting begin to make him, in his patient's eyes, a "new object"—something not encountered previously (Loewald, 1960). The neurotic patient also relates to his analyst with introjection and projection, but his process is largely in the background, whereas with the regressed individual it is in the foreground: the more regressed the patient, the more prominent the introjective–projective cycle (Volkan, 1982). For example, among schizophrenics this cycle appears in a gross and exaggerated fashion that is usually accompanied by cannibalistic fantasies; this trait is not that obvious among the borderline patients, although it is readily observable when the analyst is watching for it.

The major technical manoeuvre needed in the psychoanalysis of a borderline patient, at least at first, is the maintenance of this "new object"—sometimes called "the analytic introject" (Giovacchini, 1972). The analyst helps prevent the patient from becoming contaminated with the patient's archaic unintegrated self- and object representations. Once the analytic introject enters the introjective–projective cycle and becomes an object of identification for the patient, the patient assumes an analytical attitude on the basis of this identification and is better able to observe the cycle, as well as to retard it. Then, he can identify with the analyst's tolerance of unneutralized affects and his differentiating and integrating functions. Effective identification with the analyst's functions is necessary for the consolidation of opposing representations; it also strengthens the patient's psycho-biological push towards integrated psychic organization on a higher level. The therapeutic handling of introjective–projective relatedness in the initial phase of a regressed patient's treatment is the crucial curative factor (Volkan, 1982).

In the intimate dyadic encounter with the patient who makes him a target of split self- and object units and who inwardly needs but dreads their integration, the analyst's own sense of self and internalized object world is threatened. Fully possessed, presumably, of a cohesive sense of self and a stable internalized world, the analyst regresses therapeutically, nevertheless, in the service of the other (Olinick, 1969). Indeed, in treating a borderline patient he regresses to a level not normally available to him in his everyday experience of life, although he retains intellectual awareness of his patient's psychic structure. What happens in the psychoanalytic treatment of such a patient is more like a reactivation of the child/mother relationship than what happens in the psychoanalysis of a neurotic individual (Loewald, 1960). In the former case, the analyst/patient relationship reactivates the patient's ego-building and helps him develop new ego abilities in the service of further differentiation and integration of self- and object representations. In turn, the analyst's "long-forgotten" part-object experiences, introjective–projective relatedness, and unneutralized affects are stirred up in the course of his therapeutic regression, causing certain countertransference manifestations that are more commonly present in the treatment of a regressed patient than in that of a neurotic one.

## Countertransference

When emphasis is placed on the two preoccupations of a borderline patient early in treatment, the stage is set for studying common countertransference issues. Before proceeding with this study, however, a few general remarks on countertransference are necessary.

Freud introduced the term *countertransference* in 1910, before he wrote most of his papers about technique. The term was then thought roughly to be the converse of transference, referring to conditions under which the analyst's own feelings, thoughts, and attitudes towards people and things that had been important to him as a child are displaced onto the patient. In this conceptualization, since the analyst's residual pathological elements and conflicts are included in countertransference, they were thought to obstruct or to at least interfere with treatment. The belief was that countertransference did not appear when the analyst had been properly analysed, and that the analyst should do away with it in order to treat a patient successfully.

Countertransference is unconscious, however, so only derivative manifestations can be detected. As analysts gained more experience with regressed patients, the negative view changed. Followers of Melanie Klein in England and South America were the first to stress that *all* feelings, thoughts, and attitudes experienced by an analyst towards his patient should be considered: The concept came to include not only the unconscious conflicts of the analyst, but his reactions to his patient's personality and transference as well. Abend (1989) offers a comprehensive review of all that is involved in the term countertransference, and how its meaning has so radically altered over the years. I shall refer here only to some of the contributions on the subject.

Little (1951, 1957) was followed by Kernberg (1965) in recommending a *totalistic* view of this phenomenon, claiming that the analyst's total emotional reactions should be considered, including the following: (1) his unconscious neurotic needs, (2) his reality needs, (3) his reactions to the patient's reality, and (4) his reaction to the patient's transference. These four categories can be intermingled.

Karl Menninger (1958), writing negatively about countertransference as originally described by Freud, offered a long list of suggestions for "the detection and correction of countertransference", and he attempted to show the common ways in which it can be an obstruction. The following are some examples: seeking ways to impress the patient or to impress colleagues with the importance of one's patient; repeatedly experiencing erotic or affectionate feelings toward a patient; being tempted to engage in professional gossip about a patient; dreaming about a patient; having a recurrent impulse to ask favours of the patient, and so on.

Although most of the items on Menninger's list may reflect something like a *countertransference neurosis*, the application of a totalistic viewpoint will show that the persistent derivatives of the analyst's feelings, thoughts, and behaviour patterns about a patient can be studied in a more sophisticated way. For example, Menninger talks about the analyst's drowsiness during analytic sessions. We can speculate that this heralds the onset of countertransference, but of what kind? The patient may represent a hated sibling to the analyst, and if the latter still has a blind spot about the sibling rivalry he once experienced, he may react neurotically towards his patient. Then his drowsiness can be understood as evidence of an attempt to deny rage against his brother/patient. In this case the countertransference exemplifies the classical "negative" concept of this phenomenon and does constitute an impediment to analytic work.

On the other hand, the analyst may experience drowsiness because of his own or his patient's real situation: an obsessional patient, through endless dry intellectualizations and ruminations, may bore his analyst to the point of lethargy. Should the patient's real-life situation be extremely painful, such as when a son or daughter is seriously ill, the analyst's drowsiness may be a means of seeking relief from empathic identification with the suffering patient. The analyst's own reality, which may include worries about his health or envy of his rich patient's possessions, may account for his reaction. This will differ from analyst to analyst and obviously must be subjected to self-analysis if the treatment is to proceed smoothly.

Many analysts share a kind of drowsiness that can be considered "common". For example, Kohut (1971), Modell (1976), Kernberg (1975a), and I have independently and consistently reported feeling drowsy at times during the analysis of patients with full-blown narcissistic personality organizations, in response to their narcissistic transference. While undergoing treatment, the narcissistic patient who activates his fantasy of being self-sufficient and grandiosely above needing anyone else, and who treats his analyst as non-existent or worthless, is likely to evoke such a feeling of drowsiness. From an object-relations point of view, the narcissistic patient in this example has kept his grandiose self to himself, while experiencing the analyst as a representation of devalued self- and object representations.

## *"Common" countertransference reactions*

I consider "common" those countertransference manifestations that are evoked in analysts by transferences that are characteristic of most if not all patients of a given personality organization, as in the case of the narcissistic patient who most probably will denigrate his analyst and keep him at a distance some time during treatment. Then the analyst's drowsiness is "common", for it emanates from a shared therapeutic regression while meeting the patient on the level of the patient's personality organization, thus providing the analyst with an opportunity to experience his patient's inner world. The analyst's knowledge about and use of these "common" countertransferences can contribute significantly to the overall treatment process.

Once placed in an analytic setting, a patient with a borderline personality organization will be preoccupied with integrating his self- and object representations and resisting such a psycho-biological push. He will develop a "typical" *split transference* (Volkan, 1981), and the analyst will become aware of four players in his office rather than two: the patient's "good" self- and object representations are there, as are his "bad" self- and object representations. The patient's other preoccupation—developing introjective–projective relatedness with his analyst—will put these "four players" into motion. The patient will then experience them within himself—or within the analyst—while maintaining, most of the time, a psychological border between his analyst and himself.

The analyst who adopts a style that supports his patient's therapeutic regression and who himself regresses does not see the split transference as simply something to note intellectually; he personally experiences its effect on himself. He opens up to the patient's introjective–projective way of relating while at the same time maintaining his observing and working ego (Olinick et al., 1973) and protecting his patient's observing ego as well. He will experience "common" countertransference reactions during this interaction.

The analyst's participation in his patient's split transference and introjective–projective cycle is a "common" countertransference in the treatment of the borderline patient. Just as with the narcissistic patient, the borderline individual who despises or denies the presence of his analyst may induce a dull feeling in the latter: receiving "bad" self- or object representations, the analyst may feel heavy, irritated, and uncomfortable and may even have psychosomatic sensations such as intestinal cramps, heartburn, or breathing problems. One patient of mine fell asleep whenever I thought he was feeling anxious. While he slept and snored, sometimes for half an hour or so, I simultaneously experienced mild difficulty in my chest and felt uncomfortable in my stomach, as though I had eaten a heavy meal. Upon awakening, he would report fragmented dream images. For example, he would see a house, a room, a tree, a gun, a hangman's noose, a star, and so on. At first I forced myself to focus intellectually on these fragmented images and to elicit my patient's associations with them. He would not provide any useful associations, however. While he was lying supine on the couch, seemingly in a relaxed state, I felt uncomfortable. As time passed and such experiences were repeated, I began to fantasize that his fragmented dream images were like bits of faecal material, suggesting that my patient was having oral diarrhoea in which he sought to drown me. This patient's history included beatings by his parents in the bathroom when the patient was a child; the parents had given him enemas repeatedly, and he was unable to integrate their loving and murderous representations as well as his corresponding representations of himself.

What was important in his analysis at this time was *not* my curiosity about and attempted analysis of his dream fragments, but the experience, understanding, and interpretation of his reactivation of early bathroom experiences within the transference–countertransference axis. As his analysis progressed, we were able to reconstruct certain facts about the past—that while being beaten in the bathroom and being given enemas, he had tried to protect himself by devising a fantasy of "blasting off" both his parents with explosive diarrhoea (Volkan & Ast, in press).

The analyst is likely to feel elated at times, or bodily light, without apparent reason, if he is the recipient of his patient's "good" self- and object representations. Another of my patients, who also had been given enemas as a child, began coming to his appointments 25 minutes late. This continued for about a month without my interfering. I knew intellectually that he was splitting the sessions and me by being absent during the first half of his hour but present in the second. I was fascinated when I realized that during the second half of his hour, when he was in my office, I felt elated and had a grin on my face—for no apparent reason. I learned eventually that he spent the first 25 minutes of his assigned hour on the toilet in a bathroom near my office, and that while there he imagined me to be a monster; my "bad" representation was in the bathroom, but in my office he deposited in me an idealized/good parent, and made me "happy" (Volkan, 1975).

Any analyst treating a borderline patient may have such heavy/uncomfortable and light/happy emotional and bodily feelings that shift abruptly. No matter how different other clinical manifestations may be on the surface, and no matter what the analyst's associated thoughts and feelings may be, their meaning will remain the same, and they can be tied to the patient's depositing in his analyst "good" self- and object representations as well as "bad" ones, as the analyst is included in the patient's introjective–projective cycle.

## Training necessary for the tolerance of "common" countertransference reactions

Some analysts cannot effectively "regress in the service of the other" (Olinick, 1969), when deep regression is needed to meet the patient on a level at which unintegrated self- and object representations are actively in motion. Some analysts may be unsuited for treating patients who are already regressed when the treatment involves regression of the analyst as well, in order for a fully therapeutic relationship to evolve that parallels the child/mother relationship. All too often psychoanalytic institutes simply do not provide proper education for the psychoanalytic treatment of the regressed or undeveloped patient. In preparing psychoanalytic candidates to treat regressed patients, we should give them opportunities for supervised work with such patients who, being thought unanalysable, are seldom made available; the prospective analysts should be followed to familiarize themselves with split transference and the

introjective–projective cycle, so that they can learn to be tolerant of the consequences.

An analyst does not easily form temporary therapeutic empathic identifications with patients whose experiences in analysis are outside the range of his own customary way of life and
clinical practice. The psychoanalytic trainee who is selected for
training on the basis of his advanced personality and who is
without a high degree of primitive relatedness will not benefit
from identification with his training analyst, and he will not
"learn" how to be tolerant of being in an introjective–projective
cycle or how to be able to resolve split transferences, since
such processes are not dominant in his training analysis. This
type of trainee will require proper supervision in dealing with
the regressed and the undeveloped.

When a young analyst begins work with a borderline patient,
becoming the target of "good" and "bad" self- and object representations causes reactions; to be perceived as being loving one
day and hating the next may evoke a response of feeling like
being on a roller-coaster. Then, instead of repeatedly feeling
uncomfortable or elated and observing these feelings with tolerance, the analyst may react to the roller-coaster situation by
becoming excessively rigid, setting unreasonable limits, and
becoming an advisor or manager to his patient, thereby losing
his analytic stance. The appearance of "common" transference
relatedness early in treatment and before the novice analyst can
"adjust" to his patient therapeutically is another factor that will
have a negative effect.

It is not true that neurotic transference is strongest when
an advanced (neurotic) patient enters treatment, and that a
"real" relationship comes about at the end of treatment. Anna
Freud (1954) held that the neurotic patient enters analysis with
a reality-based attitude towards his analyst, but that this becomes secondary as full-blown transference neurosis develops.
When this is worked through, the figure of the analyst as a
"real" person emerges once again, but as long as the analysand
has a healthy part of his personality intact, he never completely
submerges his experiencing of his analyst outside his transference expectations. A similar comment can appropriately be
made about countertransference. This description cannot be
applied, however, when an analyst works with regressed and

undeveloped patients—i.e. patients with borderline personality organizations. Then, transference distortions and alternating relationships with the analyst as "good" and "bad" are extreme at the outset and, accordingly, may induce intense emotional responses in the analyst right from the start. This may create a situation unlike that in which the transference–countertransference axis develops step-by-step, in work with neurotic individuals. As the analyst gains more experience with borderline patients, he tames his "common" countertransference responses to the initial assault of split transference and the introjective–projective cycle. His experience enables him to "own" his "common" countertransference responses so that he may focus on the unconscious therapeutic stories they reflect.

## Therapeutic stories reflected in "common" countertransference reactions

Every "good" or "bad" self- and object representation has its own developmental story, and these will be reflected in the "common" transference–countertransference axis. Early in her analysis, a regressed female patient of mine reported a dream in which she was a small child choking on her oatmeal. I learned that when she was small, her mother was grieving over the condition of a sick and deformed sibling who was a year-and-a-half older than my patient. This baby died when my patient was a year-and-a-half old, sending their mother into an even deeper depression. As a toddler, my patient had been unable to integrate the images of a grieving/unpleasurable mother with that of the caring/pleasurable one for whom she longed. At the oedipal age her father began playing with her sexually; this continued until she reached puberty, and I later understood that this behaviour was related to his being rejected by a grieving wife.

A few years into her analysis I had difficulty breathing as I sat behind the couch on which my patient lay; I could hardly wait for the end of our sessions then, and when the hour was over, I would hurry to open the window to get fresh air. At first I attributed this to my cigars (I had just begun to smoke them in those days), but soon realized that I did not have this trouble when other patients were on the couch. My patient did not seem to notice my discomfort but spoke rapidly, without separating her sentences. This type of experience continued for a few weeks, until one day I realized that her new brisk way of speaking was like her shoving spoonfuls of oatmeal in my mouth until I could no longer breathe. I began to see that within the introjective–projective cycle in which we were engaged I had become the baby obliged to "eat" my patient's experiences with a grieving/depressed mother. My patient's experience with a "bad" object representation was deposited in me, and she created a "therapeutic story" by making me uncomfortable.

Once I understood this, I could tolerate being fed "bad oatmeal". My countertransference was tamed. I told her I had noticed the change in her speech pattern, and that it felt as though oatmeal were being pushed into me, as it was done in her dream. I added that in her own way she might be expressing how her anxious mother had fed her; her mother had stimulated her in disturbing ways, and she could not digest her mother's grief. I suggested that when she was ready she could talk to me in a less anxious way, by separating her sentences— that there might be more soothing ways of feeding me her thoughts. In time her speech returned to normal, and my breathing problem disappeared. Later, when the aggressively fed hungry baby representation had been taken back through the introjective–projective cycle, I noted that it was less "bad", and she was better able to tolerate having it within herself.

Much later my patient learned from her mother that she had actually fed her in an aggressive way, and that during nursing times her mother would abruptly remove her breast because she occasionally felt pain from an infection. Some time after this experience the young woman subscribed to a gourmet magazine and learned how to cook. She had developed a new ego function.

## Conclusion

"Common" countertransference reactions occur in the treatment of a borderline patient when the analyst regresses to meet his already regressed patient and opens himself up to being a target of his patient's unintegrated self- as well as object representations and their connected affects as patient and analyst are caught up in an introjective–projective cycle. Such countertransference responses become part of the analytic process, and the analyst should take care not to develop a technique based on mechanical responses to "good" or "bad" self- and object representations as though the patient could be taught to integrate them, like putting together the pieces of a puzzle. Analytic work focuses on the meaning and affects behind each "good" and "bad" self-representation. The affective appearance of such therapeutic stories in the transference–countertransference axis constitutes the crucial aspect of working through the process, while identifications with the analyst's integrative functions help the patient advance towards integration of his split self- as well as object representations.

# CHAPTER EIGHT

# Projective identification, countertransference, and hospital treatment

*Otto F. Kernberg*

M y principal purpose in this chapter is to illustrate the pivotal function of projective identification within the therapeutic milieu of the hospital. What follows is a detailed description of crises in the treatment of two patients undergoing long-term inpatient psychiatric treatment. These patients suffered from very different psychiatric illnesses; hence their cases illustrate some features of hospital treatment that cut across different types and degrees of severity of psychopathology.

## Lucia

Lucia was single and in her late twenties—an attractive and intelligent but emotionally unstable Latin-American musician who had been educated in this country [United States] and

Reprinted by permission from *Psychiatric Clinics of North America*, *Vol. 10* (1987), No. 2: 257–272 whose very wealthy parents financially supported her and her artistic career. She had a history of chronic drug and alcohol abuse, repeated serious suicide attempts, and chronic interpersonal difficulties at work and in intimate relations.

Lucia was the youngest of three children; her older brothers had left home many years earlier, and for all practical purposes her parents treated her as their only and major concern. Father was seductive rather than loving in his interactions with Lucia and basically controlled by her mother, clearly the dominant personality in the family. Mother was a highly emotional, extroverted, charming yet also intrusive person, who, in subtle ways, attempted to control Lucia's life while yet remaining strangely indifferent or even hostile to her at a deeper level. For example, Lucia suffered from an allergy that prevented her from eating certain types of sweets; mother periodically sent her packages of those very sweets from Latin America, even after the hospital psychiatrist initially assigned to the case had discussed the issue with her.

Lucia's diagnosis on admission was (1) severe personality disorder with predominantly narcissistic and borderline features; (2) mixed substance and alcohol abuse; and (3) minor depressive disorder, with a relatively unpredictable suicidal potential linked to severe emotional crises. Because of her failure to respond to repeated efforts in outpatient psychotherapy, long-term inpatient treatment and simultaneous initiation of psychoanalytic psychotherapy had been recommended.

From the very beginning, this patient's treatment had a VIP quality. The parents' vast wealth and social connections were generally known, and hospital staff sensed that the chairman of the hospital board as well as other board members were more than ordinarily interested in Lucia's treatment. The director of the hospital, Dr A, was always available to the parents when they came to visit—a most unusual circumstance. Dr A, moreover, disagreed with the diagnosis; he thought it too "harsh" and believed that Lucia was merely infantile–hysterical. Furthermore, Dr A had told the psychiatrist assigned to Lucia that he was being too critical of this unusual family. Dr A, dissatisfied with what he considered the excessively strict, rigid, and unsophisticated approach of this psychiatrist, asked me, a new unit chief in the hospital, to take on Lucia's hospital management. Because I had graduated from a psychoanalytic training program and the other unit chiefs, although ambivalent about psychoanalysis, respected hospital psychiatrists who had been psychoanalytically trained, Dr A thought that I would be able to handle this case better.

Lucia's psychotherapist (whom she was seeing four times a week while I saw her on average for fifteen to twenty minutes five times a week) preferred to maintain his treatment with her completely separate from the hospital management. He had also been trained psychoanalytically and was a close personal friend of Dr A. In our brief encounters, Lucia's psychotherapist treated me in a friendly way but clearly as a very senior person relating to a recent graduate.

Both Lucia's psychotherapist and Dr A were also part of the faculty of an institute for postgraduate psycho-dynamic psychotherapy in town, which I will call the Institute. The theoretical orientation of the Institute was somewhat different from my traditional psychoanalytic one, so I was clearly an outsider. The hospital faculty and staff, however, considered themselves better qualified than the Institute people in handling severely ill patients in long-term inpatient treatment, and so they viewed the Institute with a degree of ambivalence. They considered the non-hospital-based Institute psychotherapists as too soft, even naive, in dealing with severely regressed patients who, in their view, required firmness and a clear treatment structure. I thus became, unwittingly at first, a representative of the philosophy of the Institute as opposed to that of the hospital staff, represented by the hospital psychiatrist I was replacing.

My relationship with Lucia started out with what might be described as a therapeutic honeymoon. She quickly informed herself of my own Latin-American background and told me she considered me to represent the European-influenced Latin-American culture that corresponded to her own background. She persuaded me to agree that the "rigidity" of her previous hospital psychiatrist regarding her participation in hospital activities and work was unreasonable and counterproductive. She proposed that, instead of her daily schedule of activities, she take correspondence courses from a local university so as to answer to her educational requirements and facilitate her progress towards an advanced degree in music.

I agreed with this course of action, saw to the arrangements of her college courses, and gave the matter little further thought. Although my relations with Lucia seemed to be developing satisfactorily, casual remarks dropped by other unit chiefs and senior hospital staff suggested that these arrangements were being viewed with a certain degree of scepticism in the belief that both Lucia's psychotherapist and I were being naive and were being manipulated by the patient.

Several weeks later the correspondence courses had not arrived, but Lucia had long since withdrawn from most of her scheduled activities. Lucia had elaborate explanations for the missing courses. First, they had been lost in the mail; a replacement set was not delivered because of some error in the hospital mail office. The third set was being delayed at its source. I then went to the hospital mail office to try to trace the source of the trouble and was told that a large package had, indeed, just arrived for my patient.

When I confronted Lucia with the discrepancy between her assertion that she had not received the package and the information from the hospital mail office, she became very upset and accused me of not believing her and of becoming like her previous hospital psychiatrist. She explained that the package she had just received (and the contents of which, she said, she was willing to show me) was from her mother.

Late that evening I was called at home because Lucia was in an intense panic and insisted on seeing me. I went back to the hospital, where Lucia received me dressed in a transparent and highly revealing negligee. She was obviously trying to seduce me, and although I maintained my equanimity, I also sensed an erotic response in my affective reaction. She said she simply wanted to tell me how upset she had been by my questioning her earlier in the day, but she was most grateful for my responding to her call and felt better now that I had come. She stressed how important it was to her that our relationship be a good one.

That night I dreamed that I was in Lucia's room in the hospital, but it now looked more like a hotel room, and I was sitting on the bed with her, in what was obviously evolving into a sexual encounter. Suddenly, with a seductive smile, Lucia put her index finger into my mouth, probing deeply, and I awoke with an intense sense of anxiety. As I lay awake thinking about the dream, it suddenly occurred to me that what she had been doing to me in the dream was, in Spanish, "*meterme el dedo en la boca*", which, translated, means "putting her finger into my mouth". In the popular language of Chile where I was educated, this was a way of saying, "to make a fool of somebody". Wide awake now, I thought about the comedy of errors of the correspondence courses and decided that Lucia had probably been lying to me all along.

The following day, I confronted her with my belief that she had been lying to me, whereupon she confessed that she had received the package from the university and had thrown it away. She now became enraged and accused me of rigidly insisting that she take college courses that she was not interested in at all. I reminded her that she had taken the initiative regarding these courses, and that I had agreed with her. I expressed my regret about her inability to share with me openly her unwillingness to take up these courses and to discuss with me possible alternatives. Lucia, apparently oblivious to what I was saying, continued to upbraid me for insisting on a study plan instead of showing concern for her interests and vocation.

It was standard hospital policy to inform a patient's psychotherapist of important developments regarding their patients, so after telling Lucia I was going to inform her psychotherapist about this issue, I promptly did so. After listening to my report, her therapist told me that he had been aware of the problem of the correspondence courses all along, but he thought that I was exaggerating its importance; after all, some manipulative behaviour was to be expected from this patient. My efforts to stress the gravity, as I saw it, of Lucia's unwarranted deceitfulness led to his telling me, in a friendlier way, that he understood this was a very difficult patient and that it was very important to understand the reasons for her need to behave this way in light of the chaotic experiences she had suffered in her childhood. Our conversation ended without a meeting of our minds. I thought he was underestimating the severity of Lucia's superego pathology and the temporary displacement onto me of an aggressive deceitfulness in the transference; he thought I was over-reacting in response to a narcissistic lesion and because of a lack of experience with this kind of patient.

Later that day, I received a call from Dr A's office, and an appointment for me to see him the following week was set up. It took very little time for the other unit chiefs to let me know that the call resulted from a complaint about me that Lucia had lodged with him. I now had the strange experience of suddenly becoming "hero of the day" in the eyes of the other unit chiefs and senior hospital staff because I stood up to Lucia's manipulative behaviour. Her deceitfulness had seemed clear to them all along. I also noticed, not without apprehension, that I was now perceived as part of the "hospital front" against the Institute.

Dr A received me in a stern fashion and told me that Lucia had complained about my rigid, obsessive, "policeman-like" attitude regarding her studies. He made clear that he was disappointed with me. He told me that he had talked with Lucia's psychotherapist, who saw the situation exactly as he did. Both thought she should be treated more gently. I felt defeated and paralysed and almost relieved when Dr A told me that, in agreement with the psychotherapist, he planned to transfer Lucia to another hospital psychiatrist.

My immediate reaction was of anger and disappointment, but once that had passed I was concerned because I believed that Lucia's "triumph" in dismissing me indirectly, through manipulation of her psychotherapist and Dr A, had profoundly self-destructive implications. In brooding over these events, I had the strong support of Clara, the head nurse of my unit. Clara now told me that Lucia had always been perceived as seductive towards men in authority. I realized that she had certainly exercised her seductive powers with Dr A as well as with me. Clara also told me that she had thought my treatment of Lucia showed me to be quite naive; Clara thought the episode might turn out to be a good learning experience for me.

Lucia was transferred to another psychiatrist; she soon reverted to alcohol and drug abuse and finally left the hospital. Within the year, the hospital lost all communication with her and her family.

After several months had passed, Dr A invited me to his home. Our relationship developed into a friendship, but he never mentioned Lucia to me again, nor did I mention her name to him.

## Discussion

What I called the therapeutic honeymoon with Lucia might be described, in terms of my countertransference reaction, as my concordant identification with the patient's pathological grandiose self, her characterological narcissistic structure. My countertransference most probably reflected my being induced into the role of an admiring and potentially corruptible as well as seductive father.

In Racker's (1957) terminology, *concordant* identification in the countertransference refers to the analyst's identifying symmetrically with the patient's currently dominant psychic structure, so that the analyst's ego identifies with the patient's ego, the analyst's superego with the patient's superego, and so forth. For practical purposes, concordant identification is the basis for the therapist's empathy with the patient's dominant subjective experience, but it also creates the danger of over-identification with the patient's defensive stance. In contrast, *complementary* identification in the countertransference refers to an identification not with the patient's currently dominant self-experience, but with one complementary to it. For example, complementary identification would be with the patient's superego when the patient is identifying himself with his own id; or identifying with the patient's object representation (inner object) when the patient is identifying himself with his own self-representation; or, in a reverse situation, an identification with the patient's self while the patient identifies with his corresponding object representation.

When I recognized Lucia's deceptiveness with regard to the college course, my internal reaction with Lucia shifted sharply, from a concordant identification with her to a suspicious, persecutory stance—a complementary identification with what may be considered the dissociated, sadistic superego precursors against which her narcissistic defences had been erected, while she identified herself with her own dissociated, humiliated, and sadistically mistreated self. By the same token, it is probable that I became a primitive, sadistic mother representation, destroying the sexualized relation with father in a violent, revengeful disruption.

One might speculate that had I not been so fearful of the activation of my sexual fantasies about her, and, at the same time, had I become aware of her narcissistic seduction of me, I might have tolerated my sexual fantasies about her while becoming alerted to her seductive behaviour and the implicit control over my independent thinking that derived from it. As it was, I had been seduced by Dr A's assignment into an implicit alliance with the patient's narcissistic defences, which reduced the objectivity of my stance regarding her.

Later on, in the sudden reversal of my relationship with her, I automatically identified with the "anti-Institute" sentience of the hospital staff, so that my complementary identification with Lucia's internal "persecutors" coincided with my identification with a rebellious ideology in the hospital.

The shift from concordant to complementary identification in my countertransference may also be related to the sudden activation of projective identification in the patient's defensive repertoire. Lucia dealt with me deceptively over a period of weeks. Her dishonesty may be considered a defence against a feared "persecutory" attack from me that reflected the projection onto me of a sadistic, persecutory object representation, most probably a pre-oedipal mother image. Her description of me as a rigid, obsessive policeman was devoid of sexuality and implied a highly self-centred, callous, suspicious, primitive authority figure who disrupted the sexualized relation with male authority (father).

That the patient could project onto me a persecutory, callous, and manipulative mother while still identifying herself with such a sadistic image (reflected by her self-protective, dishonest, and manipulative control of me) indicates the operation of projective identification rather than projection. Projective identification, as I have pointed out elsewhere, is a primitive defence, consisting of (1) projecting an intolerable impulse onto an object, (2) maintaining empathy with what is projected, (3) attempting to control the object onto whom the projection has been directed (as a continuation of the defensive effort against the intolerable intrapsychic experience), and (4) unconsciously inducing the projected intrapsychic experience in the object by means of complex affective, cognitive, and behavioural manifestations in the actual interaction.

What seems to me of particular interest here is the bridging function of my countertransference reaction: it was a response both to the patient's enactment, by means of projective identification of a primitive internalized object relation, and to the hospital milieu's enactment, by means of a powerful though subtle role induction and/or facilitation in me, of a submission to Dr A and the Institute as a defence against the underlying rebellion against them. In other words, the patient's pathology of internal object relations and the hospital's latent social conflicts "clicked" in my internal reaction at the boundary between the patient and the hospital system.

Of equal interest, it seems to me, is the "withdrawal reaction" that occurred in myself, in the patient's attitude toward me and the hospital, and in the hospital's attitude to the patient. When I was dismissed, I felt an emotional withdrawal from both Lucia and Dr A. The subsequent cynical, almost gleeful withdrawal of the hospital staff from Lucia as her treatment gradually fell apart (the hospital psychiatrist who replaced me carried out his functions somewhat perfunctorily, and, while many staff members were aware of the patient's acting out, this information no longer reached either her psychotherapist or Dr A) was the third "withdrawal reaction" in the hospital system. All these developments may be subsumed under the category of a withdrawal to protect the self-esteem of "injured parties"—in other words, a defensive narcissistic withdrawal from an intense conflict around hostility. This generalized withdrawal of the hospital system from the patient, which became dramatic in the last few months before Lucia finally interrupted the treatment, may also be considered to represent a symbolic corruption of the total care that the hospital ideally should have continued to provide for her.

It is as if the patient had let me "die", and I and the hospital staff let the patient's treatment "die" in return. The hospital staff also left me alone: once my "defeat" was obvious and I was dismissed from the case, no unit chief challenged Dr A's decision in a clinical forum or ventured to re-examine the total therapeutic handling of this case. It was as if once I served a function for the hospital ideology I was "dropped" from the scene and allowed to "die".

What perhaps is more striking than anything else in this case is the replay of Lucia's family pathology within the hospital. The family's enormous wealth had created a situation that was effectively utilized by the patient's mother to support her daughter's control over the treatment, against her daughter's better interests. This development was in continuation with the family history of a teasingly seductive but unavailable father who was controlled by her mother. Dr A's "seduction" by the patient, an implicit repetition of the relation with her father, was destroyed by the collapse of the treatment, an implicit consequence of the patient's and her mother's destructive effects on the hospital system. The family's control over their own world had found a dramatic counterpart in their daughter's self-destructive manipulativeness. Their effective control of the hospital's world similarly bred an atmosphere of corruption and revenge and destroyed their daughter's treatment.

Ideally, I should have been able to explore Lucia's dominant pathology of internalized object relations as it was replayed in the hospital: her failure at work, her sexual seductiveness as a corruption of those who were there to help her, the symbolic destruction of a good relation with an oedipal father because of the destructive effects of a sadistic, internalized image of the preoedipal mother, the projection of the patient's sadistic superego precursors onto the environment, and her secondary defences against persecution by means of dishonesty. The pathogenic features of her childhood environment, however, were replayed in her unconscious seduction of her psychotherapist, Dr A, and myself, and replayed as well in the large group process activated in the hospital milieu.

## Ralph

Ralph was a single man in his early twenties, with a history of a severe behaviour disorder that had started in early adolescence, characterized by truancy, rebelliousness, school failure, and violent fights with other youngsters and teachers, all of which led to his having been expelled from several schools. In late adolescence he showed occasional violent behaviour alternating with prolonged periods of social withdrawal. He was now considered "strange", was the butt of ridicule by peers, and showed occasionally bizarre behaviour and a gradually deepening isolation from all social contacts. Ralph dropped out shortly before graduating from high school, spending days and weeks mostly in his room, developing strange rituals, which he attempted to hide from his parents. He expressed a growing pre-occupation with changes he thought were occurring in his face. Eventually he developed delusional ideas of bodily transformation and auditory hallucinations, was diagnosed as presenting a schizophrenic illness, and was hospitalized in several psychiatric hospitals for periods lasting from a few weeks to several months.

Ralph had responded to repeated treatment with high doses of neuroleptics and electroshock to the extent of being able to return to home and school. However, at such times he presented frankly antisocial behaviour; he was dishonest and aggressive and exploited and cheated fellow students and teachers; he occasionally was violent and had again to be expelled from school. He then withdrew into his own room and presented symptoms of psychosis. By the time of his admission to our hospital, after at least eight years of a progressively worsening illness, he carried the diagnosis of a chronic, undifferentiated schizophrenic illness. Because of the striking pattern of improvement with neuroleptic treatment and the subsequent development of severe antisocial behaviour, followed by renewed regression into psychosis, he was considered to present one of the rare cases of "pseudo-psychopathic schizophrenia".

Ralph's father was a European businessman who had developed new methods for large-scale recycling of industrial waste. Ecologically minded legislators and former associates in his country of origin were questioning his methods, and lengthy lawsuits had resulted in his having become embittered, in feeling under siege, and in his having to spend an inordinate amount of time and energy on legal and political rather than business matters.

Ralph's mother never emerged as a real person in the course of all the interactions of the hospital staff with the family. She rarely if ever visited him while he was in this country; it was his father, accompanied by a personal legal counsellor, who visited the hospital and made himself available for the discussion of Ralph's treatment plans. In spite of occasional visits to this country to see Ralph, several brothers and sisters also remained shadowy and distant figures during the treatment. The father candidly expressed his feeling of hopelessness regarding the treatment of Ralph; he had selected this hospital as a last resort and implied that, although he did not have much time to invest in participating in the treatment effort, he certainly would be extremely grateful if Ralph could be helped.

This case, similar to Lucia's, was surrounded by a VIP-quality climate. The father's legal and political battles, the family's enormous wealth, and the aura of power emanating from father and his counsellor led to all sorts of rumours and speculations.

I was assigned this patient by Dr B, the hospital director who replaced Dr A (who had accepted a position elsewhere) about a year after Lucia left the hospital. Dr B was much more closely linked to the "hospital philosophy" than to the "Institute philosophy"—that is, he favoured an empirical, no-nonsense approach to patients and was sceptical about applying psycho-analytic understandings to hospital treatment.

He told me he thought Ralph needed a firm hand, that he was a very difficult patient who would surely attempt to get me entangled in arguments, and he trusted that I would be able to maintain a firm structure without over-involvement in such contests. Dr B also had a different style of communication. He was friendlier and more outgoing on the surface but also had the reputation of wanting to avoid conflicts and of bending excessively to pressures from the chairman and members of the hospital board. While Dr A had been more authoritative and even authoritarian in his dealings with faculty and staff, Dr B tried to reach a consensus whenever possible. In contrast to his predecessor, however, he did not support faculty or staff when influential people exerted pressures from outside the hospital boundaries. As far as Ralph was concerned, I understood that I would have all the hospital support I needed, unless the treatment ran into hot VIP waters.

I first met Ralph in his room, staring in the mirror, scrutinizing his face, as he explained to me, because he was concerned about the development of pimples. He explained that he was using various antiseptic facial creams to deal with irregularities on the skin of his face and neck. I could not detect any abnormality on his face. The room had a slightly rancid smell that I never ceased associating with Ralph. It was filled with containers of facial cream and boxes of facial tissues, which he used to clean his fingers as well as for spreading the cream. Used and crumpled creamy tissue papers were strewn over the bed, the chairs, and the floor.

Because it was questionable whether Ralph would be able to differentiate sufficiently a psychotherapist from an administrative hospital psychiatrist, I was assigned total hospital management of the case, including psychotherapy. Clara, the head nurse referred to earlier, told me the nursing staff were in conflict about how to deal with Ralph. Should his room be cleaned up and a daily routine developed that would provide him with clear tasks, boundaries, and limits—in other words, an "ego-psychological" approach? Or should he be permitted to regress further, with assiduous exploration of the psychological meanings of his bizarre behaviours as a way to establish contact with him and permit the exploration and eventual resolution of his psychotic regression by psychotherapeutic means —in other words, a "Chestnut Lodge" approach? The history of limited improvement with intense neuroleptic treatment and electroshock and the fact that Ralph would emerge only into antisocial behaviour rather than towards a more adaptive non-psychotic state weighed heavily on my mind. I decided to postpone designing treatment strategy until I learned more about him.

Now, I must say that my first emotional reaction to Ralph was one of disgust. It was impossible for me not to react to the rancid smell around him, the greasy doorknobs and chairs in his room, and yet I was forced to see him in his room because of his refusal to leave it. In one of our early sessions, while I was sitting on a (greasy) chair and he on his bed, Ralph said: "I must seem pretty disgusting to you", and I was at a loss for words because of the accuracy of his observation. Because I was identifying with a disgusted authority figure, I was unable to acknowledge his obvious pleasure in playing with dirt, with a messy, sticky substance, with excrements. For the same reason, I was also unable to connect his pleasure in playing with dirt and waste with his conflict over whether to submit to, identify with, or rebel against his father, the "king" of transforming industrial waste into useful industrial products, and the man accused of polluting the environment with the products of his industry.

Ralph had a terrible fear of my entering his room without his having some time to "prepare" himself. He pleaded with me to knock until he opened his door (which could take several minutes), and he always looked extremely fearful and suspicious when I entered his room. I thought he was trying to clean up his room before I came in or disguise or conceal the indications of some strange ritual, but all my attempts to discover why he wanted me to knock so lengthily only elicited a sheepish and odd-sounding laughter that I eventually read as ironic and derogatory.

While I was attempting to assess the situation, Ralph's behaviour regressed further and further; he refused to leave his room under any circumstances, and any efforts on the part of the nursing staff to mobilize him generated intense rage attacks. He was a strong, large man, and female nursing staff now became afraid of approaching him. At the same time, the prolongation of the "knocking on the door" ritual led me to the fantasy that one of its functions was to portray me to the nursing staff as weak and fearful. Eventually, nursing staff did talk about Ralph's "granting audiences" to me and to selected staff members.

My efforts to help Ralph verbalize his fantasies and fears in connection with any of these issues led nowhere. He talked vaguely and evasively about his face and the disturbing intrusiveness of nursing staff, as he saw it. Eventually I devised a treatment plan with the nursing staff that would protect Ralph's privacy in his room for certain hours of the day but also include a minimal program of activities (walking in the grounds, participating in a simple work group for regressed schizophrenic patients) for a regularly scheduled time. By the same token, his room would be cleaned as were all the other hospital rooms, except that certain drawers would be reserved for whatever he wanted to keep in them, including his creams and tissues.

The plan worked, but with results that were unforeseen. A special mental health worker was assigned to Ralph for the morning period of activities and another one for the afternoon. Both mental health workers were instructed to carry out similar functions—that is, to help the patient get appropriately dressed for outdoor walks and activities and to provide him with the opportunity to discuss whatever he wished regarding his daily life in the hospital. The morning mental health worker was a black man, the afternoon mental health worker, white. Clara, the unit head nurse, was black, and the hospital director of nursing, Clara's superior, was a white woman. Ralph developed an immediate affinity with the white mental health worker, who impressed him (and me, initially) as a friendly, outgoing, enthusiastic man. Ralph also developed an immediate and intense hatred for the black mental health worker, who also impressed me, initially, as friendly, outgoing and warm, but who gradually became tense and inhibited when confronted with Ralph's verbal, and eventually physical, onslaughts.

Both Clara and I thought that this was a clear case of splitting that required psychotherapeutic exploration, but the patient's complaints about the black mental health worker soon reached the office of the director of nursing, who recommended changing him for another staff worker. Clara and I strongly resisted that recommendation: I thought it would reinforce Ralph's splitting operations and increase both his regressive omnipotence and his deeper fears of the destructive effects of his aggression. The situation was further complicated by a visit from Ralph's father and the development of friendly contacts between the patient, his father, and the white mental health worker, who, according to Ralph, had offered to provide total coverage for him and agreed that the black mental health worker was not really helpful. Ralph's father spoke to Dr B, who talked with the director of nursing, and the director of nursing exerted further pressure on Clara to remove the black mental health worker from the case.

Before long, the entire nursing staff seemed to be divided along racial lines. In addition, I had for quite some time been critical of what I considered the coldness and distance of the director of nursing (an opinion that coincided with that of most of the other unit chiefs). The director of nursing, however, had social connections with members of the board that apparently weighed powerfully in Dr B's general support of her. Emotionally, I became a total ally of Clara and the black staff; and now the entire social system of the hospital, in ever-widening circles, appeared to be split: powerful authorities on one side and rebels on the other.

In my discussions with Ralph, I attempted to help him verbalize his sense of being between two worlds, a "white" world of conformity, established authority, and protection, against a "black" world of rebellion, danger, and violence. I also attempted to relate this to his own, internal conflict between the need to submit to his powerful father by appealing to the "highest authorities" in the hospital to protect him against the rebels, and the need to rebel against his father by refusing to leave his room and by polluting the room with facial creams and tissues. While his father was recycling waste, he was producing waste material. In short, I tried to tell him that the division of his feelings between his two mental health workers represented an effort to deal with two aspects of himself. Ralph, however, responded by becoming more suspicious and distrustful of me, now clearly perceiving me as an enemy, while his relationship with the white mental health worker seemed to grow closer each day.

I finally had a call from Dr B, who discussed with me his concern lest the patient's family get upset and complain directly to the chairman of the hospital board. He suggested, in a very friendly way, that Ralph was probably a hopeless case anyhow, why not give up on it? He felt that I was functioning under enormous pressure, that my energies and knowledge could be put to better use with other cases, and he asked me how I would feel about a transfer. After a long discussion, I conceded to him, and, in fact, felt flexible and mature in so doing, acknowledging my own limitations. I felt appreciative for the friendly way he was discussing the matter with me.

I left Dr B's office in a relaxed frame of mind and soon afterward went home. Suddenly, however, while driving home, an intense reaction of alarm and suspiciousness hit me: it is probably not an exaggeration to say that I became paranoid. I had the fantasy that this friendly conversation was the first step in the process of throwing me out of the hospital. I suspected Dr B of having received instructions from higher up to get rid of me. I suddenly also remembered that that very morning Ralph had asked me whether I had talked with Dr B. I now thought that, without my knowing it, Ralph had already been told that he would be transferred to another hospital psychiatrist. I decided to drive back to the hospital right away and establish the "truth" by discussing the matter with Ralph.

Ralph denied remembering having asked me whether I had talked with Dr B. I also had a sense that the white mental health worker, who was present, was looking at me triumphantly.

That same evening, I discussed the situation with Clara, who reassured me categorically that, from all she knew through the grapevine, there was no criticism of me in the hospital. She told me point-blank that I was being paranoid in thinking I might be dismissed because of the conflict around this patient. She reconfirmed her view and mine that Ralph had activated the potential for racial tensions in the hospital and agreed with me in my assessment of Dr B as excessively compromising and unable to take a stand. She felt that the director of nursing must have had a strong voice in this matter.

Ralph was transferred to another hospital psychiatrist. After six more months of hospital treatment in our hospital, the conclusion was reached that no real progress had been achieved, and the family decided to transfer him to yet another psychiatric institution. Follow-up information several years later, provided by indirect sources, revealed that Ralph had eventually been sent to a public hospital in his country of origin, where he died accidentally during a fire that broke out there.

## Discussion

Here again a powerful and disruptive countertransference emerged early in my initial reaction of disgust and in my delay in analysing its implications. In my complementary identification with Ralph's dissociated and projected self-loathing ("I must seem pretty disgusting to you") I became inhibited by his suspicious expectation of such loathing from me, and by his controlling behaviour aimed at inducing a paralysing sense of guilt in me for my reaction of disgust. Ralph's utilization of projective identification dominated the therapeutic relationship from its start. Ralph identified himself with the depreciated,

persecutory, and persecuted enemies of his father, while fighting off his father's terrible authority projected onto me in the
ritual of delaying opening the door to his room. Simultaneously, with his tissues and creams he was also identifying himself with his father's powerful control over industrial waste. The
conflict between father's powerful (white) authority and the
dangerous (black) rebels against his father's empire was replayed in his splitting of the images of the two mental health
workers and the subsequent triggering of a similar conflict on
the larger scale of the hospital's social system.

Again, my complementary identification in the countertransference, a consequence of the patient's projective identification, induced in me an implicit identification with his
"enemies", leading to my alliance with (black) Clara and her
supporters as against the (white) director of nursing and her
supporters, which finally led to my dismissal from the treatment by the powerful alliance of Dr B, the director of nursing,
and the patient's father.

It is of interest that, even within the extremely regressive
scenario played out in this case, an oedipal constellation was
activated in my siding with Clara against the director of nursing, the cold, distant, emotionally unavailable, yet dangerous
mother figure who only much later resonated in my mind as a
symbolic replica of the patient's own mysterious, distant, unavailable mother.

I believe that Ralph's case also illustrates the implicit corruption of the hospital social system in the eventual yielding to
the patient's demands to get rid of his black mental health
worker, in the shift of therapists, and in the efforts of the hospital director to keep things "cool", given an obvious "special
patient".

In addition, this case also illustrates the repetitive, dramatic reversal of the roles of victim and persecutor so typical of
primitive transferences. Ralph's extremely paranoid reaction to
me for "irrupting" into his room, the defensive ritual of knocking on the door, his pathetic efforts to hide tissues and creams,
were like the last-ditch protection of a faecal world threatened
with destruction by the "clean and powerful". My own intense
"paranoid" reaction on driving home after Dr B suggested
transferring the case illustrates my identification with the

patient as a victim, my fear that my own world as a unit chief was being destroyed, my sense of being attacked and defeated.

Here again, then, projective identification in the patient activated a powerful countertransference reaction in me, a complementary identification reinforced by latent conflicts in the hospital, triggered by the patient's deeply regressive behaviour. In my functions on the boundary between the patient and the social system of the hospital I unconsciously contributed to "switching on" the correspondence between intrapsychic and social pathology.

Ideally, I should have quickly clarified the meanings of the patient's "disgusting" world of "industrial waste", his unconscious identification with victim and victimizer, and interpreted his efforts to split the staff as a way of externalizing the internally intolerable tension between these two sides of himself. If I had been able to identify with the patient's own pleasure in smearing the world of his powerful father, and if I had not felt so guilty over my identification with a persecutory, "disgusted" authority, I might have utilized the understanding of this primitive object relation in the transference of victim and persecutor and attempted to reduce rather than play into the split between Clara and the director of nursing. It might have been easier, under such alternative circumstances, to gradually interpret the patient's enjoyment of "faecal rebellion", his fear of being destroyed by father, the revengeful turning the hospital into a faecal mess, and the identification with his powerful father in controlling the hospital treatment.

## Concluding comments

The general frame of reference of this chapter is psychoanalytic. Within this frame, I want to highlight two specific theoretical components relevant for hospital treatment: the functions of projective identification and of the activation of large group processes in the hospital setting.

Elsewhere I have differentiated projective identification from projection (a related, but more advanced, defensive mechanism) and described the former's functions in the transference and countertransference. My earlier paper (Kernberg, 1984a) focused on technical interventions in individual psychotherapy and psychoanalysis with a variety of patients. Here, in contrast, I am attempting to describe the activation of projective identification in the context of the hospital milieu of patients who require long-term hospital treatment.

The patient's behaviour within the therapeutic milieu tends to induce interpersonal disturbances within the hospital staff that unconsciously reproduce, in the patient's social surroundings, his intrapsychic world of object relations (Main, 1957). As Stanton and Schwartz (1954) masterfully described, such patient-induced disturbances in the social system of the hospital activate potential social conflicts that predate the patient's entry into that system and contribute to a circular process wherein intrapsychic and social pathology reinforce each other. I have in this chapter spelled out how projective identification is central (1) to the patient's induction of complementary identifications in the hospital therapist's countertransference, (2) in triggering the interpersonal conflicts of the staff interacting with the patient and even of the entire hospital social system, with the final consequence that (3) the therapist's countertransference is further reinforced and its acting out potential dangerously strengthened.

The second theoretical frame utilized here is a psychoanalytic open systems-theory approach to the large group processes activated in social organizations (Kernberg, 1976). The patient's hospital psychiatrist stands at the boundary between the patient and the hospital social system, and thus is put in the position of carrying out a leadership function for the patient within the hospital and for the hospital with the patient. This leadership function has, of course, a task-oriented aspect derived from the therapist's technical, professional, and administrative authority, but it also contains a primitive "shadow", a silent but powerful aspect—that of the leader of a potentially regressive large group represented by the hospital milieu (Turquet, 1975). A further aspect is even more subtle and ever-present: playing a "leadership" role in the patient's internal scenario of pathological object relations activated and enacted in the hospital.

As the leader of these reciprocal "large-group" formations, the interface of which is precisely located in the emotional experience of the hospital therapist, he is prone to being sucked into roles that are complementary to roles enacted by the patient's self-experience and by the potential large-group processes of the hospital milieu. The patient's family pathology, projected onto his relations with the therapist and hospital staff, and the hospital staff's latent conflicts around professional, social, and ideological commitments produce a specific emotional turbulence around each patient. The hospital therapist may, as the target for the patient's projective identification, be regressively tempted to enact the patient's dominant self and object representations and, simultaneously, become the potential leader of a regressive large group in the hospital (Kernberg, 1984a). The clarity (or ambiguity) of the hospital's administrative structure and delegation of authority, the therapist's skills and knowledge, his personality, his specific countertransferences to the patient, his relationships to professional and task groups and their corresponding ideologies in the hospital, all contribute to a configuration that, typically, and uncannily, combines to amplify the patient's intrapsychic pathology in the social system and to enact dominant conflicts in the hospital social system.

Elsewhere (Kernberg, 1980, 1983), I have dealt with large-group processes and their diagnostic and therapeutic use in hospital treatment. Here I would like to stress the correspondence between patients' regressive ego states and regressive large-group processes in terms of the induction, in all the participants, of "narcissistic" or "paranoid" reactions or both. We have seen the narcissistic withdrawal syndrome of everybody involved in Lucia's treatment. We have seen the paranoid developments in Ralph's social surround. Large-group processes tend to result in a group that is self-satisfied and leans to a narcissistic leadership, or they might produce a dynamic "mob" moved by aggressive impulses toward external enemies, led by a paranoid leader (Kernberg, 1983).

Perhaps most disturbing and dramatic is the corruption of moral values that typically takes place as part of the regressive processes I am describing. Freud (1921c) originally described how the members of a mob project the ego ideal onto the idealized leader. The effect is to eliminate moral constraints as well as the superego-mediated functions of self-criticism and responsibility of each of the members. In large groups—that is, in groups of 30 to 150—who can still communicate with each other (and thus are not yet a mob), but who do not have (at least momentarily) a functional leadership, the projection of superego functions onto the leader cannot, of course, develop (Anzieu, 1984; Kernberg, 1980; Turquet, 1975).

What obtains instead is a projection of primitive superego functions onto the group itself. Instead of projecting the mature superego functions of each individual member onto the group at large, the large-group members tend to project a minimal, highly conventional morality onto the group. The rigidity and lack of discriminating characteristics of this conventional morality create a generalized fear of "how others may react", while the individual members of these groups are strangely "liberated" from their ordinary, mature superego functions and tend to attempt to "get away with what they can". The combination of a diffuse conventionality and a reduced individual sense of responsibility creates the preconditions for a general corruption of the adherence to moral values within this group setting. This is the background against which the self-indulgent group ideology fostered by a narcissistic leader and the rationalization of aggression facilitated by a paranoid leader reinforce the moral corruptibility of regressive large groups.

Zinoviev (1984) described the characteristics of groups whose egalitarian ideology fosters the projection of moral authority onto the group at large, and, finally, to protect their egalitarianism, onto external "persecutory" authority figures. He describes the prevalence, under such conditions, of careerism, selfishness, and neglect of functional tasks, the enjoyment of others' failures, a tendency to gang up against those who get ahead, a search for propitiatory victims, and a search for an authoritarian leader to mediate the threatening conflicts within the groups. Such groups also show a negative attitude towards individuality, the differentiation of individuals, and towards courage. This description, derived from the study of the egalitarian structure of group processes in factories and educational and other social organizations in the Soviet Union, dramatically replicates the studies of the psychology of large-group processes carried out in experimental settings by Rice

(1965), Turquet (1975), and Anzieu (1984). My point is that, given the great potential for activation of superego corruption in the large group under regressive conditions, a dramatic and dangerous potential exists for the replication in the hospital's social system of patients' specific superego pathology as well.

In conclusion, projective identification is a powerful primitive defensive operation that may induce intense countertransference reactions in the therapist in the form of complementary identification and, simultaneously, regressive group processes in the hospital setting by direct triggering of latent conflicts in the hospital's social system. The therapist's leadership functions for the large group thus activated create the condition of a mutual reinforcement between the patient's pathology, the group's pathology, and the therapist's countertransference, leading under the worst circumstances to an uncanny replication within the social system of the patient's social, familial, and intrapsychic pathology. When this pathology includes significant superego deterioration, a potential corruption of the social system of the hospital may replicate and amplify the corresponding aspects of the patient's intrapsychic pathology.

CHAPTER NINE

# Some thoughts on insight and its relation to countertransference

*Athina Alexandris*
*Grigoris Vaslamatzis*

## Introduction

Much has been written about insight, in both the broad and narrow sense of the term. Hatcher (1980) pointed out that insight is not a simple matter but a complex process in psychoanalytic therapy that depends on the interplay of several factors. Kris (1956) and Blum (1979) stated the view that in psychoanalytic therapy the therapist's main task is to provide and facilitate the patient's insight. Insight on the part of both patient and therapist have also been discussed, as has insight in relation to the psychoanalytic situation, interpretation, working through, goals of therapy, transference–countertransference, and the patient's individuality. In the literature, however, there are rather few clinical examples supporting the theories.

Reprinted by permission from C. N. Stefanis, A. D. Rabavilas, & C. R. Soldatos (Eds.), *Psychiatry: A World Perspective, Volume 3* (Amsterdam: Elsevier, 1990), pp. 577–584.

This paper will present clinical material from two cases of psychoanalytic therapy in an attempt to illustrate how countertransference is related to the patient's insight, but mainly how countertransference affects the kind of insight the therapist chooses to offer his patient. The clinical material is taken from cases supervised by the authors.

For this presentation, insight can be defined as the new bits and pieces, conscious and unconscious, that the patient learns about himself during a given psychoanalytic session. As far as the definition of countertransference is concerned, we will use the definition given by Paula Heimann (1950), according to which countertransference "covers all the feelings which the analyst experiences towards his patient" (p. 81) and expanded by the psychoanalytic work of Segal, Rosenfeld, Grinberg, Racker, and Kernberg.

## Case 1:   Katerina

The case to be discussed has to do with a 27-year-old woman, Katerina, who was in psychoanalytic psychotherapy at a frequency of three sessions a week. She came to her 100th session on a Monday. It should be mentioned here that her therapist had cancelled her regular Friday appointment because, as he explained to her, it was a holiday and he was going away. Katerina began the session by telling her therapist that on Friday afternoon, while she was napping at her boyfriend's house, she had a nightmare, which went as follows:

> "I was in the big house that we lived in when I was small. I was sitting with all my family. The doorbell rang and my mother went to open the door. It was my boyfriend. I got up, he went to the bathroom. I looked in and was not sure whether he was my boyfriend or my grandfather." Here she burst into tears and proceeded to sob heavily. She continued: "He was wearing a long black coat but he was not human; he was like a Vampire. He was alive again. I felt paralysed." Katerina was still crying as she continued: "Now I am sure he was my grandfather. Now I remember everything."

And she went on to give all the details of how she had been taking care of her sick grandfather for some time. She added her thoughts about her parents and the rest of the relatives who had neglected the grandfather. They had left him completely in her care. She remembered that there were times when she too had neglected her beloved grandfather.

THERAPIST:  What was the matter with your grandfather?

PATIENT:  He had become paralysed and then bedridden.

THERAPIST:  I can imagine how difficult it was for you to have to undertake the full care of your grandfather, given his condition.

PATIENT:  Yes.

(Then she went on to say how indifferent the rest of the family were towards the grandfather.)

THERAPIST:  How come you slept that Friday afternoon? Why were you alone? Where was your boyfriend?

PATIENT:  He went to visit his mother, who is paralysed and bedridden in a hospital.

Katerina went on to describe the quarrel she had with her boyfriend when he begged her to accompany him to the hospital. She refused, even though she knew that it was very stressful for him to visit his sick mother. Instead, she had a nap. The patient continued crying.

THERAPIST:  Friday is the day that I usually see you. But this time it was a holiday, so I was absent too.

PATIENT:  Yes, I thought of that when I woke up. Of course, it makes sense that you went on holiday. Your life is none of my business, but I felt that I needed to see you this particular Friday.

Her mood changed suddenly. She giggled and jokingly replied: "O.K. Doctor. Good bye. Good bye." And she walked away.

We have chosen to follow one line of thought that emerges from this session, with reference to countertransference and the insight gained by the patient in this particular session. The therapist unconsciously chose to respond to the patient's unconscious need, which was to relieve her guilt in connection with her grandfather, by telling her that the obligation put on her by her parents to look after her grandfather was very great, thus implying that the patient's demand that the therapist should not go on holiday but should stay and look after her was also great. In other words, the therapist relieved the guilt of both of them, as though he were saying: "We are both innocent, overburdened by the demands of people, and we sometimes overlook things." Therefore the therapist's choice of this level of work and the comments he made were based mainly on the guilt projected on him by his patient—in other words, the patient managed to make her therapist feel guilty and forced him to respond to her unconscious demand to relieve her guilt and put aside the vampire part of herself and himself as well. If we continue this line of thought, what would have been the insight of the patient? She might have felt relief from her guilt, or she might have felt a magical triumph at having succeeded in making her therapist feel guilty, sad, and responsible for her emotional state.

Another possibility is that the therapist might have been afraid of a vampire attack by his patient against him and his own vampire counterattack against her. Consequently, the role that the patient assigned to her therapist (to satisfy her unconscious need for relief of the guilt she felt about her negligence of her grandfather/boyfriend) suited them both, patient and therapist. The therapist implied: "Neither of us is a vampire, we are both good people." It is as if both therapist and patient have agreed to put aside the vampire part of themselves. In this case, the patient's insight would have been in accordance with the therapist's countertransference feelings and the way he dealt with them—that is, she would have felt that her therapist was afraid to face the vampire part in each of them, and so it suited him to satisfy her need, in other words, to pacify her.

Let us now examine another possibility. Had the therapist not counter-identified with his patient, as León Grinberg would have said, but he had instead tolerated, sustained, and contained the effects of the patient's projections on him, consulting his feelings and using his countertransference as a tool to understand further his patient's unconscious, how could he have responded to his patient in this particular instance? The therapist might still have decided that the best thing for his patient was to respond in the same way and thus satisfy her unconscious need, which means that he would have chosen to work on the same level and make the same comments. In this case, the difference would have lain in the way the therapist dealt with the effects of his countertransference, which led him to decide to pacify his patient—as a good mother pacifies her child by meeting the child's needs "in time", as Winnicott would have said, by putting aside everything else for the moment, such as vampire attacks, and so forth. Here, the therapist would be acting as what the Kleinians would have called a "good container". Obviously the patient's insight would have been in accordance with countertransference feelings: "My therapist treats me like a good mother would have treated me when I was little. My therapist tolerates, contains all my feelings, fears, anxieties, aggressive attacks, frustrations, protests. He is not afraid or affected by a little girl's attacks. He provides a safe harbour for her."

Let us look at yet another possibility. Rather than pacifying his patient, the therapist could have interpreted her projections of her own feelings onto him as aiming to make him feel sad, guilty and responsible for her emotional state because he had cancelled her regular Friday appointment. He might have continued further to interpret that her parents had assigned her to look after her grandfather, as they had assigned the therapist to look after her. But there were times when she neglected her grandfather and her boyfriend, as her therapist had neglected her by cancelling her appointment, so that both had to be punished for their negligence. That was why her grandfather appeared as a vampire, to punish her.

Thus the therapist's countertransference feelings are quite different in this case. He would have believed he had helped the patient by means of interpretations, feeling that the patient was receptive to his understanding and would find his interpretation meaningful.

In this instance, the patient's insight should read as follows: she would have been made aware of her unconscious psychological mechanisms and the links between her feelings, of how and why she reacted to her therapist's cancellation of their regular Friday appointment.

## Case 2:   Stavros

Stavros, a 25-year-old man, spent all of the first five sessions telling his therapist who he really is. He said that he came for psychoanalytic therapy at the urging of his mother, that he found it difficult to find a job, either because of missed opportunities or because he would work for a short period in a job, then he would belittle it, undermine his superiors, and ultimately leave. He also stated that he did the same thing to the various psychiatrists he had visited since the age of twenty. He was eager to report that, from the age of nine on, following his parents' divorce, he had lived with his mother. When he was twelve, Stavros was informed of his father's remarriage and was shocked because he had been told nothing about it previously. After his father's remarriage, he began to act up at school, until he was finally expelled.

During these sessions in which the patient presented himself, he kept an ironic smile on his face, his sentences were incomplete, his speech was incoherent, with long silences. Thoughts were left hanging in the air: "I don't know. [Pause.] Do I have to say something? [Pause.] It is like I don't have the need to say anything." As he listened, the therapist's thoughts ran as follows: "The patient comes to therapy because he is being pushed or feels he has to. The patient wants to control the situation, he does not want to let the therapist understand him; he is not motivated to start therapy, does not have the capacity for insight, and is unsuitable for psychoanalytic therapy."

At this point the therapist wondered whether the best solution for the patient might be to propose that he discontinue therapy for a period of time and come back of his own free will when he was ready to cooperate.

However, while the therapist was thinking in this way, Stavros came to his next (sixth) session and said that the written project that he had submitted to a company for approval had been rejected, because when he was asked to support it orally, stony silence took over. He was unable to speak.

The therapist was intensely troubled by his patient's account, and especially by the word "rejection". The therapist intervened, telling the patient that he had done the same thing in therapy.

Stavros confirmed this observation by saying: "Yes, this is my problem. It is my insecurity that makes me silent." At this point the therapist became aware of his own feelings of rejection towards the patient, which had been provoked by the latter's behaviour, and that his own ideas—that the patient is unsuitable for therapy, and so on—were a defence against his feelings of rejection towards the patient.

The therapist's intervention described above resulted in Stavros' being able to speak freely during the rest of the session, without pauses and silences. The latter then went on to talk about his relationship with his father and how much he enjoyed their visits together. They used to talk about all sorts of subjects, and he never understood why his father remarried without telling him. The patient said that he took revenge on his father for this by remaining silent over most of their visit together after the father's remarriage.

If we try to understand what happened between therapist and patient, on the level of transference and countertransference, we might say that the patient, in presenting himself to the therapist, had warned him that he would either abandon his therapist abruptly (without notice), as his father had abandoned him and as he (the patient) had abandoned previous therapists, or provoke his therapist to reject him, as he had provoked his school teachers, resulting in his expulsion. The patient had thus warned the therapist about his tendency to re-enact with him the old conflictual situation—namely, his compulsion to repeat.

Following this line of thought, it could be said that the patient unconsciously managed to make his therapist want to reject him, and that is why the therapist felt like doing so. Instead of understanding his patient, the therapist felt like responding to his patient's unconscious need to be rejected by him (countertransference).

The patient had unconsciously perceived his therapist's (countertransference) feelings of wanting to reject him. This caused the patient, at the following session, to bring up the subject of his project being rejected, thus forcing the therapist to become aware of his own unconscious feelings of rejection towards his patient and his defences against these feelings.

When the therapist became aware that his feelings of rejection had been provoked by his patient (countertransference effects), he was then able to interpret that fact to him (as presented above) and in doing so opened the way for further understanding of the patient's compulsion to repeat. In this way, the therapist's insight led to the patient's insight.

However, if the therapist had acted out his feelings of rejection and had discontinued the therapy or continued therapy but remained detached, what kind of insight would the patient have gained? He might have walked away feeling that the therapist was like his father who had rejected him, or he might have felt that he had managed to make his therapist reject him. In either case, the patient would have had to go to another therapist, where he would attempt to repeat the same situation. It goes without saying that if the therapist had not been defensive in the first instance but had been in touch with his own feelings of rejection (effects of countertransference) and the defences against them, the insight he would have chosen to offer his patient would have reflected the way the therapist had dealt with the effects of the countertransference.

## Discussion and conclusions

The clinical material presented here indicates how the insight gained by the patient in a session is related to the therapist's countertransference. The kind of insight the therapist chooses to offer his patient depends mainly on the way he deals with the effects of the countertransference, rather than on the countertransference itself. The better the therapist can handle his own countertransference feelings, the more effectively will he be able to function in the best therapeutic interests of his patient.

The relationship between countertransference and insight is unaffected by the differences in therapeutic techniques. The insight of the patient depends on the insight of the therapist; but it is fair to say that often the patient leads the way to understanding of the unconscious for both therapist and patient alike.

In conclusion, the emphasis given in this chapter to the relation between countertransference and insight, without underestimating the other factors that influence the psychotherapeutic process and its outcome, meets the preoccupations of Heimann (1950), Racker (1957), Grinberg (1962), Kernberg (1975a), and Segal (1977), who are of the opinion that the therapist's countertransference is an instrument for understanding the patient's unconscious and that the therapist can utilize countertransference for his analytic work. In the two cases cited here, it has been evident that the therapist tended to satisfy the unconscious demand of the patient, even when the demand was rejection. That would be seen as "complementary identification" according to Racker's (1957) definition.

This approach implies that psychoanalytic therapy is primarily a relation between two persons. Thus, the therapist is asked, above all, to deal with the effects of his countertransference in such a way as to be able to offer the appropriate insight to his patient at the right time.

# CHAPTER TEN

# The patient–therapist fit and countertransference reaction in the light of frame theory

*Hector Warnes*

B ion has captured the concept of the frame in his meta-phor of the artist in whose painting "something has remained unaltered and on this something recognition depends" (Bion, 1977, p. 1). The invariants of a painting by an impressionist and a realist would convey different meanings. The frame has been compared by Bleger (1966) to the mere background of a Gestalt that may evolve into a figure. The background would be the constant, the invariant factor or the non-process, and the figure the transformation, the variable or the process. The frame is therefore the invariant element that is "the receiver of the symbiosis" (p. 513) and in that sense ex-presses the maternal configuration. The analytic process itself is pregnant with ambiguity and multiple meanings and does not contain the symbiotic experience. The frame acts as a sup-port of the analytic process but does not accept its ambiguity. It is similar to the child's symbiosis with the mother, which enables him to develop his ego in a background of safety and support. Within the frame or the container, there is a space and an analytic atmosphere, which may have certain characteris-tics—that is, optimal distance, refusal to play a role, neutrality, self-effacement, and benevolence. The analytic frame is deliberately unbalanced in order to activate unconscious meanings. The frame of transference expectations usually finds sufficient fit with what is transpiring in the analytic frame.

Clinically the analyst is the repository of the patient's frame, which may conflict with the specific analytic "frame". The analytic space or frame is made up of boundaries and rules, within which the patient expresses his multiple states of mind. The analyst should accept the patient's frame because it contains the non-solved symbiotic part of the personality. The frame can only be analysed within the frame. If it is successfully negotiated, it may be transformed into a process. The frame is the most primitive non-verbal part of the personality, the undifferentiated fusion of ego-body world. The frame is part of a factic ego whose syncretism is related to fusion in perception and thought of incompatible elements—for example, the analyst is at once mother and analyst.

During the beginning of an analysis, the earliest manifestations of frame pathology are experienced by the analyst in the sense that the patient insists on disavowing, on symbiotic relatedness, on sameness, on need-satisfaction, or on "perfect symmetry". The analyst's compliance with the patient's impingements and pressures to alter the frame spells out a difficult course. More interruption or disruption of the analytic process is due to excess of gratification rather than to frustration. Frame pathology represents the strongest resistance to treatment because it is not repressed but remains something split off and a never differentiated area. If the patient succeeds in imposing his own primitive frame to the analyst, it may lead to what the Barangers and Mom(1983) and Grinberg et al. (1967), inspired by Bion, called "bastion" and "parasitism". Parasitism is an extreme form of a "bastion" that stagnates the analytic field and leads to a collusion between the patient's and the analyst's resistances. The analytic frame will be attacked because it threatens the fragile narcissistic omnipotence of the patient, which constitutes the "last-ditch" defence against psychic pain and suffering. In this situation "the basic asymmetry of the analytic pact is lost and another, far more symmetrical structuring predominates in which the unconscious attachment between analyst and analysand becomes an involuntary complicity against the analytic process" (Baranger et al., 1983, p. 2). For instance, defences against fear of rejection and closeness, against fear of regression to dependency, or against fear of seduction and/or depression are stirred up within a given frame or context and threaten the narcissistic wished-for components of a potential patient–analyst fit, which sharpens further the asymmetry and difference. A complementary relationship (such as sadomasochism) would be a bastion against these anxieties. For Langs (1976), the frame has a pervasive influence on the therapeutic interaction particularly its holding function, its containing function, and its role in creating a distinctive boundary between inside and outside, fantasy and reality, and a potential space for the analytic process to unfold. The patient's inability to make use of symbols and to enter into a potential space or a playground (namely the area of illusion, play, and tolerance of ambiguity and paradox), which has been aptly explored by Ogden (1985), are related to his incapacity to tolerate the analytic frame.

Frame pathology, in the sense given by Arvanitakis (1987), is observed in some pre-psychotic and many psychotic ego-structures. In these cases a failure to internalize the analytic frame "as an interface structure whose function is to differentiate and to transform archaic anxieties" (p. 528) can be observed. Darcourt (1986) refers to these patients' fragile structure:

> Ces sujets sont aussi très sensibles aux moindres changements du cadre des séances, ils remarquent les bruits extérieures, les objets déplacés. Ils sont très sensibles à la moindre intonation ou à la moindre expression de l' analyste.

> [These individials are also very sensitive to the slightest change in the session's frame, they observe noises from outside, the displacement of objects (in the office). They are also very sensitive to the slightest change in the analyst's intonation and expression.] [p. 185]

For these patients, who cannot use the analytic setting or frame, the analysis of the container or frame must take precedence over the analysis of intrapsychic contents.

The global non-verbal aspects of the patient–analyst relationship are reflected in the frame, which defines the "screen" or the potential space out of which the patient projects his intrapsychic fantasy. The management of the frame generates projective identification and introjective identification of both patient and analyst, which causes disturbances and influences the "fit". Whether the disturbance of the frame leads to disturbances of fit or vice versa is to be understood in each interactional impasse.

Spruiell (1983) raises the question of "why can some people construct an analytic frame more or less spontaneously, and others not, or at least not without considerable work on the part of the analyst to help set up and maintain the frame?" (p. 19). In the discussion of the factors that enter into a framework, he listed: archaic conflicts; developmental factors; ego-prescriptive; superego-proscriptive rules; a world of reality represented by the metaphorical phallic father and shared notions of social reality. The role of the analyst in altering or managing that very frame is understated, although quite clearly the analyst acts as a stimulus or "key" to actualize past frames.

In discussing Spruiell's paper, McLaughlin (1983) writes: "For him [Spruiell] the analytic situation, in its structured and carefully maintained imbalance, coupled with the unique ambiguity of real–not real experiencing its shaping affords, provides a frame in which all those other experiential frames of present and past may find an actualizing 'fit'" (p. 169). It is this actualizing "fit" that emerges from the interaction of the patient's frame and the analytic frame which stirs up unconscious meaning.

There are, however, severe narcissistic or borderline patients who are able to maintain the analytic frame, as there are "those cases in which the match between the basically reliable analysands and analysts" (Bachrach, 1983, p. 200) takes on an unanticipated course. The alteration of context, the similarities and differences of the patient and the analyst's frames, and the alteration of mood that occurs during analytic regression permits the transference expectation to find "a sufficient fit with what is transpiring in the analytic frame" (McLaughlin, 1983, p. 170).

## Clinical vignettes

What follows are four brief clinical vignettes of female patients who developed a maternal transference early in therapy with manifestations of regression, including a sense of victimization by their mothers and attempts to modify the analytic frame in keeping with a desire for vindication for real or imagined maternal and environmental failures. These patients had mothers who were depressed and severely narcissistic and forced on the children a precocious pseudo-maturity and a caretaker role. Soon after beginning therapy it became clear that the analytic setting was quite threatening. They showed mistrust and vulnerability to frame issues, fear of falling into dependency, and fear of masochistic submission leading to reactive aggression, exacting narcissistic demands, conflicting perceptions of the therapist as too intrusive or too distant and indifferent, manifest anxiety over being engulfed and controlled or being abandoned, and an inordinate need for confirmation and validation of their experiences, with little tolerance of ambiguity. The setting was experienced as an engulfing and disturbing reality, without the distance required for analytic work. They had a limited ability to relate to the "as if" qualities of the psychoanalytic setting and were extremely sensitive to minute changes, especially in the analyst's clothes, attitudes, or manners. It felt as if they wanted to become familiar with every detail of the analytic frame and took nothing "at face value". They would test and "inspect" the analyst, his reliability, and the setting before risking any true feelings. From the material one could discern that they experienced themselves in a symbiotic bond with their mothers and were unable to triangulate. The prospect of change was experienced as dangerous, which defensively increased their symbiotic needs. Because of their boundary problems, the analyst rapidly became the personification of that negatively invested maternal introject. The treatment of these patients confirmed the widely held view that the development of the symbolizing capacity is dependent on the subject's ability to tolerate differences and separateness from others. These patients had difficulties in separating what pertained to the therapist's feelings and thoughts from what pertained to the self and the maternal introject. They expected and demanded to be soothed, nurtured, and understood by an idealized object that was nowhere to be found. The frame was felt to be non-gratifying, non-holding, and non-responsive.

Guntrip (1969) is of the opinion that the kind of patient I am describing—which he calls schizoid—is always impelled into a relationship by urgent needs and at once driven out again by the fear either of exhausting the love-object by the demands she makes or else losing her own individuality by over-dependence and identification. Dread of regression to dependency during therapy activated the painful experiences with a "not-good-enough" mother. The father was experienced as unavailable by both mother and child. Either he was excluded by mother and/or daughter, or he excluded himself. The outcome of therapy was successful with two cases and unsuccessful with the two others, despite considerable symptomatic improvement.

## Patient A

This female patient in her thirties sought therapy because of doubts about being a good parent. She presented herself as having a nurturing and good father and a non-nurturing, bad mother in her childhood. In her life she felt confused about "the goodness and badness" in herself. Her first therapist confirmed "the goodness" in her, which allowed her "to shut the door on mother. He (the therapist) only provided a safe environment". In her second therapy, however, the split of object relationship with the bad mother returned in full force. At first she had told the analyst, associating to a dream of having a tooth pulled, that she went to countless dentists but could not find the "special one" who would "be patient, work slowly, and cater to her". The patient herself felt "like an evil person" in her relationship with one of her children and in therapy: "I feel damaged in the presence of some people and not others"; "I pick up something that puts me in my mother's mode". The patient had "to fight mother's crazy-making environment" and feared that I was going to drive her crazy. The characteristics of the "crazy-making environment"—a hospital office in the department of psychiatry, a waiting-room where she felt exposed, a sense of feeling intruded upon by being seen, and so on—only increased her sense of vulnerability. She perceived that the analyst or the environment was infringing on her protective shield. Her anger at the analyst was experienced like the anger she felt her mother had towards her. In response to her angry devaluation, the analyst had told her that she wanted him to experience the way the mother and her unreliability made her feel. It became clear that a warded-off identification with the aggressor was being enacted, and in her fear of being mistreated by the environment and mother she mistreated the analyst. She further said about her mother: "Nothing I was doing was right; she set me up for failure." Because of the maternal transference she feared that if she should regress, the analyst would be unable to handle it, and "something damaging would happen".

The therapist was placed in the role of the mother who set her up for failure, to which she reacted with rage. "There is a fear that you cannot contain my rage and that I have to protect you from it." This very issue led her to flee from analysis. Early in therapy the analyst, not understanding the significance that the setting had for her, made the mistake of pointing out that she was preoccupied by minute details of external reality because she felt frightened and wanted to avoid something of her internal reality. She reacted with anger and felt judged and devalued as a person, insofar as the analyst failed to validate her experience of the setting. She wanted to maintain a front of control and normality, and any interpretations were felt to be tampering with her views of reality and her self-sufficiency. After a couple of years, significantly following the summer holidays, she took flight from treatment with a clear statement: "Living with mother, I spent years wondering who was crazy and who wasn't. I don't need to go back to that struggle of who's inside and who is outside." From her point of view, discontinuing therapy allowed her to gain control over her life, establish again distance from her maternal introject, and largely improve her relationship with her child. She could not tolerate the experience of looking at that disavowed and split-off mode of relatedness with her mother which was actualized without change during her analysis. The pathological frame she brought into therapy found ample resonance in the analyst's office, which offered her no safety or protection.

## Patient B

Another female patient in her twenties sought analysis because of dissatisfaction with her marriage. She had no physical attraction for her husband, who, it turned out, reminded her of her mother and felt guilty because he loved her. For other men, she was able to feel "passion". Soon after beginning therapy, she was accidentally kept waiting; after 15 minutes she left in a huff. On her next visit, she brought a dream: "I am walking near the school of my childhood when a woman brandishing a knife comes out to kill me. I feel totally helpless, but suddenly she directs the knife to herself and cuts her own throat." The woman was herself raging at the analyst and her mother. Reflecting further, she recalled how upset her mother felt when she learned that the patient had entered therapy. Mother reproached her for not calling every day. The patient cannot recall a time when her mother was not depressed to the point that the patient feared for the safety. It reminded her of another dream: She was "imprisoned in a South-American country, and in order to survive, I had to scratch the earth and eat insects". Her fear of succumbing to resourceless dependency at the mercy of a South-American doctor who did not respect the frame was the calamitous frame issue. Her dependency on the analyst felt like a prison. Because of her exacting demands, the analyst felt himself to be imprisoned. Concurrently she felt that she did not want to impose on the analyst, and she felt that he would not be able to take care of her, much as her depressed and critical mother; there were other people who needed the analyst more than she did, and he was most likely bored with her. It occurred to the analyst that his lateness confirmed her feelings that she was unwanted and did not have the right to exist, which was also linked to sibling rivalry at one level and envy of the analyst's maternal functions at another level. "I don't have the right to take a place that doesn't belong to me. I was so afraid of losing you and of shocking you." Being kept waiting was the stimulus that reactivated this early feeling that her mother not only did not pay her attention, but also did not confirm her existence. Entering therapy felt to her as if she "started to dress with mother's clothes". A clear expression of her experience of identification with her mother is psychic reality. The dream and the associations triggered by the disruption of the frame amplified the subconscious and unconscious conflicts, led to a new level of understanding and consolidated the therapeutic alliance. She has successfully terminated psychoanalytic psychotherapy. Unlike the previous patient, Patient B was able to tolerate some unavoidable disturbances of the frame and was capable of self-soothing and of responding to interpretations without the fear of attack and engulfment that characterized the Patient A. It should also be pointed out that the countertransference reaction towards Patient B was quite different from that towards Patient A, who rejected defensively no matter what was given because the basic analytic frame became the reality of her maternal failures.

In the case of Patient A, the split-off bad mother was projected onto the therapist who in part assumed her attributes (which caused the patient to feel invalidated and angry) and in part defended himself from being perceived as a bad object (in which case the patient would be forced to take back the projected badness onto herself and feel depressed). With Patient B the analyst felt imprisoned by the exacting demands of the patient. He experienced anger at having to "walk on a tightrope" and also experienced devaluation in his capacity to care. What was at stake for Patient A was her self-preservation and for Patient B was her narcissistic demands for perfection. The frame becomes the repository of past maternal failures and as such is the cradle of primary transference–countertransference conclusions.

## Patient C

The process of therapy at the non-verbal, mute, and symbiotic level of development may go unnoticed and break out suddenly with an explosion of anger, a catastrophic dream, an episode of acting out, or a refusal to continue, such as Patient C, who presented herself with pseudo-compliance: "I feel like a victim, and I try to please you by bringing into the session the subject matter you would approve of." At the same time she felt she was not succeeding in winning the analyst's favours. If she were to become totally submissive, he would take care of her, and no harm would come out of the relationship. The frame was related to the basic assumption that symbiotic relatedness was the only safe manoeuvre to ward off increment of conflict or anger either in the self or in the object. "I feel rejected, and I manage to provoke rejection." What she was able to express was her fear of rejection in a slavish style. The analyst detected a false-self quality that obviously annoyed him, because his voice and certain interpretations showed his impatience with her chameleon-like behaviour. She reported that he (the therapist) was like her mother, "critical and controlling", which only increased her hostile silence and her rebellion underneath a façade of submissiveness.

Thus she externalized an internal object (the critical and controlling mother) for him to contain it and better manage it. She herself did not realize at first how critical and controlling she was. After about a year of therapy she brought a dream from which she woke up "furious" and realized, not that the analyst *reminded her* of her mother, but that he *was* her mother. Yet she felt relieved to be able to act out her transference rage and leave therapy, not without sending him a letter expressing how "deeply impressed she was with her experience of therapy" but that she had to express her anger in defeating the therapist as she wanted to defeat her mother. During therapy she was able to develop a heterosexual relationship of an intimate and fulfilling kind that she had not known before, while she kept an ongoing latent conflict with her therapist, which erupted with explosive suddenness. The major contribution to the flight from therapy was her fear of fusion with the archaic mother and the therapist's premature interpretation of her wish to control and to avoid conflict or separateness by total submission. It could also be stated that the analyst was not "a good fit" for her insofar as he could not handle or manage the parasitic intrusions of her demands for a non-interpretable and silent merger.

## Patient D

During the course of a year's analysis a pregnant female patient in her late twenties experienced a confusion of the analytic frame with the obstetrical frame. She experienced in a dream the consulting room filled with "25 couches" while I sat behind a desk. In the office the analyst, acting like an obstetrician, told her that she had lost weight and reached for her right breast and squeezed it. The physical world and a spiritual one were also depicted in the dream. In the physical realm the analyst was measuring her with a tape. In the spiritual world she heard a beautiful voice singing, which made her feel sad. It represented the poetic aspects of her professional life. When she felt warmly towards the analyst, she realized in the dream that it was her analyst and not her lover, but when she saw the analyst washing his hands, she became afraid. Later on she went for a walk in the cemetery. In the associations to the dream she resented that the analyst was not her obstetrician because he was not able to take care of her during delivery and further that he would abandon her and, like the obstetrician, had too many patients. She also associated childbirth with death and loss. The baby came to represent an aspect of herself emerging in therapy. The analyst gave birth to a "new person". There were four intersecting frames: (1) the mixing of the obstetrician with the analyst, the physical versus the spiritual dimensions of care; (2) the baby in the analyst versus the mother in her, (3) the mother in the analyst versus the baby in her, and, finally (4) the lover versus the analyst. Regarding these four intersecting frames, I would elaborate as follows:

(1) The obstetrician and the analyst are both able to give birth to the real, the imaginary, and the symbolic infant. (2) The whole area of the physical vs. the psychological dimension of care: the more the maternal deprivation, the more the physical dimension becomes imperative for the patient and the less the "as if" illusion or the symbolic substitute is present. (3) Often in these situations there is an alternation between the patient's desire to be as a baby and be looked after by an all-loving mother or herself becoming the all-loving mother and looking after the analyst–baby. (4) At a more advanced developmental level, the patient may lose track of the reality of the setting and impose her own psychic setting. A strong and overwhelming desire to invade and replace the analyst's psychic reality with her own psychic reality becomes evident (e.g. to become her lover, to have his child). The analyst is often prey to tantalizing attributions, but likewise the patient is exquisitely sensitive to

the analyst's moods and unresolved conflicts. Under these circumstances a stagnation of the psychoanalytic process may occur. Countertransference becomes the only way out of the impasse and the only key to set the process in motion again.

During her pregnancy this patient became acutely sensitive to frame issues, particularly vis-à-vis other patients and not being comforted or held physically, which were not as intense while she was not pregnant. On the contrary, while she was not pregnant, she was acutely sensitive to the analyst's shades of fatigue, pitch of voice, or moods. Often she expressed a need to relieve the analyst of a burden or be able to look after him. Later she was able to express anger at the perceived role reversal.

## Discussion

Therapists have come to recognize that some patients are trusting or non-trusting, reliable or unreliable with particular therapists and not with others. What are the ingredients in the particular patient–therapist interaction that account for these differences? From this perspective there are three classes of patients. The first are those reflective persons with ego strength who tend to adapt to the range of differences among therapists and make the best of it. The second are those persons with significant ego weaknesses that hinder them to varying extents from participating in a psychoanalytic psychotherapy; these patients would be considered difficult by any astute therapist. The third is a "borderline" or a narcissistic group and some particularly difficult patients, for whom the fate or therapy depends more upon the person and special talents of the analyst (Bachrach, 1983). In other words, in a treatment situation some patients extract well what the therapist has to offer. For them, the psychotherapeutic process and techniques override the effect and the parameters of the therapist's *Weltanschauung*, personality, style, and degree of attunement. Other patients need to be helped to use the therapist and the therapeutic frame, whereas yet others cannot use that particular therapist, his technique, or his frame, no matter how much he extends himself. The Blancks (1979) traced back the patient–therapist match or mismatch to the mother–infant dyad, very much like the environment of the good mother that is the basis of a secure frame. A goodness of fit may be established under certain circumstances in the sense of a good maternal or therapeutic environment. As Thomas and Chess (1984) put it: Goodness of fit results when the properties of the environment and its expectations and demands are in accord with the organism's own capacities, motivations, and style of behaving.

Difficulties in the unfolding of the therapeutic process have been ascribed to an incorrect diagnostic evaluation; to inadequate technique; to countertransference–transference resistances; to "poor fit"; or to disturbances of the frame. The latter comprises a set of bilateral expectations, both conscious and unconscious, which constrains selectively the course and outcome of analytic therapy.

The therapist constructs an analytic space or "frame" with particular constant boundaries within which the process or a set of variables takes place. Constants or setting include the characteristic of the analyst, his technique, the contract, the fixing and keeping of time, interruptions, and so forth. The frame is anchored in reality and permits the world of illusion and fantasy to unfold.

The frame is related to those aspects of the therapeutic alliance that are the symbiotic part of the patient's personality and to Winnicott's "holding environment". It allows the psychoanalytic process to proceed within the context of a silent symbiotic fantasy. The importance of the frame reveals itself when it breaks or is on the verge of disruption. The frame is also part of the patient's body image in relation to mother's care-taking and holding functions; it is the body space and the pre-verbal body state of non-differentiation: "For the neurotic, the couch, its warmth and comfort, can be symbolical of the mother's love; for the psychotic, it would be more true to say these things are the analyst's physical expression of love. The couch is the analyst's lap or womb and the warmth is the live warmth of the analyst's body, and so on" (Winnicott, 1949, p. 199). Impingement of the frame may be due to external factors, including the therapist's mistakes or inadvertent failures, the unconscious attempt on the part of the patient to test the analyst's solidity or reliability, or an overwhelming activation of an archaic object in relation to an impulse or bodily need. When this occurs, a state of misfit of the patient's needs and the analyst's provisions increases the patient's distress before defences in the ego can be organized against it—for instance, a female patient felt that she was in a boundless space and that all details of the office were effaced and estranged. Every time the analyst sat behind her, she would become terrified that her mother–analyst would murder her (her own association). In this particular patient, an overwhelming activation of an archaic object occurred while she was lying down on the couch and could not directly see her therapist's face. On leaving the office, she could not recall any details of the setting or the analyst's face. After several months of non-communication, she was able to talk about the feeling of imminent chaos and loss of identity that the "infinite" analytic space provoked, and at that time she was able to evoke a more benign image of the analyst. In this instance, the constancy of the analytic setting fostered the development of object constancy.

The frame is established long before analysis commences. A patient in a waiting list for analysis reported a dream that she came to her appointment at 8 a.m., but she discovered to her horror that it had been postponed to 12 noon. She showed up for her appointment at 12:50 p.m., and to her relief she discovered that the analyst was not even there. He would not dare to reprimand her, because he was at fault as well. Should she submit to the frame he was imposing? Would he ever start seeing her? Her negative expectation is already shaping a stormy course.

The resolution of an impasse does not rest primarily on an analysis of the patient's intrapsychic conflicts but on the analyst's ability to recognize the patient's unconscious perception of the analytic frame, the nature of the patient's presuppositions of the unconscious past frame that he wishes to impose on the analyst, and the area of intersection of both.

The four patients shared common features of not having experienced "good-enough mothering" and of rapidly re-experiencing in therapy a "poor fit" and a heightened vulnerability to the analytic frame, which required special therapeutic skill. The need–fear dilemma of the kind of patient I am referring to was well understood by Kohut (1971) in discussing the person-alities of addicts: the trauma that they suffered is most fre-quently the severe disappointment in a mother who, because of her defective empathy with the child's needs . . . , did not appropriately fulfil the functions (as stimulus barrier; as an optimal provider of needed stimuli; as a supplier of tension relieving gratification, etc.) which the mature psychic appara-tus should later be able to perform (or initiate) predominantly on its own. Traumatic disappointments suffered during these archaic states of the development of the idealized self-object deprive the child of the gradual internalization of early experi-ences of being optimally soothed or being aided in going to sleep.

Bleger (1966) considers the frame to be an "addiction" in the sense of a basic stable symbiotic institution that, if interpreted prematurely, might stir the psychotic part of the personality (pp. 516–517). The constancy and reliability of the frame would ward off these psychotic anxieties. Fear of intrusions, penetra-tion, and loss of the self are activated along with defensive splitting, denial, and projective identification.

There are many components that are responsible for the "goodness of fit" between patient and therapist. Its alterations contribute to the various degrees of patient–therapist match or mismatch. Some authors would refer to "the frame" rather than to the "fit"—that area of non-process of therapy made up of constants which appears to be related to the problem of sym-biosis, only revealing itself on the verge of rupture or in a crisis. From this perspective the therapist's ability or inability to maintain a secure frame is crucial. All four patients expressed, at some period of their therapy, confusion on the question of who was helping whom, and that harm may result from the relationship. In order to control this calamitous feeling, they attempted to impose defensively on the therapist an exacting and stereotyped frame. Their experience of not having had "good-enough mothering" made them doubt their own ability to mother or made them feel that the analyst would require moth-ering and he could not function as a container. Whether he is aware or not, the therapist's feeling about the patient, his re-spect for the ground rules, and the form of interaction from the very beginning of therapy are crucial in the shaping of the therapeutic process. A secured frame may be utilized defensively by the patient to maintain a level of symbiosis that precludes analysis of the more disturbed aspects of the patient's personality. The analytic character may be an example of the narcissistic defensive use of the analytic frame.

Of all the meanings of the concept of countertransference listed by Langs (1979) and Sandler et al. (1970), I would like to underscore for the purpose of my chapter the one defined as the specific limitations in the psychoanalyst brought out by particular patients and including the specific reaction of the analyst to the patient's transference. The patient's projective role fantasy—for example, that the therapist is a figure of the past—pressures the therapist to discharge tensions, to be "seduced" into the role of a parental object, to behave or to verbalize in ways that are anti-therapeutic. It can further be said that some patients are very sensitive to the therapist's unsolved conflicts and errors. When the therapist as a person is under constant attack or he comes to feel drained, the potentially good fit or the very frame becomes fragile and shaky. The emotional onslaught expressed in some sessions raises the anxiety level of the therapist, which in turn mobilizes his defence and alters his communicational or interpersonal skills. The analytic situation is "*une système de miroirs deformantes*" [a system of distorting mirrors] (Viderman, 1982, p. 44):

> . . . *une situation saturée d'affects, d'une sensibilité emotionnelle intense, mouvante, en remaniement constant— situation ou il serait illusoire (et dommageable très sûrement tout autant) d'exiger que l'analyste pour sa part gardât toujours la tête et le coeur froids*
>
> [a situation saturated with affects, of intense emotional sensitivity, shifting, constantly changing—a situation where it will be illusory (and surely as hurtful) to demand from the analyst that he should keep his head and his heart cool.] [p. 49]

In working with the kind of patients described above, the therapist often feels he "is walking on eggs" and must carefully select the gentlest interpretation. Some patients provide inadequate cues or none to their dependency, and their grievances render them vulnerable to be rejected, to psychological assault, or to be let down when they dare to reveal their state of mind. As a result of the negative expectation consciously or unconsciously they distort cues, as if they expected the therapist to be so immersed in their experiential world that he ought to know without them telling him (Buie, 1981).

Searles (1978–79) is of the opinion that a phase of therapeutic symbiosis, the basis of a good frame, is necessary during psychotherapy or psychoanalysis with neurotic, borderline, or psychotic patients. In essence the therapeutic symbiosis constitutes a constructive and pre-ambivalent fusion to forestall increments of rage and frustration that are likely to disrupt the frame and hence the therapeutic alliance. In order to understand the therapeutic symbiosis, Searles was able to appreciate the extent to which the patient is able to function as therapist in relationship to his therapist, the goal being that of compensating for the therapist's deficiencies or inadequacies—not unlike the child who is able to mother its own mother. A patient with a conviction that her hostile feelings might damage those she cares for might attribute the same fragility to her therapist as she experienced in her mother.

A fantasy of the reversal of generations may be actualized in therapy when the patient looks after the therapist, as he once looked after one parent. Alterations of the frame and of the patient's unconscious perception of the sick part of the analyst are the stimuli that often trigger such a fantasy. In this context Jones (1950) wrote that it is quite common to find a mother trying to mould a boy along her father's lines or a father trying to mould a girl along his mother's—that is, making the child incorporate in itself its grandparent's character—and later on Jones described the negative version of the same reversal: a woman who hated her mother and then hated her daughter, or a man who hated his father and then hated his son. A mother trying to mould her son or a patient trying to mould her therapist are curative or reparative attempts. Ferenczi (1955) wrote in this regard: the fear of the inhibited, almost mad adult, changes the child, so to speak, into a psychiatrist. The therapeutic symbiosis of Searles and the fantasy of reversal of generations described by Jones and Ferenczi are based on similar dynamics. The analyst in an uncanny role-responsiveness to the patient's past frames finds himself thrown in one or another of these positions either feeling like the patient, or playing the role of an object of the patient's past environment, or periodically feeling out of commission in the performance of his therapeutic task in response to the patient's transference or projective identification. The therapist's ability to navigate through these "troubled waters" secures the frame and is a major component of the interactional "fit". It should be noted that the patient or the therapist may display split attitudes regarding "fit" at conscious and unconscious levels and that the nature of the analyst's communications, be they symbolic, non-verbal, gestural or affective, would affect the frame significantly.

It is particularly diagnostic, in dealing with patients who, as one of them put it, "within a short time I felt like having no skin and no borders" if the therapist experiences "rather soon in treatment, intense emotional reactions having more to do with the patient's premature, intense and chaotic transference and the therapist's capacity to withstand psychological stress and anxiety, than with any specific problem in the therapist's past" (Kernberg, 1975b). One can always find, however, a stimulus or key in the analyst's conscious or unconscious communications or in the setting that have provoked this chaotic situation.

In working with these types of patients, Balint (1968) advised that the therapist should try to avoid penetrating defences or undoing splits by incisive and correct interpretations (the unobtrusive analyst), as these might be felt as disbelieving the justification or validity of the patient's grievances, recriminations, and resentments as real and valid, and he should allow ample time for his patient to change his violent resentment to regret. This process must not be hurried by interpretations, however correct, since they may be felt as undue interference, as an attempt at devaluing the justification of their complaint, and they, instead of speeding up, will slow down the therapeutic process (Balint, 1968). Not only the process will come to a halt, but the past frame or container will become the "bulwark" against further progress. In other words, the experienced therapist becomes more tolerant of his patient's suffering, instead of trying to analyse the material to prove his therapeutic omnipotence. Prolonged silence may also be experienced as very threatening by these patients, who are more likely to place the

therapist in the critical, judgemental superego role. It is important to realize that the therapist, under these conditions, is
under strain to maintain a professional attitude. This latter is
built up of defences, training about techniques, and inhibitions
of an obsessional type. For Winnicott (1960a) the "psychotherapist must remain vulnerable and yet retain his professional role
in his actual working hours. I guess that the well-behaving
professional analyst is easier to come by than the analyst who
(while behaving well) retains the vulnerability that belongs to a
flexible defence organization" (p. 18).

# PART THREE

# ASPECTS
# OF COUNTERTRANSFERENCE–
# TRANSFERENCE INTERACTION
# IN SUPERVISION

# CHAPTER ELEVEN

# Transference–countertransference interactions in the supervisory situation: some observations

*Theodore J. Jacobs*

A lthough it has long been recognized that transference–countertransference interactions play a role of importance in supervision as they do in analytic therapy, this aspect of the supervisory situation has received comparatively little attention in the literature. Racker (1968) has observed that one source of a therapist's countertransference reactions in the treatment situation is his relationship with his supervisors and teachers. The therapist's emotional responses to these figures of authority, Racker noted, often colour and influence his perception of his patient. For this complex set of interactions, Racker coined the term "indirect countertransference".

In their pioneering study of psychoanalytic supervision, Fleming and Benedek (1983) noted that learning is inevitably affected by the transferences that develop between student and teacher, and they expressed the view that "disturbances of equilibrium in the learning alliance need to receive as much self-examination by a supervisor as is expected from a student" (p. 80). By way of illustration, the authors cited an example in which a supervisor, working with a candidate who made

221

repeated errors and seemed not to be able to make effective use of supervision, found herself feeling increasingly frustrated and helpless. She could neither treat the patient nor analyse the candidate. As a consequence, the supervisor's manner of teaching was decisively influenced by her emotional reactions to the student. Her supervisory style became more vigorous than usual, her tone sharp as she used the force of her personality to underline her remarks. This way of teaching intimidated the student and created problems in the learning alliance. Until the supervisor understood and could modify her approach, little effective learning could take place.

In a more recent study of the supervisory process, Dewald (1987) made a number of observations concerning the transference–countertransference interactions of student and teacher and the way in which such transactions affect both learning and treatment. Noting that countertransference reactions are not rare in supervisors, Dewald points out that a parallel process with regard to countertransference responses in candidates and supervisor may occur. This reaction is characterized by the development in the supervisor of countertransference feelings towards the student, which parallel the student's countertransference reactions to his patient. Dewald also observed that the self-esteem needs of the supervisor may have a distorting effect on the supervisory process and on his ability to assess the clinical material. Not infrequently the supervisor's countertransference will be manifested by feelings of pride in the achievements both of the patient and the student–analyst, since, in part, their progress reflects his input as a teacher. Such reactions, Dewald noted, are signs that the supervisor has become unduly invested in obtaining confirmation of the value of his own efforts.

Discussing the issue of termination, Dewald noted that the supervisor may be affected in significant ways by the ending of supervision. Unless he is aware of such reactions in himself, much of what the supervisor communicates to the student about the termination process may be coloured in significant ways by the emotions stirred up in him as the supervision comes to a close. To illustrate this point, Dewald cited an example in which he found himself intervening rather abruptly to offer support to a candidate who was experiencing a deep sense of loss during the final weeks of a long analysis. Dewald realized that his readiness to support the student by explaining that analysts, as well as patients, often undergo a process of mourning during the termination phase of analysis was a reflection of the sadness that he was feeling at the ending of his work with the candidate.

Such vignettes are illuminating as they bring to life the kinds of interplay between student and teacher that are a regular feature of the supervisory situation and that have a significant impact on its course and development. They are not easily found in the literature, however, and still less common are more comprehensive descriptions of the way in which such transactions have affected the supervisory process.

In this chapter I describe two supervisory experiences in which transference–countertransference issues played significant roles, affecting both the learning process and the course of treatment. When speaking of countertransference in the supervisory setting, I am referring to unconscious influences on the student and supervisor that affect their thinking and behaviour. These include not only their interactions with each other and their responses to the patient, but influences that derive from self and object representations stimulated by the supervisory situation as well as from reactions to teachers, colleagues, other patients, present and former analysts, and figures in the patient's world.

Some years ago I undertook the supervision of a young psychologist who was treating a rather rigid, obsessional man in analytic psychotherapy. Looking for all the world like a Damon Runyon character who had strayed from his natural Times Square habitat, G, as I shall call him, was a person who was given to action. He liked to talk and to move, and as he described his patient to me in our initial meeting he found it difficult to sit still. With arms and hands in continual motion, he punctuated his description with a parade of movements to which, at unpredictable intervals, he added a sudden facial grimace.

Before I had met G, I had heard something about him. Through the grapevine I had learned that from early on in his training he had gained a reputation for having a flamboyant personality and a flair for the dramatic. It came as no surprise, then, to learn that G had a keen interest in family therapy, that he was taking special training in that field, and that he had become a disciple of the head of that program who was himself a dramatic, action-oriented individual.

All of this gave me trouble. My own training had been primarily in individual therapy and analysis, and the particular style of family therapy that was then in vogue at our centre, with its emphasis on action, confrontation, and the deliberate use of the therapist's personality to influence and guide behaviour was the very antithesis of the approach that I utilized in treatment and of the values that informed my work. Moreover, the brief attempt that I had made in years past to work with the head of the family training program in a joint teaching project had not proved successful. Holding views that were theoretically, technically, and philosophically incompatible, unable to respect each other's position, and being rather opinionated individuals, we clashed repeatedly and found no way of working together.

The prospect of supervising someone who looked and talked like P. T. Barnum seemed a thankless, if not hopeless task. Nevertheless this was my assignment, and to request a change of supervisee on the basis of these clearly prejudicial feelings seemed indefensible.

I was quite aware, however, given my biases, that the supervision could easily get off on the wrong foot. It would be all too easy to pigeonhole G as part of the family training group, to identify him with his mentor, and to regard him as one of those individuals who, by temperament and inclination, was ill suited to the task of doing psychotherapy.

Without realizing it, I could easily slip into an adversarial stance vis-à-vis G and perceive him, not as a younger colleague, but as an interloper from the enemy camp. I made a determined effort, therefore, to approach my new student with as open a mind as possible.

In this effort I was not entirely unsuccessful. On guard against allowing a jaundiced eye to colour my view of G, I began, in fact, to see him quite differently than I had imagined. It is true that he was by nature irrepressible. Reserve, introspection, and self-restraint were not his strong points. Quick-witted and spontaneous, he could also be impulsive.

It was also true, however, that G had other qualities: ones that I had not heard about and whose discovery came as a welcome surprise. Intelligent and sensitive, he also demonstrated a grasp of dynamics and a natural talent for understanding unconscious mental processes that exceeded the capacities of most of the students I had taught. There was no doubt, given these gifts, that G had the potential to become a highly accomplished therapist.

It came as a surprise and a disappointment, then, to realize after some months that G showed no signs whatever of living up to his potential. In fact it was clear that he was making little progress in learning to be a therapist. He had trouble following the material, and both in his understanding and in his interventions he was often off the mark.

Why it was that G had such difficulty mastering the fundamentals of psychotherapy was not clear. Although initially he and I were wary of one another and viewed the idea of working together in supervision with hesitancy and suspicion, within a short time we had come to like and respect each other. Not having had adequate training in individual therapy, G seemed eager to learn what I had to teach.

Try as he might, however, G was unable to orient himself properly and to take an appropriate therapeutic stance. It was extremely difficult for him to remain neutral, to focus on the inner world of the patient, and to listen in a non-judgmental way. We would talk about these problems, and invariably after a supervisory session G would leave my office resolved to adopt an exploratory attitude, to refrain from making judgements and offering opinions, and to focus on his patient's conflicts and not on the problems of other family members.

In the heat of the therapy, however, his resolve would be lost. Learning, for instance, that his patient had been ill-treated by his family, G would become incensed, would point out the pathology of the offenders, and, either directly or by unsubtle implication, would suggest the correct manner of dealing with such miscreants.

It was difficult, too, for G not to intervene when his patient seemed headed for trouble. His patient was an anxious and compulsive fellow, rigid in his character structure, and terrified of spontaneous feelings. Highly controlled and given to endless

obsessional ruminations, he could also be stubborn, argumen-
tative, and secretly rebellious. For the most part deliberate and
cautious in all that he did, he would on occasion act in impulsive ways.

On one such occasion, the patient became involved with
a woman of questionable character, whom G viewed as a de-
cidedly inappropriate choice. Abandoning even the pretence of
neutrality, he handled the situation with the subtlety of Mike
Tyson throwing a left hook to the jaw. The woman, he said, was
strictly a user—someone who thought solely of herself, freely
manipulated others, and who, as a prospective mate, ranked
only slightly behind Eva Peron and Lady Macbeth.

G's method was effective. Alarmed and stung by the force-
fulness of his therapist's words, the patient backed away from
the relationship and soon thereafter dropped it.

He was not always so compliant, however. Stubbornness
and negativity were deeply rooted in his character, and he had
a lifelong history of responding to authority with oppositional
behaviour. G's confrontational style often came through to the
patient as dictatorial, very much in the style of his arbitrary
and often irrational father. To such commands he often responded with defiance that took the form, not of open rebellion,
but of passive resistance.

In short order, a battle was joined. Responding to the
pressure he felt coming from G, the patient dug in his heels.
Although outwardly co-operative and appearing interested in
altering certain troublesome character traits, he did not budge.
In fact, in the face of some of G's interventions, certain of these
traits were intensified.

Confronted with such tenacious resistance, G redoubled his
efforts to effect change, and his interventions, always direct,
took on an insistent quality. A stand-off ensued, and within
months the treatment, which had never really taken wing,
ground to a halt.

A number of interlocking factors contributed to this unhappy state of affairs. Clearly G's flamboyant personality, his
prior work in family therapy, his identification with powerful
and influential figures in that field, and his inexperience as an
individual therapist all played roles. In supervision these issues were talked about at length, and finally, realizing that

long-standing troubles of his own were fuelling the situation, G made the decision to enter therapy.

During the next half-year there was considerable improvement in G's work. Though it did not come easily to him, he was able to shift his focus from a concentration on the external world and the problems it presented to his patient's inner realities. He was also able, for the most part, to maintain a stance of neutrality despite a strong inclination to do otherwise. In the course of supervision, G shared with me some of the conflicts stirred up in him by our supervisory situation and by my attitude toward the patient, both of which resonated with certain personal experiences of his own and which intensified his already strong countertransference feelings.

From the outset, G explained, he was ambivalent about working with me. Although I came well recommended as a supervisor who could help him learn the techniques of psychotherapy, he felt disloyal to the family training group, both because of his interest in individual work and because he had requested me as a supervisor. His mentor in the family section had made a number of disparaging remarks about his working with me, and G knew that he was none too happy about that arrangement. This openly expressed disapproval heightened G's conflicts and his feelings of disloyalty and made him both anxious and angry.

Something about me, too, troubled him. He experienced me as a thoughtful and sensitive person whose approach to life was eminently rational. While he appreciated these traits, they also bothered him. They reminded him of certain qualities in his stepfather, the man who had raised him after his father died. A considerate and kindly individual, the stepfather was also a reserved and highly controlled person who was difficult to know in any but the most superficial ways.

G felt frustrated by his inability to make emotional contact with his stepfather, and out of hurt and anger he turned to an uncle for support and guidance. This individual was the family success story. Flamboyant in style and manner, he was a star salesman for a jewellery concern. His trademark was showmanship, and he could be seen regularly on the streets of his home-town wearing the latest Armani fashions and driving a Porsche.

Seeking his uncle's love and approval, G endorsed his lifestyle and, through identification, took on many of his traits.
Thus he, too, became a showman, impelled to put on a performance wherever he went. In the residency, G had immediately been drawn to the extroverted and dramatic style of the
family therapists. Family therapy, in fact, seemed to be his
métier. a field in which his propensity for action and drama
could find sanctioned expression.

In time, however, G's fascination with flamboyant and extroverted personalities began to change. This had happened in
his relationship with his uncle, whose vanity and shallowness
had eventually put G off. Disillusioned with the uncle in late
adolescence, he made an effort to turn back to the stepfather,
whose modesty and thoughtfulness he had come to admire.
This effort, however, was not successful. G was met with a
coolness and reserve on the part of his stepfather that he could
not help but interpret as rejection. Wounded, he shunned the
stepfather from that time on, and with renewed vigour em-
braced the lifestyle of his uncle.

A similar scenario had developed in the residency program.
As G became better acquainted with the family therapy approach that initially held such appeal for him, he recognized the
limitations of this method. He realized that in large measure
family therapy relied for its effects on influence, persuasion, and
manipulation. No in-depth understanding of individual family
members was possible, and, in fact, G's efforts to integrate
individual dynamics with the dynamics of the family were discouraged by his teachers. Increasingly interested in individual
psychology and dissatisfied with what family therapy had to
offer, G wished to have training in analytic therapy. He had
heard me speak on one occasion and recalled thinking at the
time that he would very much like to have me as a supervisor.
Since he associated me with the quiet and reserved, but also
rejecting, stepfather, however, he was wary about asking to
work with me. Although he thought repeatedly of making such
a request, his fear of rejection was such that it took him more
than a year to actually do so.

G was afraid that I would regard him as an outsider, an
emissary of the enemy, and someone woefully lacking in talent.
Then, to avoid disappointment when he finally undertook train-

ing in psychotherapy, he kept part of himself aloof and did not commit himself to learning the techniques of individual therapy. He straddled the fence, seeing individuals but clinging to the family therapy model and utilizing many of its techniques. The result was that he used a mixture of methods that, being neither fish nor fowl, led to a buckshot approach that lacked clarity of focus. It was only after many months of supervision, during which time G repeatedly tested my tolerance for him and the genuineness of my interest in his development, that he could risk making a genuine effort to become a psychotherapist—an effort that he knew would open him up to the possibility of another painful rejection.

The psychological factors that contributed to the stalemated treatment and to G's difficulty in making use of what I could offer him did not, however, lie entirely in his side of the supervisory equation. I, too, contributed to them. Working with G had, outside of my awareness, awakened certain memories and conflicts in myself. The stirring of these old ghosts had influenced my interaction with G and had led to my transmitting covert messages to him that often contradicted and subverted the conscious ones that were contained in my supervisory interventions.

G had something in common with my father. Although often depressed, my father could, when in good spirits, be a showman. Fond of telling long and elaborate stories full of invention and artifice, he, like G, enjoyed playing the role of the entertainer. As a child I was enthralled by my father's stories and never tired of hearing them. For me they constituted a treat, one that occurred all too infrequently and that lasted for too short a time. When, telling one of his tales, my father approached its end, I would encourage him through body language, facial expression, and the quality of my listening, as well as by more direct appeals, to go on, to invent more, and to keep the narrative flowing.

For me these performances were more than a source of pleasure. They embodied the creative and imaginative side of my father—the side of him that I admired and wished to emulate. Bright, original, and imaginative, my father the performer was someone of whom I could be proud. And by focusing on what was interesting and creative in him I could forget the side of my father that I found threatening—the side characterized by depression, silence, and withdrawal.

Listening to G aroused memories of listening to my father hold forth at the dinner table, and, unconsciously, I responded to him in ways that were old and familiar. G was exasperating, but, like my father, he was also intriguing. What he did and said as a therapist was often wrong and wrong-headed, and as his supervisor I told him so. But there was something fascinating in his verve, his spirit, his energy, and his audacity. Bold, forthright, original, and often clever. G presented his work with a mixture of wit, defiance, and puckish charm. One could be mesmerized by G, and I found myself captivated by his accounts of his therapeutic hours as, forty years before, I had been captivated by my father's stories.

As a result I sent mixed signals to G. Overtly, my words conveyed the message that he was on the wrong track, that the force of his personality was influencing the patient, and that such a stance was incompatible with insight therapy, while covertly and unconsciously my tone, manner, and body language conveyed something else: that I was intrigued by G's account and that vicariously I experienced pleasure at hearing about his boldness, originality, and willingness to throw away the book. Thus, non-verbally and through metacommunications, I was subtly encouraging G to continue to play the renegade. G got the message. Along with a number of other contributing factors, it exerted a subtle but strong influence on him not to change his approach.

My interactions with G, however, were shaped not only by memories of my father's behaviour, but by encoded responses to others as well. G was about the age of a very close friend of mine, and although in most respects he was quite a different person, he shared with this friend a certain delight in being original, challenging, and mischievous. I was the quieter and more contained of the two of us, and often I envied my friend his good spirits, his social ease, and his seeming enjoyment of life. It gave me pleasure to hear about some of his more audacious exploits, and, living vicariously through his adventures, I have no doubt that I encouraged him to do the "bad" things that I dared not attempt. The fact that as a result of his actions he might get into trouble and be scolded by parents or teachers

probably also played some part in my subtle—and not so subtle—encouragement of his misbehaviour. These factors, too,
were operative in my work with G. On the one hand, he was
doing what some part of me also wanted to do: to play the rebel,
to kick over the traces, to abandon a stringent analytic stance,
and to use the full force of my personality to reach my patients
and to effect change. The fact that as a result of acting in just
this way—and my encouraging him to do so—G was soundly
criticized by his teachers and branded as an incorrigible and
unreachable student unconsciously served a purpose for me.
He became my proxy, acting out not only certain secret wishes
of mine, but being the recipient of the punishment that I felt I
deserved for those wishes.

My own experiences as a therapist, too, played a role in
influencing my communications to G. As a young therapist, I
had attempted to work with patients of the kind he was treating. Often I found them to be exasperating, the work slow and
painful, and the results often less than satisfactory. Highly
intellectualized and Talmudic in their approach to life, such
patients used rationality and a tenacious adherence to reality
as rock-ribbed defences. Clever and skilled in debate, they
sought to engage me in endless and unproductive arguments.
Every interpretation of mine was disputed, and, if finally
accepted, it was only after numerous corrections and emen-
dations had been made. Progress with such patients was extremely slow and sometimes barely perceptible. In not a few
cases, the traditional approach of analysing defences and focusing on the transference proved futile. In such instances it
was often necessary to confront the patient directly with his
concealed aggression and with the efforts at manipulation that
lay behind the manifest symptoms. Sometimes it was necessary to shift gears and to utilize an active approach that
directed the patient's attention to certain characteristic behaviour patterns and their consequences to himself and others.

Listening to G's account of his patient's obsessional style,
his passive–aggressive behaviour, and his endless procrastina-
tions, I began unconsciously to identify with him in his efforts
to deal with this frustrating individual. Remembering my own
struggles with such patients and the feelings of helplessness
when my efforts to work with them analytically encountered

unbreachable resistances, I unconsciously endorsed a more active, confrontational approach. While the model I taught in supervision was basically analytic, with emphasis on the importance of neutrality, the analysis of resistances, interpretation in the here and now of the transference, and the need for working through, privately I questioned whether even the most technically correct analytic approach could prove effective with a patient like G's. My own experiences with similar cases gave me pause on this score, and my doubts must have been conveyed to G. For this reason, the message I gave him was an ambivalent one. My words conveyed an adherence to, and a belief in, the analytic method; through tone, manner, and other non-verbal means, however, I conveyed another message: that to reach such a patient would require a more direct and active approach, one that challenged his long-standing mode of operating in the world and that shook up his iron-clad system of defences. I was, in short, giving G permission *sub rosa* to employ his unconventional style and to use the force of his personality to reach his patient. As a neophyte therapist with a predilection for active interventions and heavily influenced by his family therapy training, G responded to this ambivalence by holding on to and utilizing the method that he knew best and that had worked for him in treating families. Thus a number of factors coalesced in myself and contributed to the mixed messages that I sent to G—messages that, along with motivations derived from his own conflicts, prompted him to employ a brand of therapy—part individual, part family—that, if not particularly effective, was unquestionably unique.

As it turned out, the patient proved to be more flexible and less encased in concrete than I had supposed. In time and with careful handling he was able to make good use of an analytic approach and to achieve substantial gains. For some time, however, he was treated with a mixed bag of techniques that led to no improvement. Both therapist and supervisor, each for their own reasons but working in concert, blocked the employment of the most useful therapeutic approach. And it was only when each of us had explored, and had come to better terms, with our own conflicts that both the supervision and the treatment could get back on track.

* * *

My second example will not be a lengthy one. It concerns the supervision of a student who was beginning analytic work, and I cite it to illustrate the manifold influences that may impinge on the supervisory situation and that may affect the supervisor's judgement and capacity to work with a candidate. Like the analyst, the supervisor must maintain a stance of neutrality vis-à-vis the patient as he listens to the material. This supervisory neutrality has two faces. Its outer one is manifested in the attitude towards the patient that he conveys to the student. The supervisor's comments, his way of thinking, and the model interpretations that he offers reflect this attitude. Its inner face reflects the quality of the supervisor's receptivity as he listens to and processes the material. His capacity to listen in an open-ended, neutral way depends no less than does the analyst's receptivity on the attainment of a state of mind that is relatively free of personal biases, pre-set theoretical positions, or disruptive emotional reactions.

Such influences, however, operate regularly and constitute as much of a threat to the supervisor's ability to hear what the patient is communicating as they do in the analytic situation. Unlike analysts, however, who in the clinical situation are taught to be aware of the importance of countertransference in shaping their thinking and their responses, supervisors often overlook the critical role that such phenomena play in supervision. In fact, it is not uncommon for an analyst to be well attuned to the emotions stirred up in him in his work with patients and to be quite blind to similar feelings evoked in the supervisory situation. Since it is uncommon in the teaching of supervision for stress to be placed on the importance of the supervisor's emotional reactions to the student, the analytic material, the Institute, and other influences on his perceptions and thinking, the message conveyed by implication is that countertransference does not have the same significance in supervision as it does in treatment. Since the process of self-scrutiny is never an easy one and inevitably encounters strong resistance, this attitude reinforces the tendency among many supervisors to overlook their own responses as they work in supervision and to concentrate quite exclusively on the material that is being presented. Part of my motivation in describing the following example is not only to illustrate the importance of countertransference phenomena in the supervisory situation, but to demonstrate the way in which multiple intersecting forces contribute to those phenomena.

Although not a desirable state of affairs, it happens with some frequency that for his first analytic case a candidate chooses, or is assigned, a patient who turns out to be quite troubled. This always presents problems for both analyst and supervisor, not the least of which is the necessity of determining whether or not to continue the analytic work with such individuals. This difficult situation is made more complex if the supervisor's judgement and ability to process the clinical material are compromised by emotional responses that derive from conflicts and experiences of his own.

Such was the situation in my supervision of Dr F, a bright and thoughtful candidate, whose first analytic patient proved to be a disturbed individual with little impulse control and a strong inclination to act on and to dramatize his conflicts. It became clear after several years of work that this patient could make little effective use of the analytic method and that the best way to treat him was by means of a more directly supportive approach. This conclusion, which should have been evident in the early months of treatment when the extent of the patient's pathology became clear, was long delayed by the development of scotomas in supervisor and analyst. It was, however, the blind spots in the supervisor that, in large measure, contributed to the analyst's distortions and to his persistent efforts to turn an unsuitable patient into a workable analytic case.

From the time that I first learned of the patient and read over the initial intake evaluations, countertransference responses played an important role in my responses to her. One of the evaluators was a former teacher and supervisor of mine from whom I had learned a great deal and whom I held in the highest esteem. This colleague had recommended that the patient be accepted for analysis. Although much about the patient's character and history caused me to have reservations about his analysability, I suppressed these doubts and went along with what I thought to be the superior judgement of an experienced clinician. Later, as I reviewed my decision to supervise the case, I became aware of the fact that my need to suppress my doubts about the judgement of my former teacher was not a new experience. As a child I had frequently responded in this way when I disagreed with my father. Out of fear of his wrath I often abandoned my position in order to avoid a conflict and to remain in the good graces of a man who I valued and wanted to please. In bowing to the views of my old teacher with regard to the patient's analysability, I had been in the grip of an old reaction, an old pattern.

There were other factors, too, that contributed to my misreading of the clinical situation. As one of my first psychotherapy cases, I had undertaken the treatment of a troubled and vulnerable young woman whose rage lay millimetres beneath her shy, waif-like manner. The treatment did not last long. Feeling buffeted by her passive–aggressive behaviour, which often took the form of prolonged silences, frequent missed sessions, and a stubborn negativism, I found reasons to end the therapy. Subsequently, the patient did not do well. She had difficulty holding a job, made repeated suicide attempts, and ended up being hospitalized. For years afterwards, as I realized that the reasons I gave myself for terminating the treatment were rationalizations for unmanageable countertransference reactions, I regretted having done so. To make up for this error, I wished to have a second chance at treating such a patient. I found this opportunity in the form of Dr F's case. A shy, needy individual who latched on to others and sought their protection, his impulsive, manipulative side was not detectable for some time. Hearing about him, I found myself responding primarily to the patient's vulnerability, a trait that evoked memories of my former patient. And when it became clear that Dr F's patient could not work in analysis, I did not want to give up. I had done this once before, and I had learned my lesson. It would be important, I thought, to stick it out, to stay with the treatment, and not abandon ship. The fact that both patient and analyst were sinking escaped me, however. I was too busy trying to rework an old case and to redeem myself in my own eyes to perceive clearly what was happening in Dr F's treatment.

Dr F, too, stirred up strong feelings in me. A bright and able student, he was eager to help, eager to cure. In his enthusiasms he reminded me of my brother, in his naiveté of myself as a beginning candidate. Having something of the psychology of the rescuer, he was convinced—as I had been as a student—that armed with the powerful instrument of analysis he could help the most troubled individuals.

Dr F had invested much in this case, his first, and was anxious to test both his capacities as an analyst and the effectiveness of the method. I sensed, too, that he was someone who was insecure about his professional abilities. If this case did not work out, rationally he would accept the fact that analysis was not a suitable method for this patient. Not far from the surface, however, he would experience deep disappointment, feel that he was a failure, and suffer considerable erosion of his self-confidence.

While in fact my judgement about Dr F might have been correct, my perceptions of him were coloured by my own experiences as a student. For my first patient I had been assigned a man who proved to be about as analysable as Saddam Hussein. Not wanting to lose the case, however, for many years I persisted in my efforts to analyse this individual, alternately feeling angry at the Institute for accepting him and at myself for agreeing to work with such a patient. While this experience was not entirely a negative one for me, there was much frustration, much disappointment along the way.

As I listened to Dr F tell me about his first case, memories of my work with this difficult first patient began to surface, and with them the old and familiar angers directed both at myself and at certain individuals—now colleagues—who were responsible for sending me such a case. Such feelings, however, were troublesome, and to keep them at bay I focused on problems of technique in Dr F's case and not on the fact that his patient, like mine, was inappropriately selected for analysis.

Since I identified with Dr F who very much wanted the analysis to succeed, I colluded with him to persist in a hopeless cause. Afterwards I wondered if I was driven by another motive. As a candidate who was assigned a most difficult patient, I had undergone a rough passage—a rite of initiation, so to speak. Should Dr F be spared his own initiation? Perhaps I, like others before me, had unconsciously wanted my student to experience what I had experienced and be obliged to travel the same rocky road.

Other factors, too, coloured my view of the clinical situation. In his youth a friend of mine, who was a deeply troubled person, had received inadequate psychiatric care. Eventually, he killed himself. At some point in his therapy his psychiatrist had stopped the treatment, and this action, I believed, played an important role in what had happened. I was a medical student at the time, and then and there I resolved not to treat patients in that way. Yet it was I who also had given up on a difficult patient. As a supervisor I did not intend to allow a student of mine to repeat this error.

Initially the candidate, too, wanted to persist in the treatment. He, like I, had fantasies of curing the patient through analysis. Both of us had been impressed by reports in the literature of lengthy and successful treatments of troubled individuals. Moreover, at a number of clinical conferences at our institute the effective analysis of cases of seemingly unreachable patients had been presented. The analysts in those cases had received much praise for their persistence in working for 8, 10, or 12 years with these unpromising cases. Their never-say-die attitudes, it seemed, had paid off. Perhaps this was what was required, we thought, to achieve results with such patients. And if we stayed the course, perhaps one day we, too, would be able to impress our colleagues by presenting the successful treatment of a deeply troubled individual.

Hearing about the case, the candidate's analyst began to interpret the student's hero-and-rescue fantasies and, indirectly, conveyed the view that the patient was not analysable. The candidate was then caught between the conflicting messages sent by supervisor and analyst. Because he liked me and was at the time caught up in negative transference feelings towards his analyst, the candidate favoured my position and wanted to believe that it was the correct one.

He was not the only one whose negative feelings towards his analyst affected his judgement. This analyst had been a teacher at the institute, and in his course, in my view, had been a disaster. In tone and manner, if not in words, I let my feelings be known, and some antagonism developed between us. I did not think much of this colleague's clinical judgement either, and when the candidate reported that his analyst was questioning the viability of his case, I reacted by supplying reasons for him to carry on the treatment. Thus an old struggle, flaring anew, affected by perceptions in this case, just as had the feeling of affection and loyalty that I experienced towards the teacher that I so admired. In fact, it was in part to please him that I found myself believing that the case could be effectively treated in analysis. Not only did I not want to contradict his judgement by refusing the patient or declaring him unanalysable, I also wanted to impress him with my skills as a supervisor. He had often said that I would make a good supervisor, and he looked forward to the time when I would have that status. Now word would get back to him that my first supervisory case was a failure and that the patient had to be switched to psychotherapy. Rationally he would understand that not every case works out; but perhaps he would question my handling of the situation. After all, he had recommended analysis. Would not a skilled supervisor, understanding the reasons for the recommendation, be able to help his student work through the presenting difficulties? Perhaps he had been wrong about me, and I was not good supervisory material after all. I have no doubt that the discomfort that accompanied this fantasy also contributed to my decision to continue the analytic work.

* * *

I have presented these two cases to illustrate a simple, but often neglected fact: that transference and countertransference operate as powerful forces in supervision, just as they do in treatment. Well recognized as important influences in the clinical situation, they are often overlooked in the supervisory one. Such phenomena often have multiple roots and derive from such diverse sources as the supervisor's unconscious responses to the patient, to the candidate, to the candidate's analyst and other teachers, to his own former teachers and supervisors, and to the institute. Memories, fantasies, and self- and object representations stimulated by the material can also arouse countertransference responses. Unrecognized and uncorrected, such phenomena lead to distortions in the supervisor's ability to listen to and to process the analytic material. And such difficulties inevitably distort not only the teaching and learning processes, but the treatment as well.

# CHAPTER TWELVE

# Some transference–countertransference issues of the supervisory situation: a dream about the supervisor

*Grigoris Vaslamatzis*

A supervisee's dream about the supervisor is presented in this chapter. The dream coincides with the patient's reverting to her earlier symptoms during the termination phase. As a result of this the psychotherapy had to be prolonged.

Unfortunately, little is seen in the literature on the dynamics and dysfunctions of supervision. In his important paper, Pedder (1986) indicates the difficulties that may arise when transference problems occur in psychotherapy supervision towards the supervisor. Heising (1976) and Sandell (1985) also pointed out the threat of the negative influence that supervision might have on the therapeutic outcome.

The objective of this study is to elucidate further the transference–countertransference issues that arise between trainees

This is a modified version of "A Dream About the Supervisor: Personal View", *British Journal of Psychotherapy, 6* (1990) No. 4. By permission of the author. My appreciation goes to Chrysanthi Rodinou and Dr Theodore Bazas for their comments and assistance on the English version of this paper.

and supervisors, as well as their consequences on the psycho-therapy.

## The supervision

Dr D was a third-year psychiatric resident, married, in her mid-thirties. She was considered a very intelligent young physician, and everyone felt that she was pleased to present the material of her cases. She was very enthusiastic to have her first patient in psychotherapy, and after the termination she asked to be assigned a second case of brief psychoanalytic psychotherapy (Vaslamatzis & Verveniotis, 1985). Her second case was a female patient who presented with anxiety attacks and somatic symptoms. She was single and clung to relationships with motherly-behaving older men. The patient's mother had died three years previously, and it was at that time that her symptoms had first appeared. The evaluator had been the supervisor himself, who had decided about the patient's suitability for brief psychotherapy (up to 30 sessions). The patient had agreed to this limit.

From the first therapeutic sessions the therapist had difficulty in dealing with the patient's anger, either in its overt or concealed form (e.g. delays, absences, etc.). Throughout the course of therapy, she did not have any difficulty during the supervision in discerning the patient's transference, but she failed to focus and manage its meaning at the right time and correctly in the therapy. This was particularly prevalent in issues that were more indicative of the patient's dependence or anger over the temporariness of the relationship. Another manifestation of which the supervisor gradually became aware was that she often sought to prolong the supervisory hour—for example, she suddenly remembered an interesting dream of her patient, she wanted to clarify some issues, and so on.

After the twentieth session, the supervisor understood that the therapist's difficulty was related to the anticipated termination of her supervision—which also coincided with the end of her training. The supervisor very tactfully pointed out this association.

On the night that followed the twenty-eighth session, during which the patient had clearly reverted to her depression and presented acting-out behaviour (she had lost her wallet with her whole month's salary on her way to the session), the therapist had the following dream: "I was locked in a flat; I looked out the window pane and saw a girl falling off the balcony from a building across the street, and a man's hand pulling her back. That movement was repeated many times." She added, "I knew that the hand was yours" (i.e., the supervisor's). The supervisor asked at that point what the supervisee was thinking of, concerning the dream. Dr D answered in a rather direct way that the dream seemed to express anger that was aimed at both patient and supervisor. The latter ought to be more active and help her out with the therapy. The supervisor commented that her request was that he himself would undertake the psychotherapy—something that was quite impossible. If she thought it might be helpful, she could provide for an extension in order to work better with the patient's transference as well as her own countertransference. Should she not feel ready to do that, she could refer her patient to another therapist.

Finally, with the aim of overcoming the crisis the patient was in regarding the termination and loss, the therapy was continued for another 12 sessions. During that time Dr D managed to unblock her feelings of inner conflict by deciding and managing to work on the terminal phase of the treatment. These additional sessions proved quite productive, and treatment ended with an increase of the patient's insight regarding the importance of separation and loss in her life.

## Discussion

Through her dream, Dr D unconsciously communicates to her supervisor issues that were present throughout the supervisory period but had not become the object of attention and analysis—the sexual wish, for instance, as it is symbolized in her dream with the repeated movement of a man's hand that grasps the woman–representative of the therapist's self. The intense prohibitions and defences—"locked" behind the window pane, a paralysed therapist. One could either see in that dream the subject of the primal scene or speculate on the therapist's wish to live a "holding" experience in the supervision. During the supervisory session, the supervisor perceived his own defensive behaviour against the eroticization of the supervision. He understood that he failed to notice that although the therapist had accepted all his remarks about the patient's unconscious anger, she did not work on that subject during the therapeutic sessions; or that the student therapist often sought to prolong the supervisory hour. The question raised here is whether we can maintain that the supervisor had unconsciously accepted the eroticization, misinterpreting it as a "learning alliance" behaviour. My reply to the above question is yes.

The above supervisory example confirms once again that the supervisory situation is not a simple one. Transference-countertransference interactions cannot easily be put aside. The supervisor has to face and deal with the transference of the trainee therapist and his/her own countertransference, so that the supervision fulfils its goals. However, before further elaborating on the issue, I wish briefly to review the theoretical point of view.

"It is easy for the supervisor to forget the complicated stresses acting on the student in the training scheme", says Blomfield (1985, p. 407). It might be added that the supervisor should have an overall idea about what his/her supervisee is like as well as of the supervisory situation itself.

According to Wagner (1957), when supervision is patient-centred, the supervisor teaches technique. If the supervision is therapist-centred, attention is given to the therapist's reactions, blind spots, and countertransference. If supervision is process-centred, the supervisor attempts to make use of the analogy that both the patient and the therapist are seeking help. In the latter case supervision includes the supervisory process. Although in the studies following Wagner's, further remarks were written on the subject of supervision, we did not see any particular elaboration of the point. The recent article by Szecsödy (1990) and Theodore Jacobs' chapter eleven in this book could be some exceptions to the rule. Fleming and Benedek (1983) had also reported that it is useful to think of the supervisory situation as a triadic system composed of sub-systems in a complex process of communication with each other. One may perhaps deduce that psychotherapy proceeds not merely under supervision, but through the supervisory relationship.

In our case the supervisor appears in the dream. The report is indirect ("I knew that . . .") but clear. Harris (1962) reports the uniformity and the increased incidence of dreams about the analyst undisguised during the terminal phase of treatment, as well as the reactivation of separation anxiety, which would cause the patient to cling to the analyst as a timid or frightened child would cling to the mother. Our student–therapist through her associations offers such an interpretation; however, the need for the continuation of libidinal and scopophilic satisfaction is also apparent in her dream. The dream is a compromise formation among various wishes, prohibitions, and defences—a fact that shows the development of a "supervisory" transference. The supervisor, feeling the pressure that is exercised by the symbolism of the dream, reacted with a defensive effort of avoiding to comprehend and analyse through supervision the over-determined dynamics of the relationship. At this point the patient's treatment was threatened—on the one hand, due to the therapist's tendency to use it as the field of her transference projections towards the supervisor and, on the other, as a result of the supervisor's defensive behaviour. This use of the therapy is confirmed by the fact that the therapist understands and elaborates during the early supervisory sessions the material brought by her patient, she cannot use this understanding in the course of the psychotherapy. The insight gained in the supervision is warded off, as it arouses anxieties related to the meaning of the termination of both psychotherapy and supervision. Her identification with the dependent part of her patient's self has to be abandoned, and the libidinal satisfaction gained in the supervisory relationship is becoming more threatening to her.

The supervisor did not face this issue in the context of transference–countertransference, partly because he consciously believed that it would not interfere with the psychotherapy and would end with its termination. Unconsciously, however, in denying this issue, the supervisor was satisfying certain wishes on the transference–countertransference level.

The supervisor's behaviour was supported by the notion that the trainee therapist should be referred to his or her own analyst when such difficulties arise. The question to be asked here is: Is this the only alternative? Should not supervision be, perhaps, analytically understood and managed by the supervisor, and the transference issues discussed tactfully and directly within the supervisory session? In the latter case, complementing the process with a supervisor's supervision would definitely have been of help.

This is the way that I understand the old aphorism, quoted by Pedder, that supervision is "more than education and less than psychotherapy". Theodore Jacobs' chapter is an attempt to advance further the psychoanalytic understanding of the supervision, which might be interpreted as paying attention to the transference–countertransference themes of the supervisory relationship.

Full exploration of these issues is beyond the scope of this chapter; however, any research and specific suggestions that could facilitate the discussion of the neglected transferences of trainees in psychotherapy towards their supervisors, as well as the ensuing countertransference reactions of the latter, should be encouraged.

# REFERENCES

Abend, S. M. (1989). Countertransference and psychoanalytic technique. The *Psychoanalytic Quarterly*, *43*: 374–395.

Anzieu D. (1984). *The Group and the Unconscious*. London: Routledge & Kegan Paul.

Arvanitakis, K. (1987). The analytic frame in the treatment of schizophrenia and its relation to depression. *International Journal of Psycho-Analysis*, *68*: 525–533.

Bachrach, H. M. (1983). On the concept of analyzability. *Psychoanalytic Quarterly*, *52*: 180–204.

Balint, M. (1968). *The Basic Fault*. London: Tavistock.

Baranger, M., Baranger, W., & Mom, J. (1983). Process and non-process in analytic work. *International Journal of Psycho-Analysis*, *64*: 1–15.

Beres, D., & Arlow, J. A. (1974). Fantasy and identification in empathy. *Psychoanalytic Quarterly*, *43*: 26–50.

Bion, W. R. (1959). *Experiences in Groups*. New York: Basic Books.

———. (1962a). *Learning from Experience*. London: Heinemann. [Reprinted London: Karnac Books, 1984.]

———. (1962b). A theory of thinking. *International Journal of Psycho-Analysis 43*. Reprinted in *Second Thoughts* (pp. 110–119). London: Heinemann. [Reprinted London: Karnac Books, 1984.]

245

_____. (1967). *Second Thoughts*. London: Heinemann. [Reprinted London: Karnac Books, 1984.]

_____. (1970). *Attention and Interpretation*. London: Heinemann. [Reprinted London: Karnac Books, 1984.]

_____. (1977). Transformations in *Seven Servants*. New York: Jason Aronson.

Blanck, G., & Blanck, R. (1979). *Ego Psychology, II*. New York: Columbia University Press.

Bleger, J. (1966). Psychoanalysis of the psychoanalytic frame. *International Journal of Psycho-Analysis, 48*: 511–519.

Blomfield, O. H. D. (1985). Psychoanalytic supervision—an overview. *International Review of Psycho-Analysis 12*: 401–409.

Blum, H. (1979). The curative and creative aspects of insight. *Journal of the American Psychoanalytic Association 27*: 41–69.

Boyer, L. B. (1961). Provisional evaluation of psycho-analysis with few parameters in the treatment of schizophrenics. *International Journal of Psycho-Analysis, 42*: 389–403.

_____. (1990). Countertransference and technique. In: L. B. Boyer & P. L. Giovacchini (Eds.), *Master Clinicians on Treating the Regressed Patient* (pp. 303–324). North Vale, NJ: Jason Aronson.

Boyer, L. B., & Giovacchini, P. L. (1967). *Psychoanalytic Treatment of Characterological and Schizophrenic Disorders*. New York: Science House.

Buie, D. H. (1981). Empathy: Its nature and limitations. *Journal of American Psychoanalytic Association, 29*: 281–307.

Darcourt, G. (1986). Moments-limites en cures analytiques. In: J. Bergeret & W. Reid (Eds.), *Narcissisme et etats-limites*. Presses de l'Universite de Montreal, Dunod.

Dewald, D. A. (1987). *Learning Process in Psychoanalytic Supervision: Complexities and Challenges*. Madison, CT: International Universities Press.

Erikson, E. H. (1956). The problem of ego identity. *Journal of the American Psychoanalytic Association, 1*: 56–121.

Ferenczi, S. (1955). Confusion of tongues between adult and the child. (1933). In: S. Ferenczi, *Final Contribution to the Problems and Methods of Psychoanalysis*. New York: Brunner/Mazel. [Reprinted London: Karnac Books, 1980.]

Fleming, J. & Benedek, T. F. (1983). *Psychoanalytic Supervision* (2nd ed.). New York: International Universities Press.

Fliess, R. (1942). Metapsychology of the analyst. *Psychoanalytic Quarterly, 11.*

Freud, A. (1954). The widening scope of indications for psycho-analysis: Discussion. In: *Writings of Anna Freud, 4:* 356–376, New York: International Universities Press.

Freud, S. (1900a). *Interpretation of Dreams. S.E., 4, 5.*

_____. (1910d). The future prospects of psycho-analytic therapy. *S.E., 11:* 139–157.

_____. (1912–13). *Totem and Taboo. S.E., 13.*

_____. (1912a). The dynamics of transference. *S.E., 12.*

_____. (1912b). Recommendations to physicians practicing psychoanalysis. *S.E., 12.*

_____. (1913c). On beginning the treatment. *S.E., 12.*

_____. (1913d). The occurence in dreams of material from fairy tales, *S.E., 12.*

_____. (1913i). The disposition to obsessional neurosis, *S.E., 12.*

_____. (1914c). On narcissism: An introduction. *S.E., 14.*

_____. (1914d). On the history of the psycho-analytic movement. *S.E., 14.*

_____. (1914g). Remembering, repeating and working through. *S.E., 12.*

_____. (1915a). Observations on transference-love. *S.E., 12.*

_____. (1917e). Mourning and melancholia. *S.E., 14.*

_____. (1920g). *Beyond the Pleasure Principle. S.E., 18.*

_____. (1921c). *Group Psychology and the Analysis of the Ego. S.E., 18.*

_____. (1923b). *The Ego and the Id. S.E., 19.*

_____. (1924d). The dissolution of Oedipal complex. *S.E., 19.*

_____. (1926d [1925]). *Inhibitions, Symptoms and Anxiety. S.E., 20.*

_____. (1933). *New Introductory Lectures on Psycho-Analysis. S.E., 22.*

_____. (1939a [1937–39]). *Moses and Monotheism. S.E., 23.*

Furman, E. (1986). On trauma. When is the death of a parent traumatic? *The Psychoanalytic Study of the Child, 41:* 191–208. New York: International Universities Press.

Giovacchini, P. L. (1972). Interpretation and the definition of the analytic setting. In: P. L. Giovacchini (Ed.), *Tactics and Techniques in Psychoanalytic Therapy* (pp. 291–304). New York: Science House.

_____. (1977). Countertransference with primitive mental states. In: L. Epstein & A. Feiner (Eds.), *Countertransference* (pp. 235–266). New York: Jason Aronson, 1979.

Goldstein, W. N. (1991). Clarification of projective identification. *The American Journal of Psychiatry, 148*: 153–161.

Greenacre, P. (1953). *Trauma, Growth and Personality.* International Psychoanal. Library, 46. London: The Hogarth Press. [Reprinted London: Karnac Books, 1987.]

Grinberg, L. (1956). Sobre algunos problemas de técnica psicoanalitica determinados por la identificación y contra-identificación proyectivas. *Revista de Psicoanálisis, 14.*

_____. (1957). Perturbaciones en la interpretacion motivadas por la contraidentificación proyectiva. *Revista de Psicoanálisis, 14.*

_____. (1958). Aspectos magicos en la transferencia y en la contratransferencia. Identificación y contraideidentificación proyectivas. *Revista de Psicoanálisis, 15.*

_____. (1962). On a specific aspect of countertransference due to the patient's projective identification. *International Journal of Psycho-Analysis, 43*: 436–440.

_____. (1963). Psicopatologia de la identificación y contraidentificación proyectivas y de la contratransferencia. *Revista de Psicoanálisis, 20.*

_____. (1976). 'An approach to the understanding of borderline patients'. (Presented to the Panel on borderline conditions. The Menninger Foundation, Topeka, Kansas.)

_____. (1979). Countertransference and projective counter-identification. *Contemporary Psychoanalysis, 15.*

_____. (1981). El "filo de la navaja" en las depresiones y en los duelos. In: L. Grinberg, *Psicoanalisis: Aspectos teóricos y clínicos.* Buenos Aires: Paidós.

_____. (1982). 'Mas allá de la contraidentification proyectiva'. Read at the Latin-American Psychoanalytic Congress, Buenos Aires.

_____. (1990). *The Goals of Psychoanalysis. Identification, Identity, and Supervision.* London: Karnac Books.

_____. (1991). Countertransference and projective counteridentification in non-verbal communication. (Presented at the Ninth Conference of the E.P.F., Stockholm, March, 1991.)

Grinberg, L., Langer, M., Liberman, D., et al. (1967). The psychoanalytic process. *International Journal of Psycho-Analysis, 48*: 496–503.

Guntrip, H. (1969). *Schizoid Phenomena, Object Relations and the Self.* New York: International Universities Press.

Harris, I. (1962). Dreams about the analyst. *International Journal of Psycho-Analysis 43*, 151–158.

Hatcher, R. L. (1980). Insight and self-observation. In: S. Slipp (Ed.), *Curative Factors in Dynamic Psychotherapy* (pp. 71–90). New York: McGraw-Hill.

Heimann, P. (1950). On countertransference. *International Journal of Psycho-Analysis, 31*: 81–84.

_____. (1960). Countertransference. *British Journal of Medical Psychology, 33*: 9–15.

Heising, G. (1976). Zur Psychodynamik der Supervision. *Praxis Psychother. 21*: 185–191.

Jacobson, E. (1964). *The Self and the Object World.* New York: International Universities Press.

Jones, E. (1950). *Papers on Psychoanalysis.* Baltimore, MD: Williams and Wilkins.

Joseph, B. (1988). Projective identification: Clinical aspects. In: J. Sandler (Ed.), *Projection, Identification, Projective Identification* (pp. 93–115). London: Karnac Books, 1988.

Katan, A. (1973). Children who were raped. *The Psychoanalytic Study of the Child, 28*: 208–224. New York: International Universities Press.

Kerenyi, K. (1966). *Die Mythologie der Griechen.*

Kernberg, O. F. (1965). Notes on countertransference. *Journal of the American Psychoanalytic Association, 13*: 38–56.

_____. (1967). Borderline personality organization. *Journal of the American Psychoanalytic Association, 5.*

_____. (1975). *Borderline Conditions and Pathological Narcissism.* New York: Jason Aronson.

_____. (1975). *Transference and Countertransference in the Treatment of Borderline Patients.* (Stecker Monograph Series no. 12). Philadelphia: Institute of the Pennsylvania Hospital, pp. 16–17.

_____. (1976). Transference and countertransference in the treatment of borderline patients. In: *Object Relations Theory and Clinical Psychoanalysis.* New York: Jason Aronson.

_____. (1980). *Internal World and External Reality.* New York: Aronson.

_____. (1983). Psychoanalytic studies of group processes: Theory and applications. In: *Psychiatry 1983: APA Annual Review* (pp. 21–36). Washington, DC: American Psychiatric Press.

_____. (1984a). The influence of projective identification on countertransference. (Presented at the first Conference of the Sigmund Freud Centre of the Hebrew University of Jerusalem.) In: J. Sandler (Ed.), *Projection, Identification, Projective Identification*. London: Karnac Books, 1988.

_____. (1984b). *Severe Personality Disorders*. New Haven, CT: Yale University Press.

_____. (1987). An ego psychology–object relations theory approach to the transference. *Psychoanalytic Quarterly, 56*: 197–221.

_____. (1988). Projection and projective identification: Developmental and clinical aspects. In: J. Sandler (Ed.), *Projection, Identification, Projective Identification* (pp. 93–115). London: Karnac Books, 1988.

Kernberg, P. (1989). Narcissistic personality disorder in childhood. The Psychiatric Clinics of North America. In: O. F. Kernberg (Ed.), *Narcissistic Personality Disorder*, 12: 671–694.

Khan, M. M. R. (1964). Ego-distortion, cumulative trauma and the role of reconstruction in the analytic situation. In: *The Privacy of the Self* (pp. 59–68). New York: International Universities Press, 1974.

_____. (1969). On symbiotic omnipotence. In: *The Privacy of the Self* (pp. 82–92). New York: International Universities Press, 1974.

Klein, M. (1946). Notes on some schizoid mechanisms. In: *Envy and Gratitude and Other Works* (pp. 1–24). London: Hogarth Press, 1975.

_____. (1955). On identification. In: M. Klein, P. Heimann, & R. E. Money-Kyrle (Eds.), *New Directions in Psycho-Analysis*. London: Tavistock. [Reprinted London: Karnac Books, 1985.] Also in: *Envy and Gratitude and Other Works* (pp. 141–175). London: Hogarth Press, 1975.

Kohut, H. (1971). *The Analysis of the Self*. New York: International Universities Press.

Kramer, S. (1986). Identification and its vicissitudes as observed in children: A developmental approach. *International Journal of Psycho-Analysis, 67*: 161–172.

Kris, E. (1956). On some vicissitudes of insight in psychoanalysis. *International Journal of Psycho-Analysis*, 37: 445–455.

Langs, R. (1976a). *The Bipersonal Field.* New York: Jason Aronson.

———. (1976b). *The Therapeutic Interaction. Vol 2.* New York: Jason Aronson.

———. (1979). *The Interactional Dimension of Countertransference in Countertransference* (edited by L. Epstein & A. Feiner). New York: Jason Aronson.

Little, M. I. (1951). Counter-transference and the patient's response to it. *International Journal of Psycho-Analysis*, 32: 32–40.

———. (1957). "R"—the analyst's total response to his patient's needs. *International Journal of Psycho-Analysis*, 38: 240–254.

Loewald, H. (1960). On the therapeutic action of psychoanalysis. *International Journal of Psycho-Analysis*, 41: 16–33.

Mahler, M. S. (1968). *On Human Symbiosis and the Vicissititudes of Individuation.* New York: International Universities Press.

Main, T. (1957). The ailment. *British Journal Medical Psychology*, 30: 129–145.

Malin, A., & Grotstein, J. (1966). Projective identification in the therapeutic process. *International Journal of Psycho-Analysis*, 47: 26–31.

McDougall, J. (1975). Le contre-transfert et la communication primitive. *Topique, No. 16.*

———. (1979). Primitive communication and the use of counter-transference. In: H. Feiner & L. Epstein (Eds.), *Counter-transference.* New York: Jason Aronson.

———. (1980). *Plea for a Measure of Abnormality.* Madison, WI: International Universities Press.

McLaughlin, J. T. (1983). Some observations on the application of frame theory to the psychoanalytic situation and process. *Psychoanalytic Quarterly*, 52: 167–179.

Menninger, K. (1958). *The Theory of Psychoanalytic Technique.* New York: Basic Books.

Modell, A. H. (1973). Affects and psychoanalytic knowledge. In: *Annual of Psychoanalysis, 1*: 117–124. New York: Quadrangle.

———. (1976). The "holding environment" and the therapeutic action of psychoanalysis. *Journal of the American Psychoanalytic Association*, 24: 285–307.

Money-Kyrle, R. (1956). Normal countertransference and some of its deviations. *International Journal of Psycho-Analysis 37*: 360–366.

Ogden, T. (1979). On projective identification. *International Journal of Psycho-Analysis, 60*: 357–373.

_____. (1982). *Projective Identification and Psychotherapeutic Technique.* New York: Jason Aronson.

_____. (1985). On potential space. *International Journal of Psycho-Analysis, 66*: 129–141.

Olinick, S. L. (1969). Empathy and regression. In: *The Psychotherapeutic Instrument* (pp. 3–16). New York: Jason Aronson, 1980.

Olinick, S. L., Poland, W. S., Grigg, K. A., & Granatir, W. L. (1973). The psycho-analytic work ego: Process and interpretation. *International Journal of Psycho-Analysis, 54*: 143–151.

Pedder, J. (1986). Reflections on the theory and practice of supervision. *Psychoanalytic Psychotherapy, 2* (1): 1–12.

Pindar. *The Odes.* Loed Classical Library. (1968).

Racker, H. (1953). A contribution to the problem of countertransference. *International Journal of Psycho-Analysis, 34.*

_____. (1957). The meanings and uses of countertransference. *Psychoanalytic Quarterly, 26*: 303–357.

_____. (1960). *Estudios sobre Técnica Psicoanalitica.* Buenos Aires: Paidós.

_____. (1968). *Transference and Countertransference.* New York: International Universities Press. [Reprinted London: Karnac Books, 1985.]

Rice, A. K. (1965). *Learning for Leadership.* London: Tavistock Publications.

Richepin J. (1954). *Greek Mythology* (translated by N. Tetene). Athens: Pertaminai.

Rieu, E. V. (1971). Apollonius of Rhodes. In: E. V. Rieu, *The Voyage of Argo.* Harmondsworth Middlesex: Penguin Classics.

Rosen, V. (1967). Disorders of communication in psychoanalysis. *Journal of the American Psychoanalytic Association, 15*: 467–490.

Rosenfeld, H. (1965). *Psychotic States. A Psychoanalytical Approach.* New York: International Universities Press. [Reprinted London: Karnac Books, 1985.]

_____. (1978). Notes on the psychopathology and the psychoanalytic treatment of some borderline patients. *International Journal of Psychoanalysis, 59*: 215–221.

_____. (1983). Primitive object relations and mechanisms. *International Journal Psychoanalysis, 64*: 261–267.

Sandell, R. (1985). Influence of supervision, therapist's competence, and patient's ego level on the effects of time-limited psychotherapy. *Psychotherapy and Psychosomatics 44*: 103–109.

Sandler, J. (1960). On the concept of the superego. *The Psychoanalytic Study of the Child, 15*. New York: International Universities Press.

_____. (1988). The concept of projective identification. In: J. Sandler (Ed.), *Projection, Identification, Projective Identification* (pp. 13–26). London: Karnac Books.

Sandler, J., Holder, A., & Dare C. (1970). Basic psychoanalytic concepts: Countertransference. *British Journal Psychiatry, 117*: 83–88.

Schafer, R. (1959). Generative empathy in the treatment situation. *Psychoanalytic Quarterly, 28*: 347–373.

Searles, H. F. (1953). Dependency processes in the psychotherapy of schizophrenia. *Journal of the American Psychoanalytic Association, 3*: 19–66.

_____. (1963). Transference psychosis in the psychotherapy of schizophrenia. In: *Collected Papers on Schizophrenia and Related Subjects. Selected Papers* (pp. 654–716). New York: International Universities Press, 1965. [Reprinted London: Karnac Books, 1986.]

_____. (1978–79). Concerning transference and countertransference. *International Journal of Psychoanalytic Psychotherapy, 7*: 165–188.

_____. (1979). *Countertransference and Related Subjects*. New York: International Universities Press.

_____. (1986). *My Work with Borderline Patients*. North Vale, NJ: Jason Aronson.

Segal, H. (1977). Countertransference. *International Journal of Psychoanalytic Psychotherapy, 6*. Also in: *The Work of Hanna Segal; A Kleinian Approach to Clinical Practice*. New York: Jason Aronson. [Reprinted London: Karnac Books, 1986.]

_____. (1981). *The Work of Hanna Segal: A Kleinian Approach to Clinical Practice*. New York, London: Jason Aronson. [Reprinted London: Karnac Books, 1986.]

_____. (1985). The Klein–Bion model. In: A. Rothstein (Ed.), *Models of the Mind: Their Relationship to Clinical Work*. New York: International Universities Press.

Spruiell, V. (1983). The rules and frames of the psychoanalytic situation. *Psychoanalytic Quarterly, 52*: 1–33.

Stanton, A., & Schwartz, M. (1954). *The Mental Hospital*. New York: Basic Books.

Stone, L. (1961). *The Psychoanalytic Situation*. New York: International Universities Press.

Szecsödy, I. (1990). Supervision: A didactic or mutative situation. *Psychoanalytic Psychotherapy, 4* (3): 245–261.

Tansey, M. J., & Burke, W. F. (1989). *Understanding Countertransference*. Hillsdale, NJ: The Analytic Press.

Thomas, A., & Chess, S. (1984). Genesis and evolution of behavioral page disorders: From infancy to early adult life. *American Journal of Psychiatry, 141*: 1–9.

Turquet, P. (1975). Threats to identity in the large group. In: Kreeger, L. (Ed.), *The Large Group: Dynamics and Therapy* (pp. 87–144). London: Constable.

Vaslamatzis, G., & Verveniotis, S. (1985). Early dropouts in brief dynamic psychotherapy. *Psychotherapy and Psychosomatics, 44*.

Viderman, S. (1982). *La construction de l' espace analytique*. Paris: Editions Gallimard.

Volkan, V. D. (1975). Cosmic laughter. In: P. L. Giovacchini (Ed.), *Tactics and Techniques in Psychoanalytic Therapy, Vol. 2* (pp. 427–440). New York: Jason Aronson.

_____. (1976). *Primitive Internalized Object Relations*. New York: International Universities Press.

_____. (1979). The glass bubble of a narcissistic patient. In: J. LeBoit & A. Capponi (Eds.), *Advances in Psychotherapy of the Borderline Patient* (pp. 405–431). New York: Jason Aronson.

_____. (1981). Transference and countertransference: An examination from the point of view of internalized object relations. In: S. Tuttman, C. Kaye, & M. Zimmerman (Eds.), *Object and Self: A Developmental Approach* (pp. 429–451). New York: International Universities Press.

_____. (1982). Identification and related psychic events: Their appearance in therapy and their curative value. In: S. Slipp (Ed.),

*Curative Factors in Dynamic Psychotherapy* (pp. 153–176). New York: McGraw-Hill.

_____. (1987). *Six Steps in the Treatment of Borderline Personality Organization.* North Vale, NJ: Jason Aronson.

_____. (1991). *Mind and Human Interaction, 2,* (3, February): 63, 64.

Volkan, V. D., & Ast, G. (in press). *Dr. Schreber's Schatten.* Stuttgart: Klett-Cotta.

Wagner, F. (1957). Supervision of psychotherapy. *American Journal of Psychotherapy. 11,* 759–768.

Winnicott, D. W. (1949). Hate in the countertransference. *International Journal of Psycho-Analysis* 30: 69–74. In *Collected Papers* (pp. 194–203). New York: Basic Books, 1958.

_____. (1958). The theory of the parent–infant relationship. In: *The Maturational Processes and the Facilitating Environment. Studies in the Theory of Emotional Development* (pp. 37–55). New York: International Universities Press, 1965.

_____. (1960). Countertransference. *British Journal of Medical Psychology, 33*: 17: 18.

_____. (1963). Dependence in infant-care, in child-care, and in the psycho-analytic setting. In: *Maturational Processes and the Facilitating Environment. Studies in the Theory of Emotional Development* (pp. 249–260). London: Hogarth Press. [Reprinted London: Karnac Books, 1990.]

_____. (1971). The use of an object and relating through identifications. In: *Playing and Reality.* London: Tavistock Publications, pp. 86–94.

Zinoviev, A. (1984). *The Reality of Communism.* New York: Schocken Books.